RISING

FROM THE

ASHES

The Return of Indiana
University Basketball

Terry Hutchens

Blue River Press
Indianapolis, IN

ISBN:9781935628194
LCCN: 2012945454

Cover designed by Phil Velikan
Editorial assistance provided by Dorothy Chambers
Packaged by Wish Publishing

Printed in the United States of America
10 9 8 7 6 5 4 3 2 1

Published by Blue River Press
Distributed by Cardinal Publishers Group
Tom Doherty Company, Inc.
www.cardinalpub.com

Front cover photo by USPRESSWIRE.COM / Brian Spurlock

This book is dedicated to Susan, Bryan and Kevin. Each of you is a daily reminder to me that nothing is more important than family.

Preface and Acknowledgements

I always wanted to write a book about Indiana basketball. If you're going to put in the time and effort to do a book, you want to make sure that you have a passionate and engaged audience. That has never been a question when it comes to Indiana University basketball fans.

That passion was lived out in so many ways with the 2011-12 season that marked the return of Indiana basketball to the national landscape for the first time in four years. Suddenly, IU basketball was relevant again, and Hoosier fans everywhere were basking in that success.

I have called upon several sources to help me in telling the story. First of all, thanks to Tom Crean and his staff. Coach Crean has had a strong and positive impact on Indiana basketball, and his passion and enthusiasm are unrivaled. I believed from the very beginning that there were two coaches who could put IU football and basketball back on the map. In football, it was Terry Hoeppner, and unfortunately that story had a tragic ending. But in basketball, from the very beginning, you could tell that Tom Crean was the coach who could bring Indiana back from the ashes. It was just a matter of getting the players to fit into his system. Once that happened, it was no surprise to see IU basketball back on top again.

Thanks, too, to IU athletic media relations director J.D. Campbell and his staff. J.D. does a great job making players available during the season and serving as the middle man between the media and the IU basketball program. I also want to sincerely thank members of Campbell's staff, including but not limited to Jeff Keag, Kyle Kuhlman, Shana Daniels, Kyle Johnson, Ryan Sheets, Nate Wiechers, Doak Henry, Ryan Preske and Melanie Schneider.

My thanks go out to Don Fischer, Royce Waltman and Joe Smith, IU's radio team, not so much for their contributions to the book but rather for their friendship that makes covering IU basketball that much more enjoyable. I could say the same for people around the program like Scott Dolson, Chuck Crabb, Tim Garl, Dr. Larry Rink, Steve Ahlfeld, Chris Reynolds and Jayd Grossman. Thanks to current athletic director Fred Glass and his predecessor Rick Greenspan.

I want to thank and congratulate the five seniors from the 2011-12 season who were able to leave Indiana with a positive experience.

That group includes Kory Barnett, Verdell Jones III, Daniel Moore, Tom Pritchard and Matt Roth.

I want to save a special thanks for Christian Watford. I started thinking about this book seriously as I drove home the night Watford's shot beat Kentucky. That shot was the rubber stamp that provided confirmation that Indiana basketball was back. I've experienced a lot of great shots first hand, but none was bigger in terms of what it meant to so many people and a program.

I want to thank all of my colleagues at the *Indianapolis Star* and other members of the media who cover Indiana for the contributions they made to this book. Many probably didn't know that their work would be used in this book, but a story like this couldn't have been told from just one viewpoint. I wanted to share good writing from many other sources, and that's what I did.

I want to thank photographers Joe Eke and Mike Dickbernd for providing pictures that I used in the book. There were far too many outstanding images to choose from. Thanks for letting me use the ones I did.

I want to thank Jim Lefko, senior editor for sports at the *Indianapolis Star*, for permission to take on this project.

I want to thank everyone at Cardinal Publishing and especially publisher Tom Doherty, for taking on this project. This is my fourth book, and I've worked with Tom on each one.

I want to thank my family. My wife, Susan, my bride of 26 years, is always my biggest support. I could say the same for my two sons, Bryan (21) and Kevin (19). Thanks for enduring my divided attention.

Finally, I want to extend a shout-out to everyone who played even the smallest role in making this book possible. A project like this doesn't come about without the cooperation of a countless number of people.

Foreword
By Calbert Cheaney

Indiana basketball is back, and I can't tell you just how proud I am to be a part of it again.

In June 2011, Tom Crean asked me if I would be Indiana's director of basketball operations. I really appreciated that he reached out to me. I think that's one of the things that separates Tom from a lot of the other coaches in this country. He could have easily done his own thing but Indiana is all about tradition and he understands that. When he extended the job offer to me, how could I say no? The fact that I could come to Indiana and help out and contribute in any way possible was great. The fact that I could go back to my alma mater was a bonus.

People ask me sometimes about what I do in my position. My role with this team is to provide life skills to our players. I try to help them understand and deal with the mental aspects of being a student-athlete. It's hard to balance both, but it's a must.

College can be one of the highlights of theplayers' life. They get to experience things on their own. They get to meet new people. We just try to teach them how to deal with the good and bad times. We try to help them grow and be responsible men. It also allows me to take my own past experiences, whether good or bad, and help players in case they have questions.

I can't say enough about the pride I had in seeing what transpired with Indiana basketball in the 2011-12 season.

It was an unbelievable ride, and it was even more unbelievable to be a part of it. The fact that the program was in such peril made the ride all the more sweeter. Being director was a lot of fun for me, because you see how hard everyone worked. I saw the kids improving everyday. I saw them start to believe in themselves each passing day.

I saw Coach Crean, Coach Buckley, Coach Seltzer, Coach McClain, and Coach Jackson teaching and developing these kids to become not only great basketball players, but great men.

I saw our trainer, Tim Garl, making sure the kids were taking care of themselves. I saw Jayd Grossman, Beth McLaughlin, Casey Hockersmith and Stephanie Klar make sure everything ran smoothly in the front office. I saw Marni Mooney and Mattie White give it their all to make sure these kids got the education they deserve. That's what made it fun for me. That's what it's all about.

It was everyone working to achieve one common goal. Being one big, happy family!

I enjoy what I do all the time, because I have a passion for it. When you have a passion for something, like Terry does for writing, it makes what you do a lot easier. I enjoy the fact that I get to learn from great coaches along the way; The fact that I'm able to relay what I have learned to other kids; The fact that we get to watch these kids improve each and every day. The fact that we get to experience our great fans each and everyday.

Whether it be random fans walking through on any given day to see the facilities, or seeing our fans cheering the team on at Assembly Hall on a game night, or just walking around campus and witnessing the love our students have for the team. That's what it's like to live it every day. From a coach's or former player's perspective, it never gets old.

Being a former player, you would never think in a million years that the program would ever start from square one all over again. You would always assume nothing would ever happen to a program like Indiana. The five national championships, the numerous Big Ten titles, the legendary players and coaches that have made this program. But unfortunately it did happen. I guess that's the reality of life. There was one thing I learned through the whole experience: even great things can take a few steps back.

I've been asked if I was surprised by what the 2011-12 team was able to accomplish. And I say that nothing really surprised me. You could see a vast improvement in the kids at the end of the previous season. All the work the kids put in during the spring and summer was phenomenal. When you work that hard, nothing but good things will happen. Couple that with the addition of Cody Zeller, Remy Abell and Austin Etherington, and you had a team that had the potential to do great things.

I knew we were going to be pretty good when I watched the first couple of days of practice. Every kid was competing and working extremely hard. It was the type of hard work and dedication that teams get when they're tired of getting beat every night. They had the look that said they'd had enough. Coach Crean and the rest of the coaching staff had the exact same look.

The team had improved in so many different ways. Cody, in particular, boosted the team because he brought a different dynamic to the group. He also made an impact by making things easier for everybody else. When you have a player who can do that, your team already improves by leaps and bounds. From the very first couple of days in practice, you saw an improvement. Everyone was locked in. They were practicing and competing extremely hard. It was like they were saying with their play, "We're not going to have another losing season!"

As the season progressed, I thought one of the games where we made big strides was at North Carolina State. It was the first time the kids had to travel to a somewhat hostile environment. Our kids played their hearts out. There was a time late in the second half when we were down 63-56, but our kids didn't blink. They fought right back, and we ended up winning 86-75.

Another big game was at Purdue. In this rivalry, it doesn't matter if both teams are 0-20 or 20-0. Whoever wins will have bragging rights until they play again. The game was very physical from the start. Both teams had a tough time scoring the ball in the beginning of the game. Our kids showed not only physical toughness, but more importantly, mental toughness. When you're in an environment like Mackey Arena, where the Purdue fans are yelling and screaming at you with words I can't say, it takes tremendous concentration to drown all of that out and focus on the task at hand. But the kids did that, and they were able to break the Boilermakers will at the end of the game. We ended up winning the game by 17 or 18.

When we were selected to play against New Mexico State in Portland, it might have been the biggest accomplishment for the program in the last 10 years. If we had been chosen to go play in Siberia, we still would have been extremely excited. It was like a big weight was lifted off the program's shoulders. Coach Crean and his team had finally realized their goal of getting to the NCAA tournament.

New Mexico State was a very formidable foe. They had just come off winning the Western Athletic Conference tournament championship. They were riding high going into the tournament against us. They were a big, physical, athletic team. Everybody picked us to lose, because everyone thought their athleticism and physicality would cause problems for us. We were only worried about how our team would respond to playing in its first-ever NCAA Tournament game.

We knew the boys would be a little nervous, because it was their first time. Would we get off to a good start? Or would we start flat and be down 10 by the first TV timeout? Would the fact that the game was being played way out in Portland affect the team? Well, it didn't. The boys came out and played well from the tip. They played consistently well through the game and won rather easily.

The next big test would be against Virginia Commonwealth University. They beat a very good Wichita State team. Shaka Smart and his team were the darlings of the tournament last year by getting to the Final Four. They were a well-coached basketball team with tournament experience. Again, nobody picked us to win except our own faithful fans.

The great thing about our kids is they don't care about what's said about them. They're concerned about playing hard, playing smart and letting the chips fall where they may. The big improvement I saw with this team is that when they got hit in the mouth, they didn't quit. When VCU made runs against the kids, they responded in a big way.

When we were down nine late in the first half, Christian Watford led us with two threes. We were able to close the lead to two at the break. When we were down five late in the second half, Cody, Victor and Will made big plays when we needed them, and we prevailed! Our kids never quit, no matter what the circumstances. That was the story of the entire season: Our kids never quit!

When you saw the cover of this book, it had to take you back to that moment when Christian hit the shot to beat Kentucky.

That game against Kentucky was incredible. Nobody gave us a chance to win. Everybody thought Kentucky was too big, too strong, too athletic and too talented. We knew we had a talented team as well. And we knew if we stuck to our game plan, we would have a great chance of winning.

When Verdell raced up the court and found Christian for the shot, I knew the ball was going in as soon as it left his hands. Christian was right in line with me and the basket. So when he let it go, it was right on the mark. It was just a matter of being short or long. Christian made a three from the same spot earlier in the second half. So there was a great chance he would make it again.

When he made it, I didn't know what to do or think. It was like a dream, and you didn't want to wake up. When the fans rushed the court, it was like a tremendous weight had been lifted. They had suffered through several years of severe mediocrity. And for the game to be won in that manner was unbelievable.

I just stood there and took it all in. I was worried about the players getting trampled, but there were so many fans on the floor, I couldn't find our guys. There wasn't much you could do, anyway. As I started to walk to the tunnel, you could see Christian with his family. Victor was in the stands with his family. It was amazing to see.

When I got to the tunnel, I just stood there and enjoyed everything I saw. To see the best fans in the world adore their basketball team was amazing! The only memory that comes close is when we beat Michigan at Assembly Hall my freshman year. That environment was crazy. But I still think that the game against Kentucky will go down as one of the most incredible celebrations in IU history.

I still remember my feelings when I heard that Coach Crean was taking over our Indiana basketball program. I thought it was great. He had turned a Marquette program around in a matter of a few years. He had coached some great players like Dwyane Wade, Travis Diener and Steve Novak, who are still in the NBA. So you knew he would do a good job.

But I think the most important thing was that he would embrace the IU tradition, which was so important. The tradition of championships, former coaches and former players was very important, and the preservation of it extremely important to our fans. The first time I met him, I could tell immediately that the history, tradition and fans were very important to him. The fact that he came in and respected the program from the get-go was huge.

Another thing about Coach Crean is his tireless work ethic. He never stops trying to improve. There are many responsibilities that come with taking the head coaching job at IU. You're not just the head coach. You have to wear a lot of hats. He embraced that part as well.

But the most important thing about Coach is that he didn't have to come here. He had it going at Marquette, so he didn't have to take the IU job. He did because he saw the great potential of this program. I'm sure he knew he would have to start from the beginning, but I think he was up for the challenge. He knew that it was going to be a struggle, but I also think he knew it would be worth it in the end. Like he said, "IT'S INDIANA!"

I hope you enjoy this book and continue to celebrate the success this group of kids was able to achieve in the 2011-12 season. It was a great ride that year, and the ride is only going to continue.

Calbert Cheaney

PART 1:
The Shot

Christian Watford's 3-point shot that beat No. 1 Kentucky 73-72, December 10, 2011 at Assembly Hall.

Chapter 1

Christian Watford may go on to do great things in his life.

He probably will. At the time of this writing, he's heading into his senior year of college. He may have a long career ahead of him in the NBA or on the European circuit. He may become a doctor or a lawyer or one of a thousand different accomplished professions. He may get married, have children, and have countless experiences as both a husband and a father.

But *The Shot* will follow him wherever he goes.

He'll hear about it in the checkout line at the grocery store or while he's enjoying a meal at a restaurant. He may be half a world away in an airport terminal in Barcelona, and someone will recognize his face and tell him how that one simple shot was forever cemented in that person's mind.

Or in any public place, at any time, someone will walk up behind him, pat him on the back, and ask him to take them back to that moment in time when, with one flick of the wrist, he officially ushered in the return of Indiana basketball. Watford will never have to pay for a drink in a bar in the state of Indiana for the rest of his life.

Think I'm exaggerating? Just ask Keith Smart or Christian Laettner how many times they've been asked to relive the moment that their shots tickled the twine and changed their lives and that of their respective fan bases forever. Smart's baseline jumper against Syracuse in 1987 gave Indiana a 74-73 victory and its fifth national championship. Laettner's turnaround jumper from the top of the key in 1992 gave Duke a 104-103 victory over Kentucky in the NCAA East Regional final.

But everywhere they've gone for the past 20 years, those shots have been right there with them, like a bright neon glow whenever they enter a room. "Hey, Keith, great shot, man!" Smart has heard too many times to count. Or someone is always quick to say to Laettner, "Hey, Christian, I'll never forget where I was when you hit that shot."

They are life-changing moments for fans from the casual to the passionate. They look for moments like those to hang their hats on. It's part of their fabric and their DNA. And they'll carry them with them forever, and every time that 10-second video clip is shown on ESPN, they'll rush back to that moment and remember distinctly where they were and how that made them feel.

Smart and Laettner have grown to accept it. For Watford, the adulation has just begun.

ꕥ

Under normal circumstances, *The Shot* for Watford wouldn't have been considered a difficult one. It was a 3-pointer from about 21 feet away, with his size-15 sneakers just inches behind the arc from the left wing. It was your basic 3-point shot, and one that he had attempted thousands of times growing up. He had probably hoisted that same shot from that place on the Assembly Hall floor hundreds of times in practice or in games over the previous three years. In fact, he had already made a shot from the exact same spot earlier in this game.

Still, given the circumstances, *The Shot* was anything but routine. As Watford took a short pass from Verdell Jones III and lined up for that 3-pointer, the replays will show Darius Miller lunging toward him on the high side and Marquis Teague falling in his direction to his right.

What the replays don't show is the 2,000-pound gorilla wearing candy-striped warm-up pants that was playing piggyback with Watford at that moment. Look closely and use your imagination, and you can see the right arm of the gorilla just around Watford's neck. It's name: Hoosier Nation.

In Indiana, basketball is more than just a game. At IU, it's closer to a religion. It may have been just a simple 21-foot shot from the left wing, but for Indiana basketball fans it was so much more. This was an Indiana fan base that had been imprisoned the previous three seasons and was looking for a reason for hope.

A storied Indiana basketball program had fallen on hard times. Five national championship banners may hang from the rafters in the south end of Assembly Hall, but the previous three seasons had made those memories seem like a lifetime away. Some programs have had victories and trophies taken away because of NCAA violations. Indiana basketball fans just wish those three seasons could be erased all together. In terms of consecutive futile seasons, they were the worst three in an IU basketball history that spanned more than a hundred years.

A program that had always prided itself on doing things the right way had fallen victim to a coach that had taken shortcuts. And when the NCAA came down on Kelvin Sampson for skirting the rules and taking improper liberties in recruiting, IU basketball hit rock bottom.

By the time Tom Crean and his assistants arrived in April 2008, the Indiana program wasn't even a shell of its former self. If this was a new house, it hadn't even been framed yet. The foundation was being formed but the concrete was still wet. When Crean arrived in Bloomington, he must have felt that the ground was settling beneath that foundation. When Crean took the job, he was starting a program from ground zero unlike any college coach had ever experienced.

In his first three seasons, Indiana won 28 out of a possible 94 games. The first season, IU was 1-17 in Big Ten play. In three seasons, Indiana won a total of eight conference games. The once-mighty had fallen and while the Hoosiers were expected to be better in Crean's fourth season, no one had lofty expectations. Most figured it would take one more year before Indiana basketball was all the way back.

Yet as Watford lined up to take that 3-point shot on December 10, 2011 at Assembly Hall, there were some fans who were trying to believe that an Indiana turnaround could take place a year ahead of schedule. Indiana was 8-0 but it didn't really have a benchmark win. The Hoosiers had won on the road at Evansville and North Carolina State, but neither of those programs when spoken aloud caused many to tremble.

Indiana had beaten Butler, a team that played in back-to-back national championship games the past two seasons. But this Butler team wasn't close to those in terms of talent, and in fact the Bulldogs eventually wouldn't even get back to the NCAA Tournament when this season ended.

But this game was clearly different than the first eight. Indiana faced Kentucky. The fact that it was UK was probably enough for most Indiana fans. That program, along with in-state rival Purdue, are the two teams Hoosier fans want to beat more than any other. The fact that Kentucky was the No. 1 team in the nation, though, just added a little fuel to the fire.

The fan base had stayed with Indiana through the down years and they were beginning to sense that something could be special with this season. On the day of the Kentucky game, fans began lining up 10 hours prior to the tip. A few hours before game time, Crean went through the line of fans, posing for pictures, signing countless autographs, and thanking one student after another for their support of this IU team.

☯   �

The game would have gone down in Indiana-Kentucky history as a great one even if Watford hadn't had his last-second heroics. Indiana had a double-digit lead midway through the second half before the Wildcats clawed back and took a late lead. When Doron Lamb made one of two free throws with 5.6 seconds to play, Kentucky had a 72-70 lead and IU had one final chance.

Kentucky had two fouls to give, and because of that, Crean didn't think he could run a conventional, drive-the-ball-up-the-court last-second play. Instead, his idea was to throw a deep pass down the court and hopefully get off a good shot before Kentucky was able to foul.

But the Wildcats were in the frontcourt for the most part, and the second option was for Watford to get the ball to Verdell Jones III and then sprint to the other end, filling the left-side lane.

"Verdell got the ball, made a play at midcourt, and had his eyes on the rim," Crean said in the postgame press conference. "He had the presence of mind, because in a situation like that you want to have four spots filled when you're driving the ball. And Christian did a phenomenal job of being in the backcourt and finding the open gap. Verdell did a tremendous job of finding him."

So as the play unfolded, Watford in-bounded it to Jones, who dribbled it to half court with Marquis Teague guarding him. Near the midcourt stripe, freshman Cody Zeller set a screen that collected Teague and ended any hopes of the freshman guard from Indianapolis being able to foul the IU senior. Jones continued to dribble toward the center of the floor as if he was going to take it to the basket. The few Kentucky fans in the building were screaming for the Wildcats to foul. A foul not in the act of shooting would have given IU the ball out of bounds with just a few ticks left on the clock. And more than that, it would have given UK coach John Calipari another opportunity to remind his team they could foul one more time. But the first foul never came.

Instead, just after Jones crossed inside the 3-point line, he pulled up and tossed the ball out to Watford on the wing. When the shot left his hands, there was less than a second remaining.

"When I got the ball, I knew Christian was going to be sprinting down because he was taking the ball out and he was the trail-man," Jones said. "I just drove in and he was like 'V! V!' and I turned around and passed it to him, and the rest is history."

Watford was squared up to the basket, his body had the perfect alignment, and he had textbook form as the ball left his hands. "He stayed in his shot, he didn't fade, he didn't leg kick," Crean would say later. "It was picture-perfect form."

Those in the stands that had the angle looking over Watford's shoulder said they knew *The Shot* was down the moment it left the shooter's hands. A few seconds later, everyone in attendance and those watching on national television on ESPN knew the same thing themselves.

As the shot hit nothing but net and the clock showed nothing but zeroes, Indiana had shocked the world with a 73-72 victory over No. 1 Kentucky.

"Unbelievable! Unbelievable!" Dick Vitale shouted into his courtside microphone as he commentated the game along with Dan Shulman for ESPN.

Within seconds, students were pouring onto the court in record numbers. Somewhere under a pile, Watford, who is claustrophobic by nature, was having trouble catching his breath.

"I remember being trampled by the fans," Watford said. "A lot of people got on me, and I couldn't breathe. I told Tom (Pritchard) to get them off of me, and he started throwing people everywhere."

For the next 30 minutes, students sang and danced and swayed in rhythm on the Assembly Hall floor. Those who couldn't get down there because there wasn't a single space anywhere to be found stayed in their seats and just basked in the moment. The sound was deafening, and the cheers and chants and songs went on and on and on. The IU Pep Band played for another 25 minutes.

"It was just crazy, just an unbelievable feeling," Zeller said. "It's probably one of those feelings I'll never forget."

Crean said Indiana fans deserved that postgame celebration.

"Our fans deserved that," Crean said. "They deserve to storm the court, they deserve to stand on chairs and tables and be excited. They do, and our players deserve it.

"I told our guys before the game, and I don't think it was anything profound, but these guys have endured a lot. And to have an opportunity like they had today in front of them, I was 100 percent confident that they would do everything to max it out. And they did."

Victor Oladipo ran up into the stands and gave his mother a hug. It was the first home game she had been able to attend that season, and Victor wanted to show her his appreciation. Jordan Hulls, Verdell Jones III, Christian Watford and Will Sheehey stood on the scorers table, where they could completely take in the scene, and they posed for pictures and exhorted the crowd to get louder and louder. They didn't disappoint. It was a Hoosier lovefest in the truest sense of the phrase.

IU assistant Tim Buckley said the overwhelming moment was when the crowd rushed the floor.

"I took two steps to go shake hands with Kentucky and I couldn't move after that," Buckley said in an interview in 2012. "The crowd closed in that quickly. Later, to see the reactions from other places around the country on YouTube also showed the magnitude of the moment.

"I would have to say that I enjoyed the moment for a while, though. I had well over 135 text messages. However, we have always expected to win, and so I think for me, stepping back and watching the guys enjoy it as well as the rest of the staff was something I will always remember."

The celebration was memorable indeed. It was simply a celebration like never before at Assembly Hall. There had been big shots and floor-rushing pandemonium in this building before, but those were all celebrations of a single game. This was a fan base celebrating the return of its basketball program.

With one simple flick of his wrist, Christian Watford had made Indiana basketball whole again.

                                            80   03

As the shot went in and Tom Crean headed toward mid-court to shake John Calipari's hand, the IU coach had a stunned look on his face. Asked what he was thinking when the ball went through the basket, Crean admitted the word "stunned" was an accurate one.

"I wanted to make sure it counted, because I saw the referees running over to the monitor," Crean said. "So I wanted to hold in my excitement there. I talked to John (Calipari), I shook hands with a couple of guys and I just wanted to wait.

"And then when you could see on the clock that it (the ball) was off and through before the red light came on, then well, you take a moment to raise the hands and then I just really wanted to find my family and my wife."

Crean hugged his wife, Joani, her parents (the Harbaughs), his son, Riley, and his daughter, Megan, and then found a place on the side of the arena to stand back for a moment and watch the celebration. He had waited three-and-a-half years for a moment like this one. He wanted to soak it in, if only for a moment.

Crean said he has a picture from his days at Michigan State as a graduate assistant during the 1989-90 season when the Spartans won the Big Ten title. The picture showed Tom Izzo standing back while everyone else was celebrating the game.

"I always thought that was the coolest thing," Crean said. "Sometimes whether it was at Marquette or here where the crowd has erupted, you see pictures but you never quite take it all in.

"I took about two minutes to make sure I took it all in."

After a few minutes passed, he headed for the locker room. When he finally got there, he was tackled by his players and held on the floor, where he received a bath from a large bucket of water.

Crean was asked later what he told his players in the locker room following the game.

"I just told them I was really proud of them," Crean said. "We had a lot of people in there, and we really just talked about individuals a little bit.

"It was kind of a blur. I was freezing because I got doused. I got held down, and there was no way I was getting away from (strength coach) Je'Ney Jackson. They had it planned. But it's cool."

Close to an hour later, Crean was asked again about those last few moments as he waited for the officials to confirm that the shot was good and as students were storming the court behind him.

"I thought it was good," Crean said. "I would have been, like, stunned if it wasn't. But again, we're not going to get giddy and joyful and have a letdown, either.

"But I have no idea how we would have got that game finished if it wasn't."

ༀ ༀ

In the postgame press conference, Crean started off by thanking the fans. Fans had started lining up on Tuesday for the Saturday game. They were there again on Wednesday, but the university stepped in and said that for the safety of the students, with the cold temperatures, fans should stay home until game day.

But the university had a reward for those fans who had at least tried to show their support. Those fans were given passes that allowed them to be first in line when the doors opened at 3:45 p.m. for the 5 p.m. game. Fans were allowed to line up beginning at 7 a.m. on game day, and they came in droves.

"The first thing to me, and again, we've never taken anything for granted here, was to look outside Tuesday and see how many fans were waiting outside," Crean said. "To see them Wednesday, to see that passion and then to see it all today and see the people lined up from early this morning on through the afternoon, is incredible. And then to just hear that crowd.

"This is one of the most shared moments that I've ever been a part of. Maybe the most shared moment where you want to share it with everybody that's been a part of this program long before we got here, the ones who have joined in and those who have become fans over a period of time."

Crean said the crowd support was "the epitome of what Hoosier Nation is all about."

"The fans and everybody that supports this program from close and far, young and old, they deserve it, because it's one of those moments that everybody is going to remember," Crean said.

In talking about the final play, Crean was asked if he was surprised that Kentucky didn't foul with two fouls to give.

"I never put myself in another coach's position right there," Crean said. "It looked like they tried (to foul), but the screen at mid-court was good and Verdell just did a great job of putting a burst on out there. I thought he was going to take (the shot) and I would have been OK with it because he was going left and he's an excellent pull-up shooter. But he got cut off and Christian was in an open spot."

Crean talked about wanting to get the long pass but settling for Jones taking the ball up the court.

"We wanted to sneak a long pass in there where we could get the long pass and have a chance to win the game, or we'd get held on the cut and they'd foul right there," Crean said. "But they didn't come up and bite."

Instead, Jones took control and eventually made the perfect pass.

"We just ran, and for Verdell to pivot and make that pass, well, that's the biggest assist he has had at Indiana," Crean said. "And as good as Christian is playing, I can't describe enough how that was just a perfectly fundamentally formed shot. He has worked so hard to become a better shooter and he made it.

"Everybody did their job. Victor ran long and Cody, Jordan, everybody did their job. But the bottom line in something like that is belief. Yet, they were able to execute under pressure, and it turned out to be a bit of a broken play because we weren't able to go long, but when everybody fills their spots good things can happen."

Crean said he told Jones at about the three-and-a-half-minute mark, when he put him back in the game, that he needed Jones to step up and be a senior leader.

"We just needed to get settled down, and the rest of the time he really did a great job of that," Crean said. "At the end, with that timeout at the free throw situation, we knew they had fouls to give so we weren't going with our conventional five seconds to go full-court play.

"We wanted to break long but get Verdell the ball if we couldn't hit anybody long."

Zeller talked about the final possession of the game from his viewpoint.

"We were just trying to make a play," Zeller said. "Verdell hit C Wat, and I was just trying to get a good offensive rebounding position and when I saw it go through it was a pretty incredible moment. "But we wanted to get the ball to Verdell and have him make a play and that's what he did. He made a pretty unselfish play."

Zeller said the screen he set on Teague was called in the huddle at IU's final timeout. He said the idea was that he would set a screen to

Verdell Jones III hits a shot against Kentucky in December 2011.

try to get Verdell open if IU wasn't able to make the long pass down court.

Another point Zeller made was that IU's experience against North Carolina State a few weeks before, when the Hoosiers had trailed late in the game and then came back to win, helped against Kentucky when the Wildcats made a late run, erased a 10-point deficit and took the lead.

Crean said there's no doubt that the N.C. State game helped in that regard but he said you could go back even farther than that.

"I don't think there's any question, but I can say going back to the Indiana State scrimmage has helped these guys," Crean said. "Everything is a very good experience for them whether it's a plus or whether it's a minus. It's all in the way that they learn from it.

"And their week of concentration and focus was at a high, high level. If anything, I didn't think we were overanxious to play. They were very mature."

Crean said he thought Assistant Coach Tim Buckley said it the best.

"I said to Tim, 'I hope they're enjoying this,' and he said, 'If they were giddy, they might not believe they could win,'" Crean said. "He said, 'I think they believe they're going to win.' And I think that was a great mindset that our team carried throughout the week.

"And I think games like N.C. State helped that happen because the way we won. Our guys knew what it was going to take to win, and we didn't always do it, but we had the ball last."

Crean then spent a few moments talking about Watford and how he knew that his junior forward was going to play a big role in the outcome of the Kentucky game. He obviously didn't realize just how big Watford would be, but he knew for Indiana to have a chance that the play of Watford would be critical.

"I was only upset with him one time all day, and that was when he took a challenged three and they got a piece of it," Crean said. "We knew that we had some matchup problems, but we also felt that they might have one with him. And he needed to be utilized in a lot of different ways. You go back to last year, and he's one of our best 3-point shooters. And when it became harder for Jordan last year after Verdell was out for a little bit and after we lost Mo (Creek), Christian continued to make 3-point shots."

But Crean said Watford played a complete game that went beyond *The Shot* that decided the outcome.

"He made plays at the rim, he made plays in the pull-up, he made plays in the post, he made plays on the glass, and he made four 3's," Crean said. "You can't win games like this without your best players really bringing it, and he did."

Chapter 2

In the days that followed Indiana's monumental victory against Kentucky, many scribes from Indiana and across the nation weighed in on IU's accomplishment.

Here's my description in my game story that ran Sunday, December 11 in the *Indianapolis Star*.

BLOOMINGTON, Ind. – Christian Watford said he had no idea why he was that open. Maybe Kentucky forgot about him, he said.

He didn't care. All that mattered was that his 3-pointer from the left wing as time expired hit nothing but net and lifted Indiana to a stunning 73-72 victory over No. 1 Kentucky on Saturday before a frenzied capacity crowd of 17,472, many of whom rushed the floor at game's end.

As Watford stood on the scorer's table and surveyed the crowd, he said he was flooded with emotions.

"It's just indescribable. All I know is I saw Verdell (Jones III) driving and I just tried to loop behind him. He did a great job of finding me and I knocked down the shot,"Watford said.

Then he tried to dodge the mass of humanity. Eventually, he found a safe haven on the scorer's table, which was like an island in the sun. There, he stood with Jones and Will Sheehey, soaking up the moment.

His father, Ernest Watford, leaned against the scorer's table as Indiana students celebrated in the background. He said he knew the shot was in when it left his son's hands.

"I could tell it was down; there was no doubt in my mind," Ernest Watford said. "This is the reason we chose Indiana and came up here from Alabama. We've been through some really tough times, but now all of the hard work is starting to pay off."

Watford had a season-high 20 points and hit 4-of-6 3-pointers. Defensively, he limited Terrence Jones – Kentucky's leading scorer with a 15.0 average – to four points, just three attempted shots and helped to force Jones into committing six turnovers.

Indiana (9-0) knocked off a No. 1 team for the first time since the 2002 NCAA Tournament when the Hoosiers defeated Duke 74-73 in the Sweet Sixteen. The last time Indiana beat a No. 1 team at Assembly Hall was in 2001, when Kirk Haston hit a 3-pointer from the right wing to lift the Hoosiers to a 59-58 victory over Michigan State.

ℰ℧ ℭ℥

Indianapolis Star columnist Bob Kravitz wrote this in his column that ran on A-1 in Sunday's *Star*.

The calendar said Dec. 10, 2011. The calendar lied.

Inside Assembly Hall, on a day when Hoosier Hysteria was restored to something akin to its former glory, it felt and sounded like the 1970s or 1980s, when Hoosiers hoops was king.

On this night, Indiana University basketball dramatically, demonstrably announced its return. After all the crushing blows, after Kelvin Sampson destroyed the program, after Tom Crean struggled through three years of losing with under-manned rosters, the Hoosiers returned to national relevance with the kind of performance, the kind of finish, that will not be forgotten.

IU 73, No. 1 Kentucky 72.

Welcome back.

"I'm speechless," said Victor Oladipo, who is rarely left without words.

"Ridiculous," said Jordan Hulls, who grew up in Bloomington and knows a little bit about IU basketball. "A ridiculous atmosphere."

"Biggest moment of my life," said Christian Watford, whose exclamatory buzzer-beating 3-pointer brought the students streaming onto the court. "It's indescribable."

"That's one of those moments everybody is going to remember," said IU coach Tom Crean, still drying off after a tub of water was dumped on him by players and members of his staff.

This was one of those you-had-to-be-there kind of days. TV couldn't do it proper justice. The fans showed up early — like on Tuesday. And they stayed late. By the time you read this, they may still be celebrating on the Assembly Hall court, which they rushed like a bunch of kids being let out for recess.

The coaches and players did this, but they were pushed along on a wave of fan ardor. When Crean took the job and asked why he would take over a program in such a wretched state, he kept saying, 'It's Indiana.' On Saturday against Kentucky, it was Indiana, the kind of game, the kind of atmosphere that used to be commonplace back in the good old days.

"This is the reason I came to Indiana," Oladipo said. "I'm from Maryland, people ask me, why are you coming so far to a farm town?"

Hulls, the Bloomington native, chimed in. "C'mon now," he said.

Oladipo smiled. There was a lot of that going on Saturday.

"The first thing I'd say is, 'It's not a farm town,'" Oladipo said. "But it's Indiana. It gets old to say it, but it's the truth … It was so loud, my head still hurts. I need some ibuprofen or something."

Trailing by two points with 5.6 seconds remaining, the Hoosiers drew up a play called 'Cowboy' in the huddle and hoped to take the ball to the basket and get a tie. Maybe it would be Oladipo. Maybe Verdell Jones III. They wanted to attack, assuming all the while that Kentucky, with two fouls to give, would intentionally foul.

But as Jones brought the ball down, he was able to avoid the swiping hands of Kentucky's Marquis Teague. As Jones dribbled off the wing, he had a voice behind him.

"V! V!" Watford called.

Jones kicked it out.

"And the rest," Watford said, "was history."

How did they win this thing? Not with deadeye shooting; the Hoosiers shot just 43 percent although that's significantly better than anybody else has done against Kentucky's top-rated defense.

They won with toughness. They won with belief. They had more offensive rebounds than Kentucky, which is an extraordinary statistic. And they got balanced scoring — five players in double figures and one with eight points.

It's a long way from the days of Kyle Taber. The tough times make the good times even sweeter.

Someone asked Hulls: Jordy, after all the tough times you guys have been through, can you put a victory like this in some kind of perspective?

He smiled.

"No," he said quietly. "I can't."

They are coming up on finals week here at Indiana, but they might as well cancel those tests. When Watford's buzzer-beating 3-pointer fell through the net, students rushed the floor screaming and acting like they'd won a national title.

Somewhere in the middle of the madness, Watford was being mauled.

"I was afraid for him," Hulls said.

Good for them, for all those fans who refused to abandon this program through the leanest times imaginable.

Good for IU basketball, for the coaches and the players who spent three years getting their teeth kicked in by superior talent.

When the shot went through, Crean initially restrained himself, first making sure the replays confirmed that Watford's shot beat the clock. Then he joined the fray, found his family and friends, hugged and celebrated.

Finally he stopped, stood on the periphery, took a mental picture of the madness his team had just inspired — the players on the scorer's table, the students everywhere.

"When I was at Michigan State as a grad assistant, this was 1989-90 and we'd won the Big Ten title, and there was this picture of Tom (Izzo) standing back and watching while everybody was celebrating," Crean said. "And I thought that was the coolest thing. Sometimes you never really take the time to take it in. This time, I took two minutes to really take it in."

Take this snapshot and add this caption:

Indiana basketball is back.

ɞ   ȝ

Pete DiPrimio of the *Fort Wayne News-Sentinel* quickly addressed the significance of the victory in his story two days later.

Are the Hoosiers back?

The short answer is yes. The long answer will take a season — at least — to decide.

The aftermath of Indiana's stunning 73-72 upset of No. 1 Kentucky leaves a NCAA tourney return a likely reward.

Yes, we know there are a ton of games left to play, and if you've seen the last three seasons of basketball misery, you know nothing is sure except fans will pack Assembly Hall no matter what.

Later in the column, DiPrimio turned prognosticator. I can tell you from personal experience, this is always dangerous ground. Fans want predictions, but they also can't wait to tell you 'I told you so' when you're wrong. In 2007, I predicted that IU football would go 7-5 in the regular season, beat Purdue by a field goal in the last game, go to the Insight Bowl, and lose to Oklahoma State. Amazingly, all of those things came true. That prediction was made in August, and the bowl game was New Year's Eve.

My direct report at the time was Chris Wright, and he put something in the paper about it the day after IU was announced to be headed for the Insight Bowl. In the sentence below, however, he reminded people that *The Star*'s Nostradamus also the same day picked Illinois to finish 10th in the Big Ten, and the Illini were headed for the Rose Bowl.

The point is that prognostications can be of the hit-or-miss variety. Still, with IU at 9-0, DiPrimio made the following prediction. It should be revealed that IU's final record in the 2011-12 season would end up at 27-9 after a 1-1 record in the Big Ten Tournament, and the Hoosiers would garner a No. 4 seed in the NCAA Tournament.

Here's how DiPrimio closed out that column:

More big-time Hoosier moments are sure to continue. A look into the crystal ball (we know that's dangerous, but this is dangerous sports writing) suggests a 1-1 Big Ten tourney record, and an overall 26-7 mark that might earn the Hoosiers a No. 5 NCAA seed.

After that, the ball gets fuzzy.

Yes, they could mess this up by losing the hunger that got them here and return to basketball as you don't want to see it. But we're betting that won't happen. As Hulls said, "This was a huge game, but we have more big games coming up. It's another step in the process. We can continue to get better. We have lots of room to improve."

Jeff Goodman of CBS Sports.com gave a shout-out to Crean in his column the next day.

Tom Crean can celebrate however he wants after this one. He could be yelling and screaming buck naked in the lobby of Assembly Hall and it would be fine with me (OK, I take that one back).

I mocked the Indiana coach last season after he went bananas in the lobby of Assembly Hall following a home victory over Illinois. However, Saturday's victory against top-ranked Kentucky? Well, that's worthy of a full-fledged party well into the night for Crean and the Hoosiers.

This may wind up becoming a defining moment for the Indiana program in the Crean Era — one that had some fans and many around the country questioning whether the Hoosiers would be nationally relevant again.

Kentucky was more talented at every single position on the court, but Indiana took control of the game in the second half, and after blowing a 10-point lead, got a 3-pointer at the buzzer from Christian Watford for the 73-72 upset.

The Hoosiers showed mental resolve.

This Hoosiers team has officially turned the corner. They hadn't really beaten anyone of note until now (Butler and N.C State don't quite count) but should make their way into the Top 25 for the first time since Kelvin Sampson was running things and making illegal phone calls in Bloomington.

It was nice to see Assembly Hall rocking again because the fans in Bloomington are rabid — and are deserving of success. Indiana doesn't blow you away, but now Crean has enough talent and experience to compete with the big boys.

Tim Ethridge of the *Evansville Courier & Press* also said it was time to sing the praises of Crean.

For the past four years, there have been plenty of four-letter words uttered about the Indiana University basketball team.

Many were directed at Kelvin Sampson, the coach who left the program both under a cloud and in shambles. Others were aimed at in-state recruits who passed on a chance to help rebuild the Hoosiers, and at lousy luck such as the injuries that derailed Maurice Creek's promising career.

And last year, at least, Coach Tom Crean was a target, with fans complaining that the turnaround was taking too long, that players who stuck with the program weren't improving.

After Saturday's amazing 73-72 victory over top-ranked Kentucky, another four letters were bandied about — with cause — by students who crashed the court at Assembly Hall or filled the streets outside the bars along Kirkwood. How do you spell N-C-A-A?

This season, at last, it could be with red letters.

Pat Forde, writing for Yahoo Sports, also initially talked about Crean in his column the day after the win.

Tom Crean was navigating the back hallways of Assembly Hall in his characteristically quick stride as the tumult echoed from Branch McCracken Court.

It was mayhem out there — students flooding the floor and climbing on each others' shoulders, players standing on the scorer's table, middle-aged men dancing as the pep band kept playing and replaying every song in its repertoire. Glory-starved Indiana had shocked No. 1 Kentucky 73-72, and the old limestone building had come unhinged. The Hall rocked like it did back in the championship days — probably even crazier because it has been a good, long while since those days were here.

Back in the relative calm of the hallway, Joani Crean ran up alongside her husband and hugged him as he walked. They'd shared a public moment earlier amid the frenzy on the court, but this was a poignant, private celebration of a breakthrough point in the arduous rebuilding of Indiana basketball.

It lasted just a few seconds before the public caught up to the couple. There was a fan, startled to be face to face with the coach of the Hoosiers, who blurted out "Crean!" He got a high-five. There was Dick Vitale offering hugs to coach and wife. There was a fan seeking an autograph on his hat, and another seeking an autographed ticket stub, and another and another ...

Tom Crean signed and smiled.

Undoubtedly, some of these same euphoric people had been grumbling about the coach during his IU tenure. They saw a powerhouse program brought low, losing an unfathomable 66 games in Crean's first three seasons — them of them lopsided losses to the rival Wildcats. Spoiled by victory, they refused to reckon the full extent of the damage done by the Kelvin Sampson scandal — the probation, the scholarship cuts, the recruiting restrictions, the mass exodus of talent.

The impatient and impractical among them saw Butler going to improbable Final Fours and decided that Brad Stevens should take the short drive south from Indiana to Bloomington to replace Crean.

Today, Stevens' Butler team is 4-6 after Saturday's loss to Ball State. Crean's Indiana team is 9-0 and ready to roar back into the top 25 for the first time since 2008.

"This is a surreal experience," sophomore guard Victor Oladipo said. "... All the struggles we've been through to try to get the program back, to have a game like that and to win a game like that, it speaks for itself."

This moment doesn't just speak for itself. It primally screams that Indiana basketball is back, rebuilt with the sweat equity invested by Crean and his players.

"Our fans deserve that," Crean said. "They deserve to storm the court and stand on chairs and tables."

Fact is, they deserved to celebrate no matter how this one ended. The Hoosiers would be back even if Christian Watford's instantly famous 3-point shot hadn't swished at the final horn and stunned the Wildcats. In the ultimate prove-it game, taking on the most talented team in the nation, they led for all but 2 minutes and 25 seconds of the final 24:39. They were the more aggressive team. They clearly believed for a full 40 minutes that they could beat Kentucky — even as a double-digit lead melted in the final minutes.

"Our guys never wavered," Crean said.

So even if Watford's final shot had drawn iron instead of net, Indiana would have staked its claim to legitimacy. But that it went in drove home that declaration with a thunderclap heard 'round Hoopsworld.

It's early, but Watford's '3' has a chance to be the Shot of the Year in college basketball.

– –

Eamonn Brennan wrote this in his College Basketball Nation Blog at ESPN.com on Sunday, the day before IU would be ranked in the top 25 for the first time in forever.

Indiana is back. Consider this statistic: IU hasn't been ranked since March 10, 2008. That's, count 'em, 1,372 days — the longest stretch in school history — that the Hoosiers have existed outside the realm of college basketball relevance. Those days appear to be over. For IU fans, the inclusion will be deeply symbolic: Since 2008, when Kelvin Sampson's disgraced exit left Indiana with a crater where its basketball program once was, those fans have dealt with frustration and angst and nearly constant failure, at times wondering if the program would ever be relevant again. After Saturday's win over Kentucky, it is.

Is it just one win? Sure. But whatever happens with the rest of Indiana's season — an NCAA tournament berth looks like a lock now — IU still has a daunting Big Ten schedule to fight through first. It's clear Tom Crean has not only rebuilt this program but reinvigorated a long-dormant fan base. It's been a long time coming, more than 1,300 days, to be exact, but IU fans finally have something tangible to get excited about.

Ben Smith, who has been covering sports in Fort Wayne since 1986, wrote a column a few days later in the Fort Wayne Journal Gazette about how he was sitting in a bar late the night of IU's victory over Kentucky, watching the replay of Watford's shot shown for the umpteenth time.

He said the guy sitting next to him made the comment as the fans rushed the floor that they needed to act like they've been there before. Smith's point was that perhaps they had, but it has been so long ago and fans deserved that moment.

When you've hardly ever known the wilderness, the return from it becomes that much sweeter, Smith wrote. Home truth.

And so Saturday night was for 6-25 and 10-21 and before that, poor doomed Mike Davis, who courageously took on the impossible job of replacing a fired icon and was cruelly excoriated for not being up to the task. It was an in-your-face to Sampson, who ruined the program but couldn't, in the end, destroy it. And it was vindication for Tom Crean, who surely had no clue just how bad things were the day he arrived in Bloomington, talking on and on about candy-

striped warm-ups and how the reason he was here was because 'It's Indiana.'

As it turned out, it wasn't. But now, at last, it is again.

The Indiana of Bob Knight. The Indiana of Steve Alford and Quinn Buckner and Isiah Thomas, of Dan Dakich shuttin' down Michael Jordan and Keith Smart hittin' The Shot.

The Indiana of Christian Watford, hittin' The Shot, *Part Deux.*

Act like you've been there before?

Hey. They have.

So party on, dudes.

Many scribes attempted to describe the scene in Assembly Hall as Watford hit The Shot.

Kyle Tucker, the UK beat writer for the *Louisville Courier-Journal*, had this to say.

Three Saturdays, three epic games for Kentucky. Two weeks ago, the Wildcats' football team beat Tennessee for the first time in 26 years. Last Saturday, UK survived a thriller at rocking Rupp Arena, beating North Carolina 73-72 on a game-saving block by Anthony Davis in the final seven seconds.

And then came today. The packed house at Indiana's Assembly Hall surpassed a jet-engine-loud crowd at Rupp, and the Hoosiers delivered a stunning upset over the top-ranked Wildcats — by the same 73-72 score as UK's win over the Tar Heels. Weird, right?

It was a crazy (and deafening) atmosphere that only got more bonkers after Christian Watford beat the buzzer for the game-winning three-pointer. The fans here didn't just rush the court. They engulfed it. Not a single soul could fit. They were backed up onto the stairs and into the aisles.

At times the place shook. If you left without a headache, your noggin is made of iron. Mine isn't.

       ॐ   ॐ

Stephanie Kuzydym eloquently described the on-court celebration in a column for the *Indiana Daily Student*, IU's student newspaper. She wrote that as Watford hit his shot and the fans began to rush the floor," a decade of pent up frustration was freed onto Branch McCracken Court."

Fans sprinted. Some tripped and fell. Some were even trampled.

Members of the Big Red Basketball Band's first instinct was to protect their instruments from the chaos. They lifted their trombones and trumpets above their heads before dropping them to their mouths to play the fight song.

"We're No. 1," a fan shouted. "No. 1, baby."

Fans in the general admission seats became restless to join the party at center court.

They began jumping over the cinder block walls, using the scoreboard as a ladder rung.

More fans spilled over the edge. Policemen stood on the wood bleachers with their hands extended, catching fans as they jumped and sprinted the second their foot touched the wood.

"Careful," one officer said. "Here you go."

Once they hit the court, they slammed into one another in jubilation.

Fans poured across all avenues of the hall. A mother stood protecting her two young children, their eyes wide at the sight of what college basketball means to Bloomington.

Gray-haired men shouted. Friends hugged. Fans high-fived.

"We did it," a Hoosier alumna cheered before kissing her husband. "We're back."

The victory brought back an old feeling.

Saturday night brought back the faith that Butler basketball isn't what the state of Indiana should be known for.

This is Indiana basketball. It's the five banners. It's Martha the Mop Lady. It's the costumes and the candy stripes. It's the tradition.

After inheriting a program in shambles, Crean had now become the shepherd. At the edge of the court, the coach watched as the floor disappeared beneath a red sea.

Chapter 3

A few days after the victory over Kentucky, I caught up with two former Indiana players whom I believed would have a unique perspective on what the win over UK really meant. Brett Finkelmeier and Kyle Taber were the lone returning players on Tom Crean's first Indiana basketball team in 2008-09. They experienced the growing pains without ever enjoying the prize.

This is the story I wrote about them that appeared on Friday, December 16 in the *Indianapolis Star*.

Brett Finkelmeier watched the Indiana Hoosiers basketball game against Kentucky with a friend at a sports bar in Marco Island, Fla., on Saturday. He celebrated at his table like Hoosiers fans everywhere, as the significance of Christian Watford's game-winning 3-pointer began to resonate.

Indiana was back.

But the 24-year-old Carmel native is not your average member of the Hoosier Nation. Finkelmeier was a walk-on guard on Kelvin Sampson's final team. He and Kyle Taber were the only players who returned when Tom Crean inherited the mess that was IU basketball. Finkelmeier remembers the two IU basketball players who were needed simply to have more competition in practice, and the manager who had to play three games late in the season.

Sitting there watching the Hoosiers knock off Kentucky, he said he felt a sense of pride. He lived the rebuilding project on the inside. Now he was watching the transformation from afar.

"As I watched that game, I just felt like all of that time that we spent, it wasn't for nothing," said Finkelmeier, who was in Florida on winter break from the IU School of Dentistry. "I felt like that win just validated all of the work that has been done since the new coaching staff came in."

As the Hoosiers basked in the glow of knocking off the No. 1 team in the nation and being ranked in the top 25 for the first time in more than three years, Crean reflected on the journey.

He singled out the five current seniors — Verdell Jones III, Tom Pritchard, Matt Roth, Daniel Moore and Kory Barnett — who joined

Finkelmeier and Taber on his first team. He mentioned transfers Jeremiah Rivers and Devan Dumes, who were also there at the beginning.

"We had so many guys who worked extremely hard in the program," Crean said. "And as I've said so many times, none of them knew what they were really signing up for in the beginning, including us.

"I really hope those guys like Brett Finkelmeier and Kyle Taber are proud because we said through all those years that there was going to come a time when this gets turned around. And it's really special that our seniors, those who played on our first team, get to be a part of it."

Finkelmeier and Taber were members of the Eric Gordon-led 2007- 08 team that won 17 of its first 18 games and finished 25-8. That season, however, was marred by NCAA recruiting violations levied against Sampson that led to his resignation on Feb. 22, 2008.

By the time the 2008-09 season began, 12 of the 14 players and all but 1.6 points per game scoring were gone. Over the next three seasons, IU won 28 of its 94 games and had four losing streaks of nine games or more.

Taber, now an assistant basketball coach at Lake Forest (Ill.) College near Chicago, watched the IU-Kentucky game at home with his girlfriend, screaming when Watford hit the game-winner.

"I just felt a lot of relief when it was over, like finally something went our way," Taber said. "I would like to think the work we did helped out in some way, but I know this team has been working hard so all of the credit has to go to them."

Taber played just one season for Crean, coming to IU as a walk-on and earning a scholarship his junior season for Sampson.

"The best part of what they're going through now is they are finally getting the real Indiana experience, which is why we all went to IU in the first place," he said.

Fred Glass was hired as IU's athletic director early in the journey, his first day was Jan. 1, 2009. For the majority of Crean's first two seasons, Glass went on every basketball road trip to show those players they had the support of the administration.

"It was just unbelievable circumstances with which Tom found himself," Glass said. "I remember flying back from a road game where we got back late, and I got off the plane and I shook the hand

of every player, manager and coach on that team because I appreciated so much what they were doing for Indiana.

"These guys were just on this incredible journey sacrificing for Indiana. They were the ones who were asked to hold down the fort until the cavalry got here."

IU fans want to believe that IU's 9-0 start, top 25 ranking and win over the top-ranked team in the nation are signs that the cavalry has arrived.

"It has been a long ride, and we had a lot of difficult times where we felt like we were working hard and making progress but we just didn't see the results," Finkelmeier said. "But gradually the pieces have been added, and now it looks like Indiana has turned the corner again.

"It's nice to feel like I had a small part in helping it turn around."

֍   ֎

Indiana basketball has always had a family atmosphere, and an extended family when you think about all who have played and been a part of IU's storied tradition. The majority have fond memories of their experiences at Indiana and at the same time are protective of their program moving forward.

Bottom line: When IU basketball was down, the former players were down, too.

But when Watford hit that shot and IU basketball became relevant once again, former Indiana players everywhere rejoiced in that newfound success.

I talked to a good number of former players, managers and members of staff in the weeks and months after Watford's heroics against Kentucky. Everybody, it seemed, had a memory of the moment.

Dane Fife grew up in Michigan, his brother Dugan played for the Wolverines, and Dane is now an assistant coach on Tom Izzo's staff at Michigan State. But deep down, he'll always be a Hoosier.

Just one season removed from being the head coach at Indiana-Purdue Fort Wayne, Fife enjoyed his first season on a Big Ten bench. He admitted later that the atmosphere in Assembly Hall when IU hosted Michigan State late in the regular season was as crazy as he could remember it being. He said when IU plays Michigan State he wants the Hoosiers to lose more than any time he can remember. But when Indiana plays most anyone else, Fife still has its back.

As for the day of IU-Kentucky, Michigan State had a game that day, too. In fact, the Spartans were in the state of Washington, where they would take on Gonzaga later in the day. A side note is that Dan Dakich was the television analyst for ESPN on that game and remembers watching the Kentucky game there, too.

But as Fife tells the story, Michigan State was on the bus from the hotel to the arena, and the assistant coaches were keeping Tom Izzo up to date with how IU was faring against Kentucky as Izzo was more than a little interested in how his former assistant and good friend, Tom Crean, was doing. Unfortunately for Michigan State, the bus arrived in the closing seconds of the game, and everyone had to get off the bus.

"As we walked toward our locker room, we had to walk past the media hospitality room where there was a TV," Fife said. "While we did not stop to see why everyone was crowded around it, we did hear the subsequent roar a few seconds later when Watford hit the shot."

Fife said upon finding out what had happened, the Spartans had joy for different reasons.

"My Hoosiers had made me proud, Coach Izzo's friend had made him proud, and a fellow Big Ten team had made us all proud," Fife said.

Since that time, Fife said he's just happy to see the direction that Indiana basketball is moving in once again.

"I'm very happy knowing that the program and legacy of Indiana Basketball is back where it's supposed to be," Fife said. "My teammates and I worked very hard to preserve the work of those who came before us. And we fully hope that those after us understand the value of being part of something truly special and approach each day as such."

One of those teammates, Tom Coverdale, didn't see it live but did his best to follow the action on his phone. He was with his girlfriend in Chicago for a wedding and watched the first 10 minutes of the game in his hotel room. When they left for the wedding, he tried to follow the action on his phone. During the actual ceremony, his girlfriend told him he needed to put the phone away.

"I looked at her and she knew that was not going to happen," Coverdale said with a smile. "She laughed and allowed me to follow the game during the ceremony."

Coverdale said by the time he got to the wedding reception, there were about two minutes to go in the game.

"There were about four or five guys all following it around my phone and checking the score," Coverdale said. "When the score read that we were up by one after the 3-pointer, we all started cheering and high-fiving. So, I didn't get to watch it live, but it was still a great moment. I did watch the replay on Tivo the next day."

Coverdale said the Kentucky game made him feel like IU was headed in the right direction.

"I remember thinking that we are at least back to saying that we can beat anyone in the country on a given night," Coverdale said. "And that by itself was a big step up over where we had been the last couple of years."

Brian Evans was an IU All-American as a senior in 1996 when he averaged 21.2 points per game. He's the 10th-leading scorer in Indiana history with just over 1,700 points.

Evans said as he watched the final possession unfold with his father-in-law, he was still mad at Victor Oladipo for turning the ball over the possession before. He figured, especially with Kentucky having two fouls to give, that Indiana wouldn't even get off a decent shot to win. Even when Zeller set the screen at half court, Evans remembers telling his father-in-law that it was good that he had that kind of awareness, but it wasn't going to matter. IU simply wasn't going to get off a good shot. Evans was just mad that IU had an earlier 10-point lead and had given it all away.

"Then, as Verdell pitched the ball back to Christian, I recall glancing at the clock to see if he would get it off in time," Evans said. "As it went through the net, we both jumped up and hollered and screamed. After five minutes or so of high-fiving, watching the replay, and listening to Dickey V go nuts, I just felt so happy for our guys. I was so happy for Coach Crean, so happy for his staff, and I just had so much pride in Indiana Basketball."

Like a lot of Indiana basketball fans, Evans said that watching the replay today still gives him the chills.

"I'm just thrilled that our program is relevant again and proud of how our fans behaved and continued to love our ball club during those tough years we had," Evans said.

Landon Turner was, is, and always will be one of the special faces of Indiana basketball. Turner was a 6-10 junior starter on IU's 1981 national championship team that was also led by sophomores Isiah Thomas, Ted Kitchel and Randy Wittman along with senior Ray Tolbert.

Turner had really come on at the end of that season, and IU coach Bob Knight was certain that Turner would be one of the top picks in the NBA draft following his senior year.

But Indiana basketball fans know what happened instead. Four months after IU beat North Carolina to win the national championship,

Turner lost control of his 1975 Ford LTD on a wet road about eight miles east of Columbus, Indiana as he and three companions were headed to King's Island amusement park in Cincinnati. The other three people in the car would escape without serious injury, but Turner was paralyzed from the chest down.

More than 30 years later, Turner is still a fixture at Indiana basketball games. He's a popular friend to the program and is often positioned courtside in his wheelchair to watch his Hoosiers play. He said he gets to about five or six home games a year and when not there he is always watching in his home. He went to a lot more games when Coach Knight was still at IU but tries to get there in person as much as possible still today.

That was the case on December 10, 2011 when IU played Kentucky. Turner was at the game with a friend and was positioned under the basket where Watford was attempting *The Shot*.

"When the ball left his hand, I remember thinking to myself, 'That shot looks good,'" Turner said. "And then it was all net. The crowd was unreal and exciting. It reminded me of the old days when I was playing."

Turner said the 2011-12 IU basketball team made him proud.

"They played hard, and I recall thinking to myself that IU is back from the dungeon," Turner said. "It's time to start putting banners in the rafters again. Watford's shot gave that team great confidence that they could achieve and beat any team in the country."

One of Turner's IU teammates was All-American Randy Wittman, now the head coach of the NBA's Washington Wizards.

Wittman didn't see *The Shot* live, as the Wizards were in the middle of a training camp practice as the team was just coming out of the NBA lockout.

But that doesn't mean he wasn't being apprised of all that was happening. Wittman's daughter, Lauren, was a junior at IU and was at the game at Assembly Hall. At the end of the game, she sent her dad a video from her IPhone of the final play and of the fans storming the court.

Wittman also had a little friendly wager on the game as well. One of his players was former Kentucky standout, John Wall.

"Of course, after practice we all went up and watched the replay of it together," Wittman said. "Knowing my daughter got to see it live and was right in the middle of such a great moment was pretty cool."

Wittman said it's a satisfying feeling knowing that the basketball program is heading back in the right direction.

"It takes years to build the history and tradition that we have at Indiana, and I am extremely proud to be a part of building that," said Wittman, a member of the 1981 national championship team. "You just hope the people involved will never forget this because it doesn't take very long to destroy a tradition like that, as we all witnessed first hand. But I think all IU fans are just happy that the program is back in good hands, too."

Lance Stemler, who played two seasons at Indiana and was on both of Kelvin Sampson's teams, is now an assistant varsity basketball coach at Providence High School in Clarksville, Indiana, located between New Albany and Jeffersonville just north of the Ohio River. With a school in that locale, you're going to have a lot of fans from both Indiana and Kentucky. And the trash talk the week before the game is usually at a pretty high level.

"I was actually watching the game in the athletic director's office at Providence High School before our game," Stemler said. "Our team was warming up, and a crowd had built in the office watching the last few minutes of the game. It was nice to get to watch it alongside UK fans. When Christian hit the shot, the IU people went crazy, and they announced it in the gym to a long ovation."

Alan Henderson, an All-American for the Hoosiers in 1995 and the sixth-leading scorer in IU history, watched the game from his home in Naples, Florida. Henderson, who has retired after playing 12 seasons in the NBA, is now a stay-at-home dad. He has four children under the age of five.

"I was down here in south Florida, and I think one of my babies was taking a nap and I was able to settle in and watch the game," Henderson said in a phone interview in June of 2012. "It was a very exciting game, and you could just feel the emotion through the television. It was just a great win for the program. I know how hard those guys had been working for that."

Henderson said he doesn't get back to Bloomington, much but when he does, he always feels extremely welcome by the current staff. He said in the summer of 2011 he stopped by, and trainer Tim Garl gave him a tour of the Cook Hall practice facility.

"I think the thing I like most about IU basketball right now is that Coach Crean has really made a great effort to do it the right way," Henderson said. "And I think that's what makes most of the former players the proudest because we know Indiana basketball is being run the right way. As players, that was the only way we ever knew it was supposed to be done."

Eric Gordon, whose single season at Indiana coincided with Kelvin Sampson's final year with the Hoosiers in 2007-08, said he was in Los Angeles in December 2011 playing for the NBA's Los Angeles Clippers and watched the IU-Kentucky game live in his apartment.

"That was a big shot," Gordon said. "When they beat Kentucky and they had already beat N.C. State, that's when I knew they were going to be pretty good for the rest of the year. That showed me that they could beat anybody. When you win one of those kinds of games, you're never sure. But when you start beating good teams on a consistent basis, that's when you know you might have something special."

Dean Garrett, a member of Indiana's 1987 national championship team, watched the game from Las Vegas, which should be no surprise, since he is a manager in the Sportsbook at the Flamingo Hotel and Casino.

"I was lucky enough to watch the game with 20 IU fans and about 10 Wildcats fans," Garrett recalled. "When that shot went in, the entire Sportsbook burst into a loud roar. It was a great feeling."

Garrett was always hopeful that after what happened in the Kelvin Sampson years, the Hoosiers would be able to bounce back quickly.

"Being a true IU fan, I'd always hoped that the day would come sooner rather than later," Garrett said. "And soon I could turn on the TV and be proud of what I was watching again. The hiring of Coach Crean has allowed me to once again be proud to be a Hoosier."

Michael Lewis is Indiana's all-time assist leader and co-holds the school record for most assists in one game with 15. Lewis was an assistant coach at Butler in December 2010, and the Bulldogs had played a game earlier in the day at Ball State and afterwards he went out to recruit.

Lewis said because of that he didn't see the Kentucky game live, but when he walked into the game he was watching, several people stopped him and told him all about the shot. He said the first time he actually saw it was on ESPN's "SportsCenter" later that night.

"I was happy for the program, no doubt about it," Lewis said. "Anytime you beat Kentucky, it's a good day."

John Laskowski has been a familiar face at Indiana for nearly 40 years. He played for Bob Knight from 1973-75 and through the years has worked in the alumni office and has covered IU games on television as the play-by-play announcer.

He was in attendance at the Kentucky game that day with his 25-year-old son. He normally sits in the locker room during games with the managers who are taping the games for review by the coaches afterwards. He likes to do that so he can listen to the announcers and pick up on what they're saying. He said by doing this he can compare the announcer's remarks against what he would say if he was doing the game.

He said when the games are close, though, he likes to be courtside to feel the real emotion of the game. Against Kentucky he was with the managers in the back until the final 30 seconds. He was standing on the court next to where the IU team comes out from the locker room.

"When the shot went in the place was absolutely crazy," Laskowski recalled. "Students came on the floor from all directions, as they should have for such a great win. I stayed there courtside watching the pure joy in the IU players' faces, knowing what a great achievement that they had just accomplished.

"People kept coming down on the floor for 15 minutes after the game ended. The players didn't want to go in the locker room, and the fans wanted them to stay out there with them. That win was just a huge turning point for the program when they finally realized they were ready to play the best."

Laskowski said the scene in the locker room later was as happy as he has ever seen it. He said there were lots of hugs and happy faces with congratulations all around. He said Tom Crean then gathered everyone for a group prayer as he does after every game. These guys had a lot to be thankful for that day.

Bryant Mosbey was an IU manager from 2003-06. If ever there was a guy who bled the Crimson and Cream, it was Bryant. He was well respected by coaches, players and his fellow managers.

He and his wife, Alex, were with some co-workers at Buffalo Wild Wings in Evansville the day of the Kentucky game. That night was his Thompkins Middle School faculty Christmas party, where he's the eighth grade basketball coach. He said the bar was packed with 99 percent of the patrons being IU fans.

"As soon as the shot went in, the entire bar went absolutely crazy, but I stood there for a moment to take it all in," Mosbey said. "I turned to my wife with a tear in my eye that only she could understand. She had heard me talk about my time at IU with such proud memories even thought it was not always the best of times when it came to wins and losses. After she gave me a hug, I was able to fully let go. I began hugging and slapping high-five's with everyone around me."

But Mosbey said the best part came a few minutes after Watford's shot went in.

"Someone in the bar yelled if anyone knew the IU fight song," Mosbey said. "I immediately stood up on top of my stool and led 150 of my newly formed closest friends in the greatest song ever written."

Will Finch was also a manager at IU through the 2007 season. He is now a graduate manager at Marshall. Finch said he watched *The Shot* live, and he remembers a feeling of complete nervousness in the final timeout.

"I wasn't sure who was going to get the last shot," Finch said. "I thought Verdell, but it didn't surprise me when he pitched it back to Christian."

He said he knew the shot was in when it left Watford's hands. He said when the ball went through the net, his phone started ringing immediately.

"The Twitter world went nuts, and every one of my colleagues in the college basketball coaching world started calling to say, 'Did you just see that?!?!'

"What a shot, and it couldn't have happened to a better kid. I have only met Christian a couple of times, but friends of mine who are still in Bloomington say he is a great kid. I was really happy for him."

Kyle Hornsby knows what it feels like to knock down big 3-point shots both at Assembly Hall and in an Indiana uniform. His junior season in 2002, when Indiana went to the national championship game against Maryland, the guard from Anacoco, Louisiana made 72 of 161 shots from beyond the 3-point arc. He made four of eight against Maryland in the title game and four of five against Kent State in the Elite Eight victory in Lexington that sent the Hoosiers to the Final Four.

Now in medical school at Duke, Kyle and his wife, Whitney, remember the IU-Kentucky game very well. It was the night of the Duke internal medicine Christmas party at the Washington Duke Inn.

"I had already gotten ready with shirt, tie, slacks, etc..., and another married couple came over to watch the game with us at our apartment," Hornsby recalled. "They both had graduated from Purdue. They were rather ambivalent for most of the game, but I was acting like a maniac the entire game. By the end of the game, Whitney and I were going nuts and the Purdue fans were cheering for IU as loud as I was."

And then Watford hit *The Shot*.

"When the shot went down, I'm sure the whole apartment could hear us," Hornsby said. "I was actually hugging Purdue fans after the shot went down!"

Hornsby said *The Shot* returned IU basketball to a lofty status once again.

"Even at that time, I knew there was still a lot work to do and that this team had a lot of areas to improve upon, but it let the country know that Indiana was ready for the national stage again," Hornsby said. "As a side note, I think the NC State game was a pivotal game for that team, because it gave them confidence winning a close road game against a good team. Without it, I'm not sure if they beat UK.

"I was so proud of those kids, the coaches, and the fans. I was proud to be a Hoosier. We have such a distinguished tradition, and it was so painful to watch guys play their hearts out but with very little success."

Hornsby said after the IU win that night, he decided to celebrate the Hoosiers victory in grand style.

"I took off my shirt and tie that night and put on my red IU polo with my sports coat, and I took off to the Christmas party at the Washington Duke Inn in style," Hornsby said. "I even shed the jacket for part of the night, but I wasn't a jerk about it. That was a night to remember."

Todd Leary, who played at IU from 1990-94 and was later IU's color commentator for several years in the radio booth with Don Fischer, had two tickets for the game. But he didn't want to have to choose which of his three boys to take. He tried to get two more but was unsuccessful and ended up giving them away and watching it on television.

He said when the shot went down it was complete pandemonium in his house.

"My kids were screaming and running around the house and I was yelling, too," Leary said. "We were all yelling at the top of our lungs. I remember thinking, 'I thought I was the only one in my family that acted that way,' but it was obvious my boys picked it up, too."

Joe Hillman, a member of the 1987 national championship team and an outspoken critic of the Kelvin Sampson hire from Day 1, was at his 10-year-old son Jack's hockey game and didn't see the Kentucky game live.

He said he was following it on his phone, and though it was a big win, he was a little surprised at the reaction of those around him when *The Shot* went down.

"Everyone looked so surprised and I was thinking, 'This is IU. You're supposed to win these games at home,'" Hillman said. "I was just really happy for the seniors and the coaches who have put so much effort to get IU basketball back to where it's supposed to be."

Mike Roberts came to Indiana to play for Bob Knight but ended up playing four seasons for Mike Davis. Since leaving IU he has been an assistant college basketball coach at California and Rice, and he most recently took a job as the associate head coach at North Carolina Greensboro. He also spent a season at Texas Tech as a graduate assistant under Knight.

The day Indiana played Kentucky, Roberts was on a recruiting trip in Dallas while still on the staff at Rice. When Watford's shot went in, he said he received about 30 texts from friends. When he watched it on his DVR the next day he said it gave him goose bumps.

"It made me think back to the shot that Kirk (Haston) hit to beat Michigan State when they were No. 1," Roberts said.

Roberts said the first thing he thought about when IU started having success again in the 2011-12 season was how happy he felt for the players, fans and all alumni.

"I'm mostly happy for the players," Roberts said."Because when you aren't winning at IU, life is miserable."

Roberts said he enjoyed watching Indiana play.

"I am just happy to watch a team that plays unselfishly, and the guys seem to be in it for the right reasons," Roberts said. "The teams I was on early in my career took great pride in playing the right way and playing in a manner that would make the former players proud. Many of us grew up as IU fans, and even if we weren't great players, we took our roles seriously and were 100 percent committed to helping the team win. I see that with last year's team and that is encouraging."

Another person was inundated with text messages, first during the game and then later when it was over, was former IU manager and administrative assistant Dan Block. Block graduated from IU in 2001. He recently moved back to New Albany, Indiana, but on the day of the Kentucky game was living in Jacksonville, Florida, and watched the game with his wife there.

"At first the texts were from IU players and fans," Block said. "But then they started coming in from friends of mine. And most were saying the same thing, that college basketball is better when Indiana is relevant again."

Todd Meier, one of the three seniors on the 1987 national championship team, was another former player who was in Assembly Hall that day. He was sitting courtside with a booster friend, Jay Asdell, from South Bend. He said he went to the pre-game event at Cook Hall, and he remembers how amazing it was to see the long line of students wrapped around the building.

Meier said one of the ways he knew Indiana basketball was back in 2011-12 was simply the reaction from many to the program as the journey played out.

"I can tell you the pride level for me went up exponentially," Meier said. "I knew we were on our way back when I heard people complaining about how we could have played better, even when we won. It was just like the good ole' days. That was quite a difference from the last three years when we were just hoping we could even compete."

Dusty May spent three seasons at IU as the video coordinator and administrative assistant under Mike Davis from 2002-05. He later was an assistant coach under Davis at University of Alabama at Birmingham and is currently an assistant at Louisiana Tech.

When IU played Kentucky, Louisiaina Tech was in Hattiesburg, Mississippi, for a game against Southern Mississippi.

"I was able to watch the first half in the hotel," said May, an IU graduate. "My wife and oldest son were texting me updates on the way to our game and I didn't find out about *The Shot* until after our game was over when I checked my phone again. When I saw the highlights, I was amazed at the overall scene more than the shot. I have to admit it felt good knowing that Indiana was really back."

Another teammate of both Hornsby and Fife on that 2002 Indiana team was Jarrad Odle. Odle was a senior forward on that team. He said he watched the IU-Kentucky game live and felt good when Watford's shot went down.

But he said as bad as things got for the Hoosiers under Kelvin Sampson, he always felt that IU would bounce back. And he expected it to be in short order.

"It is always important to learn from the past, but all of us knew the negative years would be short lived," Odle said. "I always felt like Indiana was on the right path, but big moments like beating No. 1 always help speed up the process."

Eric Gordon echoed Odle's sentiments in many ways. He said he didn't expect IU basketball to be down for long, and so seeing what *The Shot* would eventually lead to with the 2011-12 team was not a big surprise.

"I think from the perspective of a former player, you just felt like once Tom Crean got his players on the floor that everything was going to work out," Gordon said.

"Indiana is the kind of program where you expect them to always be on top. So I thought this was about the time they could possibly be turning things back around."

One interesting observation wasn't turned in by a former player, manager or member of the coaching staff. Instead, at the time of *The*

Shot IU athletics media relations director J.D. Campbell was seated in the front row just a few seats down from the end of the IU bench.

I figured Campbell wouldn't have had much time to really enjoy the moment. He would have had to worry about the post-game interviews and the other logistics associated with winning such a big game on a national stage.

"I just watched the shot go in and immediately jumped up and went three chairs down and hopped the bench to get by Coach," Campbell said. "I was about 15 feet behind him as he walked toward the UK bench. There was no doubt in my mind that the shot was going to count.

"My immediate reaction was to stay with Coach because I knew ESPN would want him. I didn't think there was any shot I could find Christian in the mass of humanity. It seemed like 10 minutes had passed before we finally got him over to their broadcast position."

Campbell said at no time did he really think about the magnitude of the shot and what that might create in terms of work for his staff.

"I just tried to enjoy it," Campbell said. "When I watch the replay of the shot, it's like I wasn't even there. It's just another highlight that is burned in my mind, like Kirk Gibson's World Series home run, Doug Flutie's Hail Mary and Michael Jordan's shot to beat the Cavaliers in the playoffs. Those are all plays I remember watching on TV as they happened, and I feel the same way about the UK game."

IU radio play-by-play man Don Fischer, the longtime voice of the Hoosiers, had the memorable call on Watford's game-winning shot.

"Here comes Verdell Jones," Fischer said as Jones dribbled the ball across half court. "Three seconds, two seconds ... Verdell all the way ... Outside to Watford ... Three on the way ... Ohhhhhhhhh! It went in! It went in!

"And Indiana wins the ballgame. Christian Watford with a 3 and the Hoosiers have knocked off the No. 1-ranked Kentucky Wildcats. Unbelievable!"

It's a call that can be heard over and over with a simple mouse click and a YouTube search. It never gets old. And the excitement in Fischer's voice never wavers.

Looking back, Fischer is proud of the call. Generally his own worst critic, Fischer admitted that one's a keeper.

"I think what I was able to convey to the audience with that call was the surprise of the accomplishment, but more than that, it was the all of this hard work and all that this program had been through had finally paid off," Fischer said. "It was a surprise in the sense that the final shot would go down like that against a team of that magnitude."

Like many before have said, Fischer felt that when the shot went through the net, you just had a different feeling about Indiana basketball again.

"You just felt like this team was now for real," Fischer said. "Indiana basketball was back. When they beat North Carolina State, I think people thought this team is not bad at all. This is a pretty good Indiana basketball team.

"But I think the win over Kentucky really galvanized the opinion with a lot of people that this was a really, really good basketball team. It just put Indiana back into national prominence."

PART 2:
The Decline of IU
Basketball

Chapter 4

To completely understand the significance of *The Shot* and everything that Indiana basketball fans had been through, you need to comprehend the depths to which the program had slipped.

When Tom Crean took the Indiana job in March 2008, he was asked why he would consider taking on a reclamation project like the one that was before him. Crean had a good gig at Marquette and was just a few years beyond taking that program to the Final Four. A lot of people were surprised when Crean opted to leave Marquette for a program that was in shambles.

But Crean was steadfast in his belief that Indiana could be a top-level, storied program once again. His sound bite and quote have been, to some, overused. To others, it's a cliché. But to the die-hard Indiana fans, it's a refreshing verbalization of the ideals in which many have come to believe.

Crean simply said, "It's Indiana. It's Indiana."

Which is why IU basketball fans had an even more difficult time watching their once-proud program get run into the ground.

This was Indiana basketball. It's a state institution. It's a religion in and of itself among Hoosiers everywhere. This wasn't some run-of-the-mill program that had never spent much time on top.

For most of its existence, Indiana basketball had become synonymous with not only success on the court but running a clean program off of it. All of the filth that existed in college sports happened in other places. Bloomington was isolated from it. The feeling was almost as if a force field surrounded the program, and nothing bad was going to be able to penetrate its walls.

Indiana, with the exception of a major recruiting violation in 1960, had always steered clear of NCAA violations and sanctions. In college basketball terms, IU was dressed in a spotless, clean, white linen. There were no blemishes or imperfections. When people thought about IU basketball, they may have thought about the crazy sideline antics of one of its larger-than-life coaches known for his red sweaters, but they also thought of the program itself as maintaining the highest of standards.

Simply put, IU basketball was squeaky clean.

Two coaching legends in particular had placed the Hoosier program on that pedestal.

Branch McCracken, who coached IU from 1939-43 and then again from 1947-65, had a record of 364-174 and a winning percentage of .677. That percentage still ranks among the top seven in Big Ten Conference history. Twelve times his teams finished either first or second in Big Ten play. He brought IU its first four 20-win seasons in school history. His teams averaged 18.5 wins per season, and he had 20 players during his time at Indiana take home All-American honors.

But McCracken is probably best known as the man who put Indiana basketball on the map. Besides the nearly 20 wins per season and the multiple players who earned All-American honors, McCracken also had IU ranked in the top 10 in the nation a total of 64 times.

Every IU basketball fan is proud of and talks constantly about the five national championship banners that hang in the south end of Assembly Hall. Two of those belong to McCracken. The man whom the floor at Assembly Hall was dedicated on December 18, 1971 led the Hoosiers to the NCAA title in both 1940 and 1953. In both of those seasons, he was named national coach of the year.

Marv Huffman and Bill Henke were All-Americans on the 1940 team and instrumental in capturing IU's first national crown. In 1953, it was an IU team led by All-Americans Don Schlundt and Bobby 'Slick' Leonard. Schlundt scored 30 points in the national title win over Kansas.

The other Indiana icon and living legend needs no introduction. Bob Knight, who roamed the IU sidelines from 1972-2000, is the single reason many IU fans became fanatical about the Hoosiers. His record at Indiana was 662-239, a .737 winning percentage. He coached 12 Big Ten most valuable players and won 11 conference titles. In 29 seasons at Indiana, the Hoosiers made it to the NCAA Tournament 24 times, the NIT three times and the CCA once. That's 28 postseason tournament appearances in 29 seasons. In 21 of his seasons at Indiana, Knight's teams won at least 20 games. And they were successful in the classroom, too. One of Knight's proudest accomplishments is that 98 percent of his four-year players at Indiana would leave with their degrees.

Moreover, Knight had the ability to keep the best Indiana high school players in the state. Evansville's Calbert Cheaney, both the Big Ten and IU's all-time leading scorers, had 2,613 points. In four seasons with the Hoosiers, Cheaney averaged 19.8 points. Steve Alford was second all-time in scoring for the Hoosiers with 2,438 points. The pride of New Castle, Indiana, had a career average of 19.5 points. Alan

Henderson, from Indianapolis' Brebeuf, is IU's sixth-leading scorer of all-time with 1,979 points. Damon Bailey, from Bedford North Lawrence, ranks seventh. Kent Benson, from New Castle, ranks eighth. Brian Evans is 10th, Scott May, 11th, Greg Graham, 12th, and Randy Wittman, 13th. And the list goes on and on and on.

And of course, it was Knight who was the Indiana head coach when the Hoosiers won their last three NCAA titles.

The first one came in 1976, when a team featuring the likes of Kent Benson, Quinn Buckner, Scott May, Bobby Wilkerson and Tom Abernethy finished a perfect 32-0 overall and 18-0 in Big Ten play. The Hoosiers beat Michigan 86-68 to win the title. That team is the last one in college basketball history to go undefeated and win the national championship.

In 1981, the Hoosiers led by Isiah Thomas, Ted Kitchel, Ray Tolbert, Randy Wittman and Landon Turner beat North Carolina to win the title. In the championship game, a 63-50 win over the No. 6 Tar Heels, Thomas scored 23, Wittman 15, and Turner 15. The '81 team was the Big Ten champions with a 14-4 conference mark.

The fifth and final NCAA championship came six years later when Steve Alford and company beat Syracuse in the Superdome in New Orleans. Keith Smart's baseline jumper in the closing seconds was the game winner. That team finished 30-4 and was the Big Ten co-champions. That Hoosier team knocked off Duke, LSU, UNLV and Syracuse in its last four games to win the title.

                                       ಔ   ಚ

Indiana basketball was known for all the right things. The Hoosiers always had a great home-court advantage, thanks in part to the 17,000-plus screaming fans at Assembly Hall. In the history of the building, which opened in the 1971-72 season, IU has had a record of 487-95.

Tradition is one of the things that makes IU basketball special and unique. For example, people outside the program don't really understand the candy-striped warm-up pants. They think that's yesterday and that IU needs to move forward into the next century. But Indiana players will tell you differently. As one class of seniors after another reflects on their time at Indiana, you will almost always hear someone reference what it means to put on those candy-striped warm-up pants. It's a tradition that is singularly Indiana, but it's a great example of one of the traditions that is germane to the program. And the fans cling to those traditions, too. Candy-striped warm-up pants are a big seller each season in the IU Bookstore or Varsity Shop in Assembly Hall.

Another tradition is not having names on the backs of jerseys. Where that was once a standard with schools, it has evolved to where most programs have the names of the players on the back of the jersey. Many point to today's athlete and say that they crave that kind of attention and recognition. They want to see their jersey with their name on it. They want everyone to know who they are. The Indiana way has always been along the line of there's no 'I' in team, or that you play for the name on the front of your jersey and not for the one on the back. But again, it has always been one of those traditions that you know will stay with the program, as long as the person running the show believes in the importance of it.

That was certainly the case in the Branch McCracken era, and it was clearly adopted by Bob Knight. Tom Crean has shown former players at every turn that he wants them to be involved in the program. He wants them to come back and attend practices. He wants them to come to shootaround. He wants them to speak to the team after a practice or before a game, and he wants them in the locker room when the games are over. Why? Because he knows that the former players built the program and the current players can only learn valuable lessons from those in the past.

As an aside, I remember Mike Davis once telling me that a carrot he used to dangle in front of his 2002 team was that if they won the national championship, he would let them put their names on the backs of the jerseys. As it turned out, that team made it to the national championship game and was leading in the second half before bowing to Maryland in the Georgia Dome.

I've always wondered if Davis would have followed through, or more to the point, if the athletic department, alumni and fans would have let him follow through and put names on the backs of jerseys. At Indiana, you don't buck tradition.

For a long, long time, that included not messing with the tradition of running a clean program that would win a good share of its games, make it to the NCAA Tournament every year, and make its fan base and alumni proud. When that went away for a brief period, the reaction and fall out that came with the transgressions were not surprising. IU fans weren't happy.

Bottom line: Indiana basketball is about tradition, and the keepers of that tradition did not appreciate it being altered.

80   03

Some in Indiana circles believe that IU basketball took its first major hit on September 10, 2000, when then-IU-president Myles Brand announced that Bob Knight had been dismissed as the Indiana coach.

After being placed on "zero tolerance" by the board of trustees earlier in the spring, Knight had an incident in early September when IU freshman Kent Harvey passed the legendary coach and said, "Hey Knight, what's up?"

Knight thought Harvey showed a lack of respect and told him so. He grabbed him by the arm and told him he should call him "Coach Knight" or "Mr. Knight."

The rest is history. The incident created a firestorm at a time when Knight was walking on egg shells because of the zero-tolerance edict. In the end, the Harvey incident was the final straw and one that not even Knight could ultimately rise above. A few days later, Knight was fired.

I always thought it was too bad because I looked forward to seeing how Knight would adapt to zero tolerance. If anyone could have pulled it off, it would have been Bob Knight. He would have walked up to and toed that imaginary line but never would have crossed it. I'm convinced of that. The biggest problem, however, was that no one really knew what "zero tolerance" meant. Did it mean that if he got two technicals and was tossed from a game, he could technically be on the way out? Or did it mean he would have to physically assault someone or cause an incident that brought the school and the basketball program more negative media attention? The latter is the more likely of the two scenarios, and ultimately that may have been what Brand and the others deemed he had done with Kent Harvey.

After Knight was fired, the players quickly rallied around assistant coaches Mike Davis and John Treloar and met with athletic director Clarence Doninger. Some said they would leave the program if the university didn't at least try to hang on to some sort of continuity by bringing back Davis and Treloar.

Tom Geyer, a walk-on forward, was the only one who left. He said he had come to play for Knight and couldn't see himself playing for anyone else.

A few days after the players rallied around the assistants, athletic director Clarence Doninger announced that Mike Davis would be Indiana's 25th head coach on an interim basis for one year. Davis was also the first African-American head coach in IU athletics history. Doninger had actually wanted Davis and Treloar to be co-head coaches, but it was Treloar who insisted that Davis get the head coaching title. Davis had previously worked for Treloar in a Continental Basketball Association coaching capacity, and Treloar felt it was time for Davis to experience being a head coach.

Looking back, Treloar probably had a pretty good idea of how intense the heat would be in the kitchen, too, but generally his act was looked upon as being a selfless gesture to his friend.

Two months later, Davis, with no previous head coaching experience, was guiding one of the most storied basketball programs in history. In his first season, the Hoosiers finished 21-13 and advanced to their first Big Ten Tournament title game where they dropped a 63-61 decision to Iowa. At one point late in that game, television analyst Billy Packer predicted that the final minutes and the outcome of that game could ultimately determine the next permanent head coach at Indiana. If the Hoosiers won, Packer thought Davis would be the man. If Iowa won, he thought Hawkeyes coach Steve Alford could be next in line to get the job. IU lost ,and Packer turned out to be incorrect in his analysis, much to the disappointment of a large segment of Hoosier fans who had hoped Alford might be the eventual heir apparent to Knight.

With the second-place finish in the Big Ten Tournament, IU was able to garner a No. 4 seed in the West Region of the NCAA Tournament in San Diego. In Davis' first NCAA game, IU bowed out in the first round, losing to Kent State.

Still, Davis had shown enough that first season to be named IU's permanent coach on March 21, 2001. That decision angered a lot of Indiana fans who believed that even though Davis had compiled respectable results, he had done so with Knight's players. And they believed that Indiana basketball was big enough that it should attract a higher level coach than Davis. And truthfully, there was a large segment who thought that the coach should be Alford. But Doninger believed that Davis had earned the right to take the program moving forward and he named him the permanent coach.

By the end of IU's second season under Davis, there were more and more people beginning to land on Doninger's side of the argument. IU's success in the second season had many believing that Indiana basketball could rise again to the top.

The Hoosiers went 25-12 and picked up a share of the Big Ten title. After getting to the Sweet Sixteen with wins over Utah and UNC Wilmington, IU knocked off No. 1-ranked Duke in Lexington to advance to the Elite Eight. A revenge win over Kent State from the year before moved IU to the Final Four in Atlanta, where it would face Oklahoma and coach Kelvin Sampson. Indiana won that game, too, and then played for the national championship against Maryland. The Terps posted a 64-52 win in the championship game, handing IU its first-ever loss in an NCAA title game.

Still, a feel-good season had Indiana basketball fans on a high again.

It didn't last long. Even though the Hoosiers won 21 games the next season and got back to the NCAA Tournament for a third year in a row, with Davis, fair or not, there was always a feeling that he couldn't do enough. Just like they believed in season number one, the Knight supporters claimed that Davis' NCAA run in 2002 had been accomplished with Knight's players. I, myself, always thought that opinion was a bunch of crap. Let's not forget the fact that Knight's players didn't do squat under Knight the last six years that he was on the job, losing in the first round of the NCAA Tournament four times and not making it to the Sweet Sixteen.

In Davis' third NCAA appearance he got to the second round but suffered a 22-point loss to a good Pittsburgh team. Little did people know at the time, but the wheels were close to coming loose in the IU program.

The next two seasons, IU struggled. The Hoosiers had a stretch in the 2004 Big Ten season where they lost seven of eight games and fizzled. IU would finish 14-15, suffering its first losing season since 1969-70. The next year, IU was barely better, finishing 15-14. The Hoosiers got an NIT berth but lost in the first round at home to Vanderbilt.

Davis' sixth season, the 2005-06 campaign, would be his last in Bloomington. On February 15, during a road game at Penn State, news broke that Davis would resign at the end of the year. The Hoosiers finished out the season strong, winning their final four conference games and eventually getting back to the NCAA Tournament in Salt Lake City. After a first-round win over San Diego State, IU lost to Gonzaga in the second round, ending the Mike Davis era.

While the 14-15 and 15-14 campaigns back to back likely spelled the demise of Davis, he still did some good things in his first six seasons as a collegiate head coach. He had a record of 115-79, a winning percentage of .592. His Big Ten record was 55-41. He was the first Indiana coach in school history to open his tenure with three seasons of 20 or more wins. He took IU to four NCAA Tournament appearances and one NIT, and he defeated 22 nationally ranked opponents in his time with the Hoosiers.

Most importantly, the thing that Davis would be remembered for is that he didn't leave the Indiana program in a worse place than where he found it. His final year, IU still played in the NCAA Tournament, making the second round.

The same thing would never be said of his successor, who in less than two seasons would bring Indiana basketball to its knees.

Chapter 5

In hindsight, there were three or four days in particular that would rock the Indiana program.

One was October 14, 2007, when the IU department of athletics announced a series of recruiting violations against Coach Kelvin Sampson and his staff.

Another was February 13, 2008, when IU disclosed that it had received formal notice from the NCAA that allegations of potential "major recruiting violations" had been raised against Sampson and two of his assistant coaches, Jeff Meyer and Rob Senderoff.

Nine days later, Sampson resigned and Dan Dakich was named the interim coach.

Still another dark day came November 24, 2008, early in the Tom Crean era of IU hoops, when the IU men's basketball program was officially placed on three years probation by the NCAA Committee on Infractions for the actions of Sampson and former assistant coach Rob Senderoff. The committee also accepted the university's previously administered self-imposed sanctions.

But there was one day, looking back, that was definitely the worst in terms of IU basketball history.

March 29, 2006.

That was the day Kelvin Sampson was named the new IU basketball coach. That was the day IU, with the benefit of that 20-20 hindsight again, climbed into bed with the grim reaper.

Many believe that Sampson's hiring was orchestrated in large part by then-IU President Adam W. Herbert. Sampson was believed to be Herbert's man from the beginning. Athletic Director Rick Greenspan also was involved in the decision and would later take the fall and resign his position after the NCAA delivered a "failure to monitor" charge against the university in its inability to keep its basketball coach under control.

Talk to the people in the know at IU, and most believe Sampson was much more Herbert's doing than Greenspan. The president wanted to make a splash hire with a big name in the college ranks. And apparently he was willing to do so at any cost. Forget that IU was known for graduating its players and Sampson had a pathetic track record in that respect. Forget that IU had been able to steer clear of the kind of muck that was part of Sampson's pedigree at Oklahoma. Forget that Indiana hadn't had a major NCAA violation in basketball in more than 45 years.

But Greenspan cannot be without blame, either. As one person close to the program told me after the fact, if Greenspan really felt strongly that Sampson was the wrong person for the job and felt it was completely Herbert's hire and not his own, he could have washed his hands of the hire, submitted his own resignation at that moment, and walked away. It would have been a gutsy play and potentially career suicide, but if Greenspan truly had major reservations it was a move he could have made.

My guess is there were times over the next few years that this is exactly what Greenspan wishes he would have done. Instead, by rubber-stamping the hire and moving forward with Sampson as his basketball coach, Greenspan opened himself up for the criticism that ultimately would follow.

Still, when I look back and do my own due diligence (one of Greenspan's favorite terms while the A.D. at IU), I always have one significant issue with those who say that it was Greenspan who was responsible for Sampson's hire at IU. Simply put, given Greenspan's body of work, it doesn't fit.

Think of these three names: Terry Hoeppner, Kelvin Sampson and Tom Crean. How do you hit tape measure home runs with two of them and be so incredibly wrong on the other? Especially when you are known for doing your due diligence. That is why I've always come to my own conclusion, with a little help from people on the inside, that Herbert was ultimately the person to blame for the Sampson hire.

But you certainly were never going to hear those kinds of words come from Herbert's mouth. The IU president never gave any indication, after the mess was allowed to occur, that the hire was anything but a mutual decision between himself and his athletic director. In fact, in many ways, Herbert threw Greenspan under the bus.

The IU president gave an interview with the *Jacksonville Times-Union* in late February 2008, a few days after Sampson resigned, and in his own words explained how the hiring had come about. Herbert claimed in the story that it was Greenspan who had initially had Sampson on a short list of potential candidates for IU's head coaching vacancy.

Herbert said Greenspan recommended hiring Sampson and that "I concurred with that." It was another way of saying, "This wasn't my idea, but ultimately I went along with it."

"We had every confidence that the letter and spirit of (Sampson's contract) would be met," Herbert said. "We had to have a pretty high comfort level (to hire him). My view at the time was, and still is, that when you have a chance to hire someone with his track record, and whose only offense was telephone calls ... When you look in the broader scheme of things, it was worth giving him a second chance."

But when asked again where the idea to bring Sampson to Indiana had been born, Herbert repeated that it was Greenspan who first came to him with Sampson's name.

"In this case, the A.D. developed the list of candidates to be considered," Herbert said. "He initiated the appropriate background checks. He hired a consultant to help us. No one knew who was on our final list of candidates. (Greenspan) went through the process of narrowing the list to three or four people, with the help of a consultant. Because of the significance of basketball in this state and the issue raised about NCAA sanctions (in Sampson's case), I asked two members of the Board of Trustees to review the process."

The two were Jeff Cohen and Stephen Ferguson.

Herbert said in the interview with the *Jacksonville Times-Union* that he knew it would "raise eyebrows" if Sampson were hired because of the baggage he would bring from Oklahoma.

While at Oklahoma, the university was investigated for three years by the NCAA for recruiting violations. In the end, the NCAA issued a report that cited 577 impermissible phone calls made by Sampson and his staff to 17 different recruits between April of 2000 and September of 2004. The NCAA also alleged that Sampson failed to adequately monitor his staff's telephone calls to recruits during that time and Oklahoma had inadequate monitoring procedures in place.

Still, eventually Indiana pulled the trigger and hired the coach with excess baggage.

The night before IU introduced Sampson at a press conference in Bloomington, there was a meeting in Houston, Texas. The site was chosen because it was considered to be an out-of-the-way place. At that meeting was Sampson, president Herbert, Greenspan and IU board of trustee members Cohen and Ferguson.

Ferguson said he spoke with Sampson that night for about an hour before having to leave because of a business obligation.

"My main message was, if he came to Indiana University, we have high expectations, and I said, 'I want you to understand that, and are you committed to that?' " Ferguson said in a story in the *Indianapolis Star*.

According to Ferguson, Sampson answered, "I understand what you expect."

Following that meeting, Herbert said he was confident that Sampson realized he would have no margin for error while at Indiana.

"We came away from that feeling like (Sampson) was someone who understood what he went through and wasn't likely to make that same mistake again," Herbert told the newspaper. " He cared about the young men who played for him. All his players loved him. The parents were appreciative of what he did for their children. All of us wanted to feel comfortable that (NCAA charges against him) was an aberration."

𝒮𝒪　𝒸𝒮

Sampson was then hired on March 29. He initially signed what was termed a "memorandum of understanding" offer which amounted to an agreement of terms. It was a seven-year deal with an annual base salary of $500,000 per season. There was also additional compensation on a graduated scale over the seven years of the deal.

In that initial memo of understanding, there was also a clause that said, "Notwithstanding the above paragraphs regarding compensation, it is understood that the NCAA will hold an infractions hearing in April or sometime thereafter, regarding certain actions by you that occurred at your current place of employment. If the NCAA imposes sanctions against you personally for those actions, or if the NCAA requires that your prior employer's sanctions against you be enforced, Indiana University shall impose those same sanctions against you. Such sanctions may have an effect on the figures set forth above, and by signing this Memorandum of Understanding you explicitly acknowledge and agree that the University may adjust the figures above to reflect the sanctions taken."

At the end of the memo, which had been written by Rick Greenspan, was this final sentence. "I have every confidence that you will lead our athletics program with integrity and pride, and I look forward to welcoming you as a member of the Indiana University family." The memo was signed by Greenspan, Sampson and President Adam W. Herbert and dated March 29, 2006.

Not everyone shared Greenspan's initial confidence that he had expressed in the memorandum.

Rick Bozich, the columnist for the *Louisville Courier-Journal*, said the day after IU hired Sampson that the one thing the hiring showed was that Indiana was no longer considered a top five job.

I once believed that when coaches thought about Indiana University basketball, they were captivated by the five NCAA titles, the galaxy of great players and even the candy-cane warm-up pants. A few even knew Bloomington was a place where players did not get paid but did get diplomas. I thought, let the Indiana job open and coaches would crawl for an interview.

Silly me. My record at predicting interest in the IU job is as bad as Kelvin Sampson's NCAA Tournament record.

In college basketball, the earth is officially flat. You can get to the Final Four from George Mason or from Indiana. There's no reason for a proven coach or a talented young lion to work at a place with warring fans, tired facilities, a lame-duck president and other warts. And that is how Mike Davis gets replaced at Indiana by Sampson, the former Oklahoma coach whom Davis beat on the way to the 2002 NCAA final.

A panic hire.

This is a hire that tells me Indiana is no longer a top-five basketball job. If Indiana is a top-five job, Indiana gets Thad Matta, Billy Donovan, Mark Few — somebody with national juice, not a guy whose recruiting tactics were starting to make people at Barry Switzer University nervous. Think about that.

This is a hire that tells me the best and brightest coaches simply could not get excited about the knotted intestine that is Indiana basketball.

Score Kelvin Sampson as a panic hire: Indiana's version of Rich Brooks. I do. In the coaching grapevine, word was circulating that IU athletic director Rick Greenspan was getting turned down more times than a high school senior with a 900 SAT applying to the Ivy League.

Coaches understand it will be years before the ill will about Bob Knight's departure truly subsides. The fan base is more divided than the Balkans. Coaches remember how quickly folks turned on Mike Davis. Michigan State, Ohio State and Illinois have become sexier jobs. No wonder coaches started asking: Tell me again, what's so great about this Indiana job?

So Indiana gets a coach who always wanted to get away from chinstrap mania as well as a coach who just, well, needed to get away.

I put together a list of 15 active NCAA Division I coaches who have made at least 10 trips to the NCAA Tournament. Eight have won the title. It is a list of elite names, including Mike Krzyzewski, Roy Williams, Tubby Smith and Rick Pitino.

One man on the list has a losing NCAA Tournament record. His name is Kelvin Sampson. His record is 11-12. And his past six tournament defeats have been to teams with inferior seeds.

Off-court problems, too.

Basketball issues are bad. Issues with the NCAA are worse. Sampson has issues with the NCAA. They will be formally addressed when Oklahoma meets with the NCAA infractions committee next month. It seems that Sampson and his staff made more extra calls to recruits than a 14-year-old with unlimited cell phone minutes.

I heard Indiana administrators say what Indiana administrators had to say: Sampson is a solid guy, nationally respected, who'll do things the right way at Indiana.

Those were sound bites they had to deliver. But if you look behind the sound bite, you'll remember this: Sampson was the first guy to find a spot for Rashaad Carruth after the serial knucklehead decided to transfer from the University of Kentucky in 2002. Carruth was gone before the season started. But if you're willing to take Rashaad Carruth, you'll take anybody. Rashaad Carruth is no Quinn Buckner. And Indiana University is no longer the top-five basketball job it used to be.

The day that Sampson was hired, there seemed to be as many questions raised about how the process had played out than about Sampson's qualifications to lead the Indiana program.

I had a story the next day that looked at just that.

In it, Rick Greenspan wouldn't say who was contacted, and IU president Adam Herbert only said that his athletic director chose the best person for the position. Board of trustees member Jeff Cohen, however, said Iowa coach Steve Alford, a former IU All-American, was indeed a candidate. In the same breath, he said another former Hoosier great, Randy Wittman, wasn't really considered.

"Alford was given serious consideration," said Cohen, one of two trustee members involved in the interview process with Sampson on Tuesday night in Houston. "I think Alford was a great candidate, too. As for Wittman, because he had not been a college coach and he has not been in the recruiting circle, I think that probably hurt him."

Cohen said even though he was involved in the search, Greenspan was extremely secretive.

"We never had a conversation about which candidate Rick Greenspan liked," Cohen said. "I gave him my opinion. I said, 'Steve Alford would be a great candidate.' I gave him my opinions. But it wasn't until recently that we had conversations about who was out there, who was available, who was interested, what our options were, that sort of thing. It hasn't been a very long time."

Cohen challenged a published report that Gonzaga's Mark Few was offered the job but turned it down. Cohen described that as "nonsense."

"No one was given an offer, from my understanding," Cohen said. "We wanted a big-time college coach. A proven winner that has a big-time track record, and I believe Kelvin Sampson is one of five guys who I would have been happy with as the basketball coach here."

Cohen said he's certain that IU inquired about Few's interest in the position.

"I'm sure he did. We inquired into a million guys' interest," Cohen said. "Was he a candidate that we talked about? Absolutely. Was he one of my top five? No."

Greenspan did not reveal names of anyone he spoke with. He said several candidates told him that if their interest was disclosed, they would withdraw from consideration.

"I think if I started selectively indicating who I spoke to and what they said and what they didn't say, I think I've hindered a part of the process," Greenspan said. "My charge was always to do this in a fair way and a confidential way. So I guess I'm not going to answer that because I don't want to get into a 'he said, she said.' I just don't do business that way."

Ken Beckley, president of the IU Alumni Association, said hiring an "Indiana guy" wasn't a top priority with most of his constituents.

"What I heard more than anything else from people was to make sure you hire the best person for the job, and I think that's what we did," Beckley said.

Phillip B. Wilson of the *Indianapolis Star* polled several former IU players to get their reaction to the news that Sampson was expected to be named the Indiana basketball coach the next day. A couple, legendary names like Isiah Thomas and Damon Bailey said they thought it was a good hire. Several players opted not to return calls. Two, however, did go on record as saying they were not happy at all with the decision: Ted Kitchel and Joe Hillman.

As Wilson reported in the *Indianapolis Star* at that point:

Kitchel, a starter with Thomas on the 1981 national title team, did not hide his disgust.

"It's an absolute disgrace," Kitchel said. "I wouldn't hire that guy to coach my fifth-grade girls team. That guy is absolutely what we don't want at IU."

He and Hillman snickered about Sampson's reputation for poor graduation rates, relying on junior college transfers and having a boring offensive system.

"I talked to several other people today and they're not overly thrilled with this choice," said Hillman, who played on the 1987 national championship team.

Many former players thought they would be consulted first, as was suggested in a recent e-mail sent to ex-Hoosiers from athletic director Rick Greenspan.

"I thought part of this was to bring the IU basketball tradition back together," Hillman said of Sampson, who has no ties to the state, "and I'm not sure this is the guy to do it."

Kitchel said Greenspan told him he would be called. Kitchel wasn't.

But Greenspan and other department officials called some former players, including Bailey.

"I did talk to Rick a few weeks ago and he wanted my input," Bailey said. "I told him I thought that whomever they hired, it had to be someone who embraced the Indiana University tradition.

"I also did tell him it didn't necessarily have to be an Indiana guy. I don't think it was a must."

Bailey said the coach needed to be experienced and a proven winner. Sampson has a 455-257 record and took the Sooners to 12 consecutive postseason tournaments. Bailey said he was looking forward to Sampson instilling a defensive toughness lacking in recent years.

"They wanted a big-name coach, and he's definitely a big-name coach," Bailey said. "But the bottom line at Indiana is you have to win, whether you come in with a lot of support or no support at all.

"Indiana is not a program that wants to be middle of the road. They want to be on the top tier in the country and I think coach Sampson can get them there."

Thomas, a National Basketball Hall of Famer, also considers Sampson the right man.

"Clearly, he's qualified," the New York Knicks president said. "He's done a good job and he'll do a good job in Bloomington. You can't question his coaching ability or anything. He's a solid choice."

Kitchel and Hillman said they thought former Hoosiers Steve Alford and Randy Wittman deserved a look. Both spoke to Wittman on Tuesday. They said Wittman's repeated calls to Greenspan to express interest in the job were not returned.

"I guess Greenspan knows a hell of a lot more about IU basketball tradition than any of us," Kitchel said. "I don't think this is a good coach and I definitely don't think he'll be a good coach at Indiana."

Bailey acknowledged a hire for such a high-profile job was bound to cause mixed reaction.

"Everybody is not going to be happy," he said. "You can only hire one coach."

Rick Bozich wasn't the only local columnist who was "underwhelmed" by the Sampson hire. *Indianapolis Star* columnist Bob Kravitz shared the same sentiment in his column the day after Sampson was given the IU reins.

I came to be wowed. I came to be inspired. I came down Ind. 37 hoping to A) avoid another speeding ticket and B) be roused out of my cynical stupor by a bravura performance from new Indiana University basketball coach Kelvin Sampson.

I honestly, truly, desperately wanted to come to this news conference − which inauspiciously started 20 minutes late − and be convinced that all my initial impressions of this puzzling and unexpected hire were wrong.

Can I be honest here?

I was underwhelmed. This wasn't a pep rally to incite and unite the Hoosier Nation. This was a confessional. IU's administration spent more time in a defensive posture than any of Mike Davis' recent teams.

Even the smattering of students who showed up at Assembly Hall − hey, shouldn't you clowns be in class? − had to be roused to action by athletic director Rick Greenspan, who awkwardly implored the crowd to "give (Sampson) a big cheer."

For a week, Greenspan's office had been contacting former IU players, Isiah Thomas included, asking if they'd come to Bloomington and show support for a new coach. Well, roughly 10 former players showed up, the most notable being Brian Evans and Greg Graham. There was no Thomas, no Kent Benson, none of the luminaries from the Hoosiers' glory days.

Perhaps the most notable absence, though, was Robert Vaden, who continues to insist he will leave IU and follow Mike Davis wherever he goes. The rest of the team was there — a bored D.J. White looked like he'd rather be in geology class — but Vaden made the loudest statement by saying nothing.

Now, in fairness to the IU brain trust, I was impressed by the level of honesty shown by school president Adam Herbert, Greenspan and Sampson. Even before the questions about NCAA infractions and graduations could be asked Wednesday, they struck pre-emptive blows, and Sampson in particular took full ownership of his NCAA-related missteps.

"That was a mistake that we made," Sampson said. "There really is no excuse. . . . I don't know that as a staff we took that rule seriously enough. I think if you look back at the compliance of our programs over the last 19 years as a major college head coach, we've never had an issue with NCAA rules, nor will we again."

As for whether those NCAA troubles will follow Sampson to IU, let's just say Greenspan has some connections in the NCAA offices (cough, Myles Brand, cough) who've told him not to sweat further sanctions.

Still, the administration is concerned, so concerned, in fact, Herbert said there are stipulations in Sampson's contract that address NCAA compliance and graduation rates. And talking to Greenspan after the news conference, he sounded like he was slapping Sampson with the dreaded zero-tolerance policy.

"Is it (the NCAA trouble) a red flag? Absolutely," Greenspan said. "If it was a chronic history during his career, absolutely I would be concerned, and I'm still concerned as it is. And I had to overcome that, as did other people. But he (Sampson) stated it: He made a mistake. He's not hiding it."

No, he's not.

But on the subject of graduation rates, he was hiding, using an old argument that no longer applies. Years ago, when Oklahoma was scoring painfully low graduation rates, the NCAA calculation penalized a school for losing a transfer who graduated elsewhere, and gave a school no credit for graduating a kid who transferred in.

Except the math has changed. Now, it is fair. Now, it does give credit to a school for taking in a kid and seeing that he graduates. And in the NCAA's first Graduation Success Rate, which looked at four entering classes of players, Oklahoma scored 269th out of 317 schools. During that same time span, IU ranked 26th with 91 percent. If the Hoosier Nation isn't celebrating in Dunn Meadow — and they're not; I checked — they have reasonable cause.

"I understand (the mixed reaction), I really do," Greenspan said. "And there are some aspects of his program which he needs to prove himself at a higher level, perhaps, to meet our expectations. . . . I decided, probably the second day after I got the job, that whenever this (basketball) job opened, there would never be unanimity. It's the nature of the job. There are a lot of viable candidates and a lot of people who would be interested in the job, and that's going to create factions.

"I'm not naive to think that everybody thinks this is an appropriate choice."

In the past, Sampson has been described as energetic and charismatic and capable of selling liberal politics to Hoosiers. And I'm sure, over time, when he's had a little more time to think and maybe get some sleep after a whirlwind weekend, he will rouse the Hoosier Nation.

Winning, I'm guessing, will help quite a bit.

For now, though, I am left with largely the same impression I had one day earlier: I still don't quite get it. And my sense is, I'm not the only one.

ଔ ଓ

On April 20, Sampson signed his official contract which had plenty of language aimed at making sure he wouldn't have any similar behavior at IU.

The terms of the contract read that IU "may take further action, up to and including termination" if the NCAA imposes more significant penalties or sanctions than the University of Oklahoma's self-imposed sanctions. The contract also gave Indiana the right to fire

Sampson without obligation if his assistant coaches committed serious or repeated NCAA rules violations.

Article 2.02 of the contract included the heading "Employee May be Disciplined for Violations of NCAA Rules or Regulations." That passage went on to read, "Without limiting University's rights as otherwise set forth in this Employment Agreement, if the Employee is found to be in violation of any NCAA regulations, the Employee shall be subject to disciplinary or corrective action as set forth in the provisions of the NCAA enforcement procedures, including suspension without pay or termination of employment for significant or repetitive violations."

The day after Sampson signed the contract, he and Greenspan attended an NCAA hearing in Park City, Utah along with officials from Oklahoma. The hearing focused on the impermissible phone calls from 2000-04.

On May 25, 2006, the NCAA Committee on Infractions issued Sampson penalties that prohibited him from making any recruiting phone calls or taking part in any off-campus recruiting for a period of one year.

The fact that Sampson had gotten into this kind of trouble while at Oklahoma was even more ironic given that at that time, he was the president of the National Association of Basketball Coaches (NABC). While he was heading the association, the NABC formed an ethics committee to address many of the problems college basketball faced.

On August 16, 2006, that same ethics committee sanctioned Sampson for his Oklahoma recruiting violations and gave him three years of probation.

For that one-year period, Sampson appeared to be living and existing under his new rules. On May 25, 2007, the NCAA sanctions were lifted after Sampson had completed his one-year penalty.

It only took four-and-a-half months, however, to reveal that Sampson's problems from Oklahoma were not the "aberration" that Herbert and IU had hoped they would be. On October 14, 2007, IU announced that a series of recruiting sanctions and corrective actions were being imposed on Sampson and his staff after finding further phone call violations.

The preemptive strike had been made just over a week before, when on October 3, IU sent the NCAA a report conducted by Ice Miller, a law firm that was hired by the university. According to that report, Sampson had made more than 100 impermissible phone calls while at Indiana that violated the recruiting restrictions he had while at Oklahoma.

In a letter from Greenspan to Shep Cooper, the NCAA's director of the Committee on Infractions, dated October 3, 2007, the IU athletic director wrote: "As you will see in the attached report, Indiana University has identified issues with the successful fulfillment of some sanctions. Specifically, the athletics department compliance staff recently discovered a number of phone calls that the university has decided, after a careful and thorough review, are contrary to the sanctions regarding phone calls. Indiana University takes these transgressions very seriously and has imposed a number of additional sanctions on the basketball program and on individual coaches, as noted in the report, to address any impact caused by the lack of total compliance with the sanctions and to send a clear message that absolute compliance is expected from all of its coaches and staff."

The Ice Miller report included this passage under the heading "Chronology of the University's Investigation."

"As described above, the university conducted regular checks of phone records throughout the year. On July 10, 2007, during the course of the compliance staff's additional year-end review of recruiting logs and phone calls for all sports, a compliance intern noticed that one men's basketball prospective student-athlete had been called numerous times, all permissible under NCAA rules. Upon further inspection of the phone records, the director of compliance noticed that on January 29, 2007, there were two calls made by assistant men's basketball coach Rob Senderoff from his cell phone to the prospect on the same day and that both involved a three-way calling pattern to a number that was ultimately determined to be the home number of the head men's basketball coach, Kelvin Sampson. The director of compliance then searched the men's basketball coaching staff's cell and office records for other three-way calls."

And the three-way-calling Indiana Phone Gate controversy had been born.

Later in the Ice Miller report was the following statement regarding three-way calls.

"Three-way phone calls are permissible under NCAA rules and university policies, including recruiting calls when multiple coaches are on the phone. However, due to Sanction 7 of the revised sanctions, which prohibited Sampson 'from making any phone calls that relate in any way to recruiting or being present when members of his staff make such calls' from May 25, 2006 to May 24, 2007, three-way recruiting calls involving Sampson were not permissible.

"Of the 27 three-way phone calls that occurred during the period of the sanctions, approximately 10 to 18 involved an assistant men's basketball coach connecting Sampson into a phone call with a prospective student-athlete or an individual involved in the recruitment of a prospective student-athlete (e.g. relative, coach). Indiana University has determined that these calls are contrary to the intent of Sanction 7 as well as a clarification received from the committee's staff prior to June 13, 2006, regarding the impermissibility of three-way calling."

In the report, however, IU also tried to put the infractions into perspective.

"Indiana University takes these transgressions very seriously and has imposed a number of additional sanctions, many of which are already in effect, on the basketball program and on individual coaches as detailed below, to address any impact caused by the lack of total compliance with the sanctions and to send a clear message that absolute compliance is expected from all of its coaches and staff.

"The University is disappointed and does not condone the actions of the involved coaches, but it is important to place this issue in context. The men's basketball coaching staff is involved in over a thousand recruiting calls a month,9 and three-way calls at issue here total at most 18 over approximately eleven months, a fraction of one percent of all calls."

So basically, despite being restricted from making any recruiting phone calls, Sampson participated in approximately 10-18 three-way calls with recruits that violated the terms of the sanctions against him. Rob Senderoff also made 35 impermissible calls from his home. Senderoff subsequently resigned his position.

Chapter 6

The entire situation had left a bad taste in the mouths of Hoosier fans who quietly kept their fingers crossed, hoping that no new allegations would surface. After all, Indiana had a team on the floor that it appeared could challenge for a Big Ten title.

Still, with a team that featured D.J. White and Eric Gordon performing well on the hardwood for the Hoosiers that season, there was a dark cloud hovering over Sampson and the program. Sampson always insisted "they're just phone calls." Privately he would tell people that it wasn't like he had paid off a player or anything that egregious.

Indiana opened the season with four wins before losing to Xavier at the Chicago Invitational Challenge at Hoffman Estates. That loss was significant because the Hoosiers would then go on to win the next 13 games, including opening Big Ten play with six consecutive wins.

All that time, rumors were swirling that the NCAA was about to come down hard on the Hoosiers.

On February 8, the university received a Notice of Allegations from the NCAA saying Sampson knowingly violated recruiting restrictions imposed for violations at Oklahoma, failed to deport himself at IU in accordance with generally accepted standards of honesty, and failed to promote an atmosphere for rules compliance in IU's basketball program. Specifically, the NCAA letter claimed that:

1. Sampson, assistant coach Jeff Meyer and former assistant Rob Senderoff failed to comply with the sanctions that Sampson was under from his troubled times at Oklahoma. Sampson and Senderoff were alleged to have participated in telephone calls at a time when Sampson was prohibited from being present or taking part when staff members made such calls.

According to the report, Sampson knowingly participated in three-way phone calls with Senderoff and prospects Yancey Gates, William Buford Jr., DeJuan Blair, Demetri McCamey and DeAndre Thomas. Futhermore, the report stated, Sampson participated in a three-way call that included Yvonne Jackson, mother of prospective student-athlete Devin Ebanks.

The report said that Sampson participated in the three-way telephone conversations despite receiving specific clarification from the Committee on Infractions that three-way calls were prohibited.

In addition, the report said that Sampson participated by speakerphone in recruiting calls made by Senderoff to Thompson and prospect Marcus Morris. It said Sampson was present during one or more recruiting calls placed by Senderoff to prospect Kenny Frease, in which Senderoff made phone calls to the student-athlete, then handed the phone to Sampson.

Similarly, when Senderoff was in the presence of DeJuan Blair, Ayodele Coker, DeAndre Thomas and/or their parents or legal guardians during off-campus recruiting contacts, he would call Sampson and then hand the phone to the prospects or their guardians.

Sampson also spoke with the mother of prospect Bud Mackey via Senderoff's cell phone while Senderoff was with her.

2. Senderoff and Meyer placed at least 25 calls to nine potential recruits, exceeding NCAA limits even if no sanctions had been in place.

3. Sampson "acted contrary to the NCAA principles of ethical conduct when he knowingly violated recruiting restrictions imposed by the NCAA Committee on Infractions." In addition, he "failed to deport himself in accordance with the generally recognized high standard of honesty normally associated with the conduct and administration of intercollegiate athletics by providing the institution and the NCAA enforcement staff false or misleading information." Finally, it stated in the report that Sampson "failed to promote an atmosphere for compliance within the men's basketball program and failed to monitor the activities regarding compliance of one or more of his assistant coaches."

4. Senderoff "acted contrary to the NCAA principles of ethical conduct when he knowingly violated recruiting restrictions imposed by the NCAA Committee on Infractions." It said that he "failed to deport himself in accordance with the generally recognized high standard of honesty normally associated with the conduct and administration of intercollegiate athletics by providing the institution false or misleading information."

5. Sampson and Meyer engaged in an impermissible recruiting contact with recruit Derek Elston during a two-day sports camp held at Assembly Hall on June 30 and July 1, 2007. During that

event, Meyer told Elston's high school coach, Travis Daugherty, that Elston would be receiving a scholarship offer from Indiana in the near future. Elston, however, had not completed his activities in the camp, which made contact with him impermissible, and Elston returned to camp activities the following day. It was during this contact that Elston received a T-shirt and backpack in violation of NCAA rules.

Because of the last incident, Meyer released a statement later apologizing for his actions.

"In my 29 years as a college coach, I have tried to maintain a reputation for integrity, fairness and good sportsmanship values shared by Indiana University and the NCAA," Meyer said in a statement. "I regret that I may have made mistakes that are causing my and IU's conduct to be examined by the NCAA. I will continue to cooperate with both the University and the NCAA, and I will not comment on this process again before it is completed."

Also at the root of all the issues was the underlying belief that the NCAA didn't buy Sampson's claims that he didn't know IU was violating the recruiting restrictions. The report said that Sampson repeatedly provided IU and NCAA enforcement staff with false information.

The report said that specifically, during a November 13, 2007 interview with the institution and the enforcement staff, Sampson stated that at the time of the violations, he was unaware that Senderoff was using three-way calls to allow him to speak with prospective student-athletes, the prospective student-athletes' parents, legal guardians or coaches. Sampson further stated that he did not engage in three-way conversations with prospective student-athletes or their relatives during the period of recruiting restrictions. Additionally, Sampson stated that there was never an instance when he was on the phone with a prospective student-athlete when Senderoff also spoke. Finally, Sampson stated that he never spoke with William Buford.

The report went on to say that "In fact, Sampson engaged in three-way telephone conversations with multiple prospective student-athletes, the prospective student athlete's parents or legal guardians as set forth in this allegation including a June 19, 2006, three-way telephone conversation between himself, Senderoff and Buford."

In a story in the *Indianapolis Star*, IU's assistant vice president for university communications Larry MacIntyre, who was often times Indiana's official spokesperson during the Sampson debacle, defended IU's report to the NCAA. He said Sampson had told the school he didn't knowingly violate those rules.

"We had nothing showing us that that was a false statement," MacIntyre told *The Star*. "Now I don't know what evidence they have, but the NCAA is alleging that Sampson was untruthful. And that's different from what we came up with. We know who the NCAA talked to. They talked to people who were on the other end of those phone calls, which we were not able to do for a number of reasons. Partly we were not able to find them, and we didn't have the investigative resources that (the NCAA) has. And also there was no reason for those people to talk to us. But when the NCAA shows up on your door, that can be different."

Rick Greenspan was clearly distraught over what was happening before his eyes. At the same time, he was insistent on fighting until the end.

"In the last 40 or so years, I believe Indiana and Penn State are the only Big Ten programs that have not received NCAA sanctions," Greenspan said. "That's a tradition I take very seriously."

        ℘   ℅

Writers across the country penned their opinions about how Indiana should have known better before it hired Sampson in the first place.

Michael Rosenberg of the *Detroit Free Press* said it's not like IU didn't see the potential of Sampson's past problems rearing their ugly head in Bloomington.

Rosenberg wrote in a column: "Indiana's administrators told themselves that Kelvin Sampson would be a great fit at Indiana. Kelvin Sampson, whose graduation rates at Oklahoma were a joke. Kelvin Sampson, who has lived on junior college players for years. That Kelvin Sampson.

"Sampson got in trouble for breaking NCAA rules while he was at Oklahoma. He promised he learned his lesson. Apparently, he thought the lesson was 'Don't get caught.'"

Over the next two weeks, speculation continue to rise that Sampson would either be fired or resign.

One by one, local and national columnists were calling for Sampson's resignation.

In a column on February 14, Ben Smith of the Fort Wayne *Journal Gazette* listed the reasons why it should happen swiftly.

So here is why you do this now:

You do it for the coed with the crimson "I" on one cheek, the crimson "U" on the other and 9,000 or so red-and-white beads roped around her wrists and neck.

You do it for the fright wigs and the candy-stripe coveralls and the Eric Gordon jerseys, the DeAndre Thomas jerseys.

You do it for the largest and most loyal student section anywhere, according to the scoreboard PR. For that ballboy down there, knee high to a grass-stain. For that guy, and that guy over there, and for all the people who make Assembly Hall throb with sound on game nights, the good people who believed Kelvin Sampson when he promised to embrace the integrity that is a matter of doctrine here.

Sampson resigns for all of them now, if he cares at all. He walks today. And on his way out, he holds the door for athletic director Rick Greenspan, who hired Sampson even though the man was trailing an NCAA rap sheet — a fact that should have sent red flags flying, should have shouted loudly and clearly that here was a guy who would first rebuild your program, and then put it in jail.

And so this is on Greenspan, too, these latest allegations handed down by the NCAA. And to some extent it's on ex-IU president Adam Herbert, because he was clearly as much a Sampson guy as Greenspan.

Indianapolis Star columnist Bob Kravitz wrote that Sampson should have resigned after that night's game against Wisconsin. He also didn't mince words, one of Kravitz's better qualities.

This is what happens when you hire sleaze.

If basketball coach Kelvin Sampson is on the Indiana University sideline beyond this morning, then shame on the newly installed school president, Michael McRobbie, shame on the IU trustees and shame on athletic director Rick Greenspan, who will soon learn the hard way that when you hire sleaze, you get covered in the sleaze.

Since Sampson wasn't noble enough to resign after Wednesday night's 68-66 loss to Wisconsin — he should have done it for the good of the school and specifically his players — it's up to the IU administration to do it for him. The sooner Sampson is set adrift, the greater the likelihood that the NCAA will soften the blows it figures to land on this program down the line.

He betrayed the university's trust. And now, he must pay.

"The allegations that I knowingly acted contrary to the sanctions imposed on me for violations that occurred while I was at Oklahoma are not true," he said in a prepared statement. "I have never intentionally provided false or misleading information to the NCAA..."

It's too late for semantics, too late for dancing around and claiming he never "knowingly" misled investigators, just as home-run king Barry Bonds never "knowingly" took performance-enhancing drugs. Sampson said after the game he couldn't and wouldn't respond to questions regarding the allegations and remained adamant when he was asked if he considered resigning. Maybe he can tell his side of the story on the way out the door.

It's incredible, really. He made all those mistakes at Oklahoma, then came to IU, expressed utter contrition, promised to change his erring ways, then made all the same mistakes again.

Sampson is not a dumb guy. So it must be arrogance. It must be hubris.

Quickly, in the court of public opinion, it became a question of not if but when.

And then the talk moved to what kind of buyout Sampson would receive, especially since the university had placed some "termination for just cause" language in his original contract. IU president Michael McRobbie gave Rick Greenspan the charge of beginning an immediate investigation into the new allegations against Sampson. He would be assisted by IU vice president and general counsel Dottie Frapwell and IU athletics faculty representative Bruce Jaffee.

"I am announcing that I've directed the athletics director to oversee an immediate investigation of these new allegations and make an assessment as to whether they are credible and accurate," McRobbie said in a prepared statement the Friday after the NCAA report came down. "I've given him seven days as of now to complete this task."

McRobbie said in the February 15 press conference that he was disappointed for IU fans everywhere.

"First, let me say, I am deeply disappointed by these allegations — and I share that disappointment with all those who love and support Indiana University," McRobbie said. "I fully understand the desire by many people for us to move quickly to bring this situation to resolution. And we intend to do just that.

"Over the past week I have carefully examined all of the allegations contained in the NCAA's report. I have discussed them in great detail with Athletics Director Rick Greenspan, our vice president and general counsel, Dorothy Frapwell, and others. I am grateful for their input and advice. Let there be no doubt. These are serious allegations of misconduct.

"As president, I believe the most important measure of our success in intercollegiate athletics is not in the win-loss columns. Rather, it is in how well we measure up to our own high standards for good sportsmanship, academic success, the welfare of our student-athletes, and playing by the rules. It is my responsibility to take whatever actions are necessary to ensure that our men's basketball program lives up to the high level of integrity that has always been its hallmark, and I am determined to do just that."

Fans and former players alike were distraught over what was happening to their program right before their eyes.

Dean Garrett, the third-leading scorer on Indiana's 1987 national championship team, said what had transpired in such a short time was painful.

"I just hated to see the program go down," Garrett said. "With Coach Knight as coach, Indiana always did things the right way. To see someone come in and obviously not care about the tradition and history of Indiana basketball and what it stands for, and destroy it was very hurtful."

ℬℭ

Almost exactly a week later, Sampson submitted his resignation in a press conference that dragged well into the evening.

Sampson accepted a $750,000 buyout. Of that total, $550,000 came from a donor who wished to remain anonymous, and the other $200,000 was from athletic department funds. The agreement also prevented Sampson from suing the university.

"There was not a great appetite on either party's part to be involved in potentially contentious litigation," Greenspan said in the 9 p.m. news conference. "This helps the team, the players, the university to heal quicker."

Sampson didn't appear at the press conference but said in a statement that his decision to leave was "very difficult."

"While I'm saddened that I will not have the opportunity to continue to coach these student-athletes, I feel that it is in the best interest of the program for me to step aside at this time," he said. "As

IU Coach Kelvin Sampson walks off the court at Assembly Hall on February 19, 2008 following a victory over Purdue. It would be Sampson's final game as IU's coach.

I have previously stated, I welcome the opportunity to go before the Committee on Infractions in June. I look forward to getting back on the basketball court in the very near future."

Indianapolis Star reporter Mark Alesia wrote the next day that the firing of Sampson could help mitigate IU's punishment. As a voluntary membership organization without subpoena power, the NCAA depends on self-policing, and the infractions committee takes into account the extent to which schools punish themselves.

Alesia reported that IU spokesman Larry MacIntyre said the risk of losing a wrongful-termination lawsuit was the biggest reason for offering Sampson a buyout instead of firing him. MacIntyre said the school thought it could have been liable for $2 million to $3 million in a lawsuit.

"The university is basically avoiding that for $200,000," MacIntyre said.

IU president Michael McRobbie did not attend the news conference either. He said in a statement that he wanted "to put this matter behind us and allow our basketball season to move forward without these distractions."

As for the anonymous donor, MacIntyre said in Alesia's story that "only a handful" of people at the university know the person's identity. "We've had lots of anonymous gifts over time," he said. "It's not unusual. It's not up to me to speculate why the person doesn't want to be identified."

Stephen Ferguson, the board of trustee member who was one of two board members involved in the hiring of Sampson, told the *Indianapolis Star* that Sampson's resignation would open the flood gates for people to say "I told you so."

"People say 'I told you so,' and they're probably right," Ferguson said of the Sampson hire. "The question for the administration was whether it was a mistake to give him a second chance (after Sampson's NCAA violations at Oklahoma), because it seemed as if he had done everything else right. Coach Sampson assured everyone publicly that he knew the high level of expectations at Indiana University and he would abide by that. Sometimes second chances don't work out."

Alesia also quoted Ohio University professor David Ridpath, director of The Drake Group, a college sports reform organization. His words seemed to put into perspective a lot of what Indiana fans had been feeling for some time. He said Sampson's demise at IU was a sad but familiar story. He also said he was surprised that Indiana had hired Sampson in the first place, given his compliance record.

"I've always thought of Indiana as a little above the fray," Ridpath said. "And they jumped into the cesspool. I'm not surprised by what happened."

In June 2008, IU took its case before an NCAA panel in Seattle. President McRobbie did not attend but appeared by video conference with a message for the committee.

McRobbie told the infractions committee that Sampson's actions left the Indiana basketball program "in tatters."

"Indiana University took a risk in hiring Coach Sampson and giving him a second chance following his problems at Oklahoma," McRobbie said. "It is now clear that this was a risk that should not have been taken, and the university regrets doing so."

Sampson, who was hired within a few months as an assistant coach with the Milwaukee Bucks, repeatedly denied he was knowingly involved in three-way phone calls while at IU and continued to dispute the NCAA's finding that he did not come clean and tell the committee the whole truth.

McRobbie said in his statement to the infractions committee meeting in Seattle that IU officials believed "the evidence clearly demonstrates" that Sampson and an assistant coach tried to circumvent the sanctions against Sampson.

"These coaches were entrusted not just with the success of our men's basketball program, but with the good name of Indiana University," McRobbie said. "I am not just saddened, I am angry that they betrayed that trust."

Former players were angry, too. Pat Graham, who played for the Hoosiers from 1989-94, said the whole situation was embarrassing.

"We always prided ourselves in doing things the right way, and then when shortcuts were taken with Sampson it threw us in the conversation with all the other so-called 'cheaters'," Graham said.

In Bob Kravitz's column in the *Indianapolis Star* a week before Sampson resigned, he wrote about the harm that had been done to IU's once-proud program and tradition.

The damage to this program will be irreparable, and it will make future recruiting impossible. The NCAA hearing will continue throughout the summer, throughout recruiting season, and recruits will have questions: Will Sampson still be the coach in the future? Will the program be sanctioned, maybe subjected to a postseason ban? What player in his right mind would come to Bloomington?

Sampson, whose moral compass is broken beyond repair, thinks the people around him are a bunch of rubes who can be bought off by shiny recruits and 20-win seasons.

You can blame Sampson for only part of this. A lot of the blame falls on the people who scoured the country and thought the best person to take this plum job was a guy with a terrible graduation rate and an NCAA charge hanging over his head.

Greenspan will probably take the fall for this, whether he fully endorsed Sampson's hiring or not. Still, Greenspan was up there at that introductory news conference, singing Sampson's praises and making the case for his tainted hire, and if you stand with him, you fall with him.

Unfortunately, there's no way to make former school president Adam Herbert accountable for this mistake. But how about the trustees? Where were the school's top decision-makers when Sampson's checkered history was being recounted?

Here's what should happen: Sampson gets fired. Greenspan gets fired. Assistant coach Jeff Meyer gets fired. Assistant coach Dan Dakich, who arrived on the scene this season, has the Bob Knight seal of approval and hasn't been around long enough to have become covered in sleaze. Make him the interim head coach, with the emphasis on interim. IU doesn't need another Mike Davis mess.

Stay tuned.

It's going to get uglier.

As it should.

Chapter 7

With Kelvin Sampson gone, Indiana turned to one of its own to keep the team together through the final few games of the Big Ten season and on to the NCAA Tournament.

The day before Sampson resigned, Mark Montieth wrote in the *Indianapolis Star* about why Dan Dakich would be a good fit to take over the team on an interim basis. Montieth pointed to the fact that he was a well-respected name with the Indiana community, he was a former Bob Knight disciple and he would have the support of former Indiana players, too.

This is what Montieth wrote in *The Star* on February 21, the day before Sampson resigned.

Amid the turmoil in Indiana University's basketball program, there's one bit of good fortune that could help soothe a bitter fan base.

Dan Dakich, who sits three seats to the right of Coach Kelvin Sampson on the IU bench, is available to take over as interim coach should Sampson resign, be suspended, or get fired this week.

Dakich, 45, has what many consider the perfect pedigree for the job. He's from Indiana, spent 16 seasons alongside Bob Knight at IU — first as a player, then 12 years as an assistant coach — and has 10 years of head coaching experience with Bowling Green.

IU assistant Ray McCallum also grew up in Indiana and has head coaching experience at Ball State and Houston, but his longtime association with Sampson might work against him.

Two former Hoosiers who played with or for Dakich endorse him.

"Dan knows basketball and he knows toughness," said Joe Hillman, IU's team MVP in 1989 and a member of the 1987 NCAA championship team.

"I think people would rally around him. I really do."

Greg Graham, a member of IU's 1993 Big Ten title team, doesn't endorse anyone in particular to succeed Sampson if it becomes necessary, but he praised Dakich's work as an assistant with the Hoosiers.

"He was a key ingredient in helping improve my game," Graham said. "My shooting improved to the point I led the Big Ten in field goal percentage and 3-point field goal percentage as a senior. He was part of that from working with me before and after practice.

"Dan is perfectly capable of running a program and he knows Indiana."

Dakich was a pedestrian player at IU, averaging 3.6 points and 1.6 rebounds over his four-year career, which concluded in 1985 when IU lost to UCLA in the NIT championship game.

He gained greater recognition as an assistant coach, first as a graduate assistant for two seasons and then as a full-time assistant for 10 before becoming head coach at Bowling Green.

Dakich compiled a 156-140 record in 10 seasons at Bowling Green. He resigned last March, telling athletic director Greg Christopher that he wasn't interested in pursuing an extension to his expiring contract.

His most controversial moment came in April 2002 when he accepted the head coaching position at West Virginia, receiving an annual pay increase from $125,000 to $500,000. He backed out and returned to Bowling Green a week later, in part after learning of a possible NCAA rules violation within West Virginia's program.

Dakich returned to IU last June as the director of basketball operations, then moved onto the bench after Rob Senderoff resigned in October in the wake of NCAA sanctions.

Hillman considers Dakich a viable candidate to become IU's coach beyond this season if Sampson is fired.

"I don't see why he wouldn't be a candidate," Hillman said. "I don't think there's any doubt the next coach has to be somebody from within the IU family."

Graham, meanwhile, hopes a potential coaching upheaval doesn't jeopardize this team's Big Ten title hopes.

"I really like this basketball team," Graham said. "That's all I care about. This is a good team and it's a shame it has to be overshadowed by all this talk."

The next day IU athletics director Rick Greenspan accepted Kelvin Sampson's resignation, and at the same time announced that Dan

Dakich would be IU's interim head coach and Ray McCallum would be assistant head coach.

Neither of the two had been implicated for any wrongdoing in the Sampson mess.

Dakich was not available for comment that first day but instead issued a statement that was released to the media.

"Indiana University and the basketball program have played an important role in my life," Dakich said. "I want nothing but the best for these players and the institution. The challenge ahead is to maintain the positive momentum that has been built within the team and to keep everyone as focused as possible during this difficult time."

☯ ☪

A few days later I wrote a story in the *Indianapolis Star* that detailed exactly what had transpired in Kelvin Sampson's final few days as the IU coach and all that led to Dan Dakich being named the interim coach.

It pretty much filled in many of the gaps that had existed in the story. Most of the information had been provided by a trusted source and one clearly with knowledge of the situation.

Just before 11 a.m. Friday, Dan Dakich was standing in the Indiana University basketball locker room, scripting a Northwestern scouting report on a dry-erase board when he received a telephone call, summoning him to athletic director Rick Greenspan's office.

Dakich didn't know Coach Kelvin Sampson had just agreed in principle to a $750,000 resignation package. That was one of many new details a person familiar with the situation revealed Sunday. The source said that as late as Thursday night, Greenspan had asked for but not received Sampson's resignation. Players had lobbied school and athletic officials to save his job, the source said. An anonymous donation made Friday morning allowed both sides to end the irreconcilable relationship amicably.

When Dakich walked into Greenspan's office, he didn't know his fate either. Like most of the lead characters in this ongoing, off-the-court drama that played out most of Thursday and Friday, Dakich was in the dark.

As he walked across the Assembly Hall floor en route to Greenspan's office, the man who spent 16 years alongside Bob Knight as a player and coach paused at midcourt. He stared up at the championship banners. He thought about how much he loved the university and wondered if his time here could now be calculated in minutes.

"I truly did not know what I was being called up there for," Dakich said. "I thought, 'Maybe this is my last time here. I really don't know.' "

Moments later, Greenspan told Dakich that Sampson was out and that he wanted Dakich to become IU's interim head coach. The two quickly reached a handshake agreement regarding a contract, according to a person with knowledge of the situation, and Dakich returned to the locker room.

Thirty minutes later, the players learned of Sampson's fate, and 90 minutes after accepting his dream job, Dakich held his first team meeting as head coach. He encouraged his emotional players to maintain focus during a most trying time.

Dakich empathized, however. He reminded them of their 3:30 p.m. scheduled practice, but he knew they needed time to accept the change.

The previous day, players were in Greenspan's office, campaigning for Sampson to keep his job and requesting that assistant Ray McCallum take over if that weren't possible.

Now, they were dealing with an unexpected scenario.

"There was no chance that I was going to sit there and demand that (they go to practice)," Dakich said. "I have respect for 18- to 22-year-old people. I always have. I push them, I yell at them, I make them crazy. But I respect their opinions because they are bright people.

"Anybody that knows anything about my background knows that soft is not one of the things I'm known for as a coach. These kids needed time and they needed space. They probably still do. This is tough."

Seven of the 13 players showed up to the practice. The six who didn't joined the team Friday night for its walk-through.

A team torn apart slowly was coming together, a Big Ten championship and possibly more still within its grasp.

Two weeks earlier, IU released the NCAA's notice of allegations accusing the school of committing five potentially major recruiting violations and of Sampson repeatedly lying to IU and NCAA investigators about his role. Sampson said he never knowingly violated NCAA restrictions placed on him stemming from his misconduct at Oklahoma.

The final 36 hours of the Kelvin Sampson era of Indiana basketball were an up-and-down series of events that concluded with a news conference Friday night in which Greenspan announced Sampson had agreed to resign and accept a settlement of $750,000.

According to a person familiar with the situation, here's how the Sampson settlement came together:

Thursday, February 21:

Players weigh in, Sampson stands firm

Shortly after noon, IU players D.J. White, Eric Gordon, Lance Stemler, Adam Ahlfeld and Kyle Taber went to IU President Michael McRobbie's office, hoping to discuss the Sampson situation. The president was out, and the players instead spoke with McRobbie's chief of staff, Karen Adams. The players said they were confused and that no one had told them anything.

D.J. White spoke for the players. The source characterized it as "a good meeting."

Late Thursday afternoon, the five players met with Greenspan. Two hours after that meeting, the entire team met with Greenspan. They told him that if there was going to be a change, they preferred Ray McCallum to take over as interim coach because he recruited most of them and they were more familiar with him than with Dakich. Greenspan gave no indication of which way he was leaning.

As of 7 p.m., Sampson's future hadn't been decided.

"Rick (Greenspan) really didn't know how to describe anything to the players because at that time it wasn't a settled matter," the source said.

The players left around 7:45 p.m., and word began spreading that they might boycott Saturday's game if Sampson weren't the coach.

During the late afternoon and early evening, Greenspan spoke with Sampson and asked for his resignation. According to the source, Greenspan and Sampson had had many discussions since IU first self-reported the phone troubles to the NCAA in October. Sampson maintained he wanted to fight for his job.

According to the source, many university officials had been arguing since October that IU had enough to fire Sampson "with cause."

"So I think (Greenspan) was asking Kelvin, 'What do you want to do about all of this?' and Sampson was saying, 'Well, I want to fight it and I hope you guys will stand with me,' " the source said.

"Then it almost became a game of who blinks first. When it was clear that the university was not going to stand with him but was probably heading down what would potentially be a very different path, that's when exploratory discussions began looking at other options."

As of late Thursday night, however, Sampson wasn't close to resigning.

"At that point in the negotiations, there was not sufficient money on the table (for a settlement) for the coach to just resign under those circumstances," the source said.

With reporters huddled outside his office, Greenspan and associate athletic director Tim Fitzpatrick continued meeting. They stopped around midnight.

IU had a plan to deal with Sampson if he chose not to resign.

Friday morning, February 22:

Financing flurry, eminent termination

The university was preparing to resolve the situation in time for a 2 p.m. news conference. Greenspan and athletic department officials were adamant about making a recommendation by McRobbie's Friday deadline.

"At that point the assumption was that they were too far apart to have a deal, and that it wasn't going to happen," the source said. "But there was also the thought that there was no way in hell they were going to miss McRobbie's deadline."

The key moment came with a "midmorning" offer that changed how the day would play out. An anonymous donor offered $550,000 to help assist a resignation. Sampson's lawyer told Kelvin and Karen Sampson of the new deal. The couple walked out of Assembly Hall around 11 a.m.

Negotiations soon began. As they were playing out, players were learning the decision had been made.

At 11:45 a.m., they were told that Sampson would not be coaching the team and Dakich would take over.

At 3:10 p.m., just before practice began, McCallum and his wife met with Greenspan for more than two hours. The source said McCallum wanted to talk about his future with the school, and make sure he wasn't being passed over for perceptions that weren't accurate.

At 5:20 p.m., McCallum left the office and drove away.

After learning of the new deal, lawyers from both sides spent nine hours tweaking specific language. Sampson signed the settlement around 7:45 p.m., and IU called a 9 p.m. news conference to announce Sampson's resignation.

"The donor said that if money is the issue, that they could (go) up to a certain threshold level," the source said. "It all just went out the window when the call came in that reopened the resignation possibility when someone was willing to put money on the table to make that happen. It was all scripted out to be done by 2 p.m."

The source didn't say Sampson would have been fired had he not agreed to resign, but "I think you can draw your own conclusion about that," the source said. "Let me just say it should be pretty obvious as to where this was headed."

℘   ℘

Like is often the case with stories such as this one, sources are everywhere. You just have to make sure that you have the best sources and ones that you can absolutely trust.

When it comes to using sourced material at the *Indianapolis Star*, we have always taken that responsibility very seriously. In order to use an unnamed source I would need to have two credible people saying the information and then I would have to sell those people to my sports editor, who would move it on up the flag pole until the final OK was given at the highest level.

This was an ongoing story where sources were used routinely because people simply didn't want to be on the record.

On that Friday of the Sampson resignation, a source close to the team had said players had threatened to not board Saturday's flight to Evanston, Illinois, for the Northwestern game if Sampson was fired. The source said players would follow senior captain D.J. White's lead on whether to play.

"As far as them playing, it depends on D.J.," the source said. "He's the leader. He's the cornerstone. Whatever D.J. does, they're all going to do."

With all of that hovering over the program, Dakich and Assistant Jeff Meyer attempted to hold a practice at Assembly Hall Friday afternoon. Again, there were rumors everywhere that several players had planned to skip the practice.

I remember that day well, because it allowed me to take my investigative reporter skills to a different level.

As a reporter covering Indiana football and basketball the past 14 years, I've had my share of interesting stories to cover. I covered the final two seasons with Bob Knight at the Indiana helm and the subsequent circus-like atmosphere the week when he was fired. I can still remember the sea of television trucks that filled almost every open space in the Assembly Hall parking lot as the final days counted down to that decision.

While not as noteworthy, I broke a couple of big stories at the time that Michael McNeely was fired after 16 months as Indiana's athletic director in 2001 and 2002. An unpopular choice with the athletics staff, McNeely was let go after he was unable to connect with fans and media. I can't remember a time when more sources came forth with dirt on one person, all with the understanding that I wouldn't use their names.

I had also had some interesting times in covering the Mike Davis era of IU basketball. In one instance, shortly after Davis took the Hoosiers to the national championship game, he confirmed to me that IU had given him a contract extension and a hefty raise. But the numbers he told me did not match up with the contract that I had been provided by IU media relations. And the numbers were off by a total of $50,000 per season. When I told Davis that on the phone, he said he would call me back. A little while later he did and explained that he hadn't read the fine print closely enough and that a mistake had been made. The next day, IU made an addendum to the contract in which it gave Davis what was referred to as a "special three-year performance incentive," that basically covered the $300,000 he thought he was going to receive that wasn't in the contract. I always joked with Davis that I should have received a finder's fee for catching the error. Obviously, I was joking.

But the day Sampson was fired and the rumors were circulating that IU's players were not going to attend the afternoon practice, I wanted to find a way to get into Assembly Hall and see for myself. I didn't want to have to use sourced information unless I absolutely had to. This was something I wanted to see with my own eyes and be able to report with total confidence.

The problem is that practices are routinely closed at IU, so it's not as simple as walking through the main doors. And with this practice, in particular, there was even more of a veil of secrecy.

Normally at the top of the ramps that are on both the north and south ends of Assembly Hall, there's a screen that is up to prevent you from accessing the arena.

But on this particular day, one of those screens had been left slightly ajar, and that allowed me to get to the stairs that led to the balcony. Once there, I slithered like a snake on my belly up one of the ramps (I know, not a good visual), where I could peek out onto the Assembly Hall floor below.

What I found was that seven of the 13 players had shown up: Eric Gordon, Lance Stemler, Mike White, Kyle Taber, Brett Finkelmeier, Eli Holman and Adam Ahlfeld were all there.

Those not in attendance were starters D.J. White, Armon Bassett and Jamarcus Ellis, as well as reserves Jordan Crawford, DeAndre Thomas and Brandon McGee.

I didn't stay long. I had gotten the information I was looking for, and I went back to work.

Later that evening, just minutes after Sampson's resignation was announced, the three IU coaches held a walk-through at Assembly Hall. This time D.J. White showed, and his teammates followed suit. All 13 players were there.

When it ended, IU players quietly walked out of Assembly Hall and into the night with zero fanfare. Gone was the media horde that had filled the south lobby of the arena throughout the afternoon and had hounded players with questions as they came and left practice earlier in the day.

This time, at just after 10:25 p.m., the players departed Assembly Hall, still not ready to comment about the day's whirlwind events but with a calmness in their appearance.

It was the culmination of a rocky 30 hours. IU athletic director Rick Greenspan confirmed he met with five players Thursday afternoon, and then in the early evening with almost the entire team. A person close to the team said Ellis walked out of the initial meeting.

"I expressed to them my feelings about the situation and my thoughts about the unenviable position that they're in," Greenspan said. "I just felt they're really good young men, coming off of two superb wins and dealing with something that really was in no way their responsibility.

"I have great respect for the challenges and the adversity faced by Indiana University basketball players. Not just this year, but throughout. There's tremendous pressure on these young guys. I think they almost all the time represent us well. I tried to give encouragement during a time when I know they were very frustrated and concerned, and expressed that to me."

Associate Athletic Director for Student Development and Compliance M. Grace Calhoun had heard about a possible boycott, but she felt that after the team had a chance to reflect on the coaching switch, they would play against Northwestern.

"They're kids and they're hurting, and I think sometimes we lose sight of that," Calhoun said. "I think after they stepped back and thought about it, they realized how committed these coaches are to them, and they realized that they have a chance to do something special as a team.

"I just think in the end the realization of all of that was just too much for them to walk away from. I just think they have a sense of passion to see that through as a group, and that they are really committed to their teammates and the university."

The next day I got a text message from Dan Dakich as the team was taxiing on the runway about to leave for Northwestern. It read, "Off to Northwestern, and all 13 players are on board."

༄ ༄

Dan Dakich would coach seven games to close out the 2007-08 season.

The Hoosiers finished off the conference portion of the schedule with a 3-2 record to end up 14-4 in conference play.

The last few games weren't completely without incident, though. Starter Jamarcus Ellis was suspended for the season finale at Penn State for undisclosed disciplinary reasons. IU would lose that game in overtime, 68-64.

That gave the Hoosiers the third seed and a quarterfinal matchup with Minnesota in the Big Ten Tournament.

IU's stay would be a short one. D.J. White made one free throw to put Indiana up 58-57 with 1.5 seconds to play against the Gophers. Travis Busch inbounded a pass from the length of the court, and Blake Hoffarber caught it above the free throw line. He turned and hit a 16-footer at the buzzer to give Minnesota the 59-58 win.

Indiana then limped into the NCAA Tournament as a No. 8 seed and faced No. 9 Arkansas in Raleigh, North Carolina.

Again, the Hoosiers bowed out quickly. The Razorbacks raced to an 86-72 victory.

After the game, Dakich made it perfectly clear that he should be the next Indiana basketball coach.

Here's my story that ran the next day in the *Indianapolis Star*:

The Indiana University basketball team failed to seize the moment Friday night against Arkansas in the first round of the NCAA Tournament.

It was a different story for interim coach Dan Dakich, however, in the news conference following IU's 86-72 loss to the Razorbacks. Dakich, 45, was asked why he should be Indiana's permanent coach moving forward.

Dan Dakich celebrates a play during his first game as IU's interim coach, February 23, 2008, at Northwestern.

There was no hesitation. No looking for the politically correct answer. No passing the buck. Instead, Dakich let it go straight from the heart.

"There's no question I should be (the permanent coach)," Dakich said. "I understand there's a culture at Indiana, given the timing of all of this. There's a lot of things transpiring behind the scenes with where the program has to go. But IU needs somebody that understands it, or else you're going to get yourself in a situation just like we're in."

Dakich said he has everything the 10-person search committee is looking for.

"The passion, the desire to do things right, academically, socially, on the court, our style of play, are all things that are absolutely what would happen if I become the head basketball coach at Indiana over time," Dakich said. "This needs to be built. This needs to be built with a foundation of discipline and accountability. This needs to be built back to where there is a real pride among the people that know everything that's going on in the basketball program.

"We need former players that come and have pride in what is happening here in the program. And that can certainly happen with

a lot of people, but I'm just telling you, given the climate, the culture and what is happening right now, it has to be somebody that understands it."

Dakich alluded to the names being tossed out. But he thinks he has begun to build the foundation at IU again.

"A lot of that has begun over the last three weeks and it's going to continue as long as I'm the basketball coach," Dakich said. "I'm sure people can write a thousand reasons given our record here over the last month why there's something else, somebody else, a bigger name, whatever.

"I'm just telling you that the culture here is such that someone needs to do this the right way for Indiana people, Indiana fans. The Indiana nation wants it done right where there's no embarrassment, there's nothing but pride in all areas. And that's something that has to happen at IU. It doesn't have to happen everywhere, but it has to happen at Indiana University."

Dakich's biggest trouble area will be how the Hoosiers played over the past month. IU was 3-4 and lost four of its last five games, including the final three.

⁎ ⁃

Whether he was going to be retained as Indiana's next coach or not, one thing Dakich made perfectly clear in his final weeks as the interim coach was that he was going to run the program the way it should be run. And he was going to do so until they told him he no longer had the job.

That became abundantly clear on March 31 when Dakich kicked starters Armon Bassett and Jamarcus Ellis off the team.

Bassett and Ellis reportedly missed a prearranged appointment with Dakich earlier in the week, and he told them they were required to run at 6 a.m. the next day as punishment. He also told them at the time that if they didn't show up, they would be off the team.

Apparently they thought he was bluffing. He wasn't. The next morning neither showed up, and Dakich informed them later of his decision.

The timing of Dakich's decision would be debated over and over in the weeks to come. That's because two days later, Tom Crean was named the new Indiana head coach.

I remember the night that Crean was introduced as the Indiana coach, I tracked down Dakich in the IU basketball coaches office at

Assembly Hall. He was disappointed. He really thought he had a chance at keeping the job, but for reasons out of his control, it wasn't meant to be.

One thing I remember, though, is that he was packing his stuff into boxes and I looked over in the corner and saw two full hefty trash bags filled to the brim and tied at the top. I asked him what that was all about and he said, "That's Bassett's and Ellis' stuff. We cleaned out their lockers and told them to come and get their stuff, but they haven't stopped by to get it yet."

Four years later in June 2012, I reminded Dakich of that moment. When he thought about those two trash bags, he smiled. "You know, I don't know if those guys ever came back and got their stuff," Dakich said.

&〇 〇8

In that same interview in June 2012, I asked Dakich if he had it all to do over again, would he have done things the same way? Would he have held players like Ellis and Bassett accountable or just looked the other way, knowing that in a few weeks someone else would have the IU head coaching title and it would be their problem to deal with.

He paused for a moment and thought about it. He said he knew that what he was doing was clearly more of the road less traveled.

"I got advice from coaches, a variety of coaches from different sports, and they all said the same thing," Dakich said. "They said, 'You're going to try to do the right thing, the players aren't going to like it, you're not going to get the job, someone else is going to get it and make a ton of money, and you're going to be left saying you did the right thing, but nobody is going to be listening.'

"So I really don't know. I know I sleep well. I know I don't have any problems about it and that's important to me. That's really important to me. So that would have been my dilemma."

My own opinion is that some of the advice he received was flawed. The part where they told him that he would be left saying he did the right thing and nobody would be listening isn't accurate. A lot of people were listening. The IU fans and alumni who wanted the sleaze of the program to go away were listening. Sure, the Hoosiers could have won a few more games the next season, but with all the wrong players. IU was starting over anyway, so why not do it with a clean slate?

And even Dakich said later that if it was about doing the right thing, the way he proceeded was the only way to go with a clear conscious.

"That's the way I always believed Indiana should be," Dakich said. "You needed to be held accountable. You needed to go to class, you needed to attend the workouts you were supposed to attend, you were supposed to meet with tutors and do all the necessary academic things. And at the end that wasn't happening, and I didn't think it was right."

Looking back, Dakich said his seven games as IU's interim coach were a definite life lesson. He said that early on, people were being encouraging about him getting the job full time. When IU lost its final three games, though, that tune began to change.

"We started out 2-0 and we were actually 3-1 and I was talking to Rick (Greenspan) all the time," Dakich said. "But like everyone else, Rick was great when we were winning and not so much when we were losing. But that's just the way it is. I know that. I don't have any hard feelings with anybody.

"But then came the Minnesota game. Something happened that night that I won't talk about that basically ended the season. It wasn't with me, but it happened later on that night. And really no matter what transpired from that point on, our season wasn't going to last long."

Even as badly as the Sampson era ended for IU, Dakich looks back on his one-season return to Indiana as an enjoyable time. Of course, he's disappointed with what happened to the program, but in terms of his own chance to return to his alma mater, it was good.

"It was great to be back, Kelvin treated me really well and it was a good situation," Dakich said. "Now, in the end it wasn't good. We don't speak anymore. We had one last meeting after his second-to-last game, which was Michigan State at home, and he knew at that point it wasn't going to be good. And we haven't spoken since."

Dakich said being the interim IU coach, even for just seven games, was a thrill.

"I mean, obviously the way I ended up getting the job wasn't the way you would want to get it," Dakich said. "And I felt bad for a lot of people. I felt bad for Kelvin's wife (Karen), I felt bad for (his son) Kellen, I felt bad for the daughter (Lauren). And I felt bad for Kelvin.

"But I don't have bad days. I didn't have bad days back then. The only bad days I ever had was when we would lose, and they would last for a couple of days after."

Dakich said the whole experience taught him a lot.

"It made me stronger as a human being," he said. "It made me tougher as a person. I showed me a bad way of how to go about coaching college basketball, because I had never been involved in a bad way to coach college basketball. When I was a head coach at Bowling Green, we always did things the right way. When I was with coach Knight, we always did things the right way. So that was hard. But you learn life lessons in a variety of ways, and I definitely learned life lessons that season with IU basketball."

When I brought up the trash bags in the corner of his office that belonged to Bassett and Ellis, Dakich smiled again.

He said he believed Bassett and Ellis deserved their punishment, but he also felt that DeAndre Thomas wasn't far behind.

"I told him if I had one more day, that would be you tomorrow," Dakich said with a laugh. "That really happened. I had to go somewhere, and I bumped into him and told him, 'If I had one more day, your stuff would be up there, too.'"

The reality. though is that Dakich's interim tag as the Indiana coach lasted 38 days, and as he departed. the Hoosiers were about to usher in a new period in IU basketball.

The Tom Crean era had begun.

Tom Crean holds up a Crean & Crimson T-shirt at his introductory press conference at IU on April 2, 2008.

PART 3:
"It's Indiana.
It's Indiana."

Chapter 8

As far as introductory press conferences go, Tom Crean's was of the home run variety. And not just a ball that barely cleared the fence at the 378-foot mark in left-center. No, this was a towering shot that landed in places that most balls don't go.

Crean talked about a lot of things after he was introduced as Indiana's 28th head basketball coach at a press conference on April 2, 2008.

He talked about the challenges facing his new team, and the difficulties he had saying goodbye the night before to his previous team at Marquette. He talked about idolizing Kent Benson at an early age and his first experience attending one of Bob Knight's basketball clinics. He rattled off a laundry list of former IU players that he wanted people to embrace their tradition and loyalty to the program.

But if you ask someone today to recall what they remember about Crean's first press conference, there are usually two things that come up immediately. First is the image of Crean standing at the podium and holding up a t-shirt that reads, "Crean & Crimson." Second is Crean's response when he was asked why he would want to leave a comfortable situation at Marquette to take on a rebuilding project with the Hoosiers.

"It's Indiana," Crean said. "It's Indiana."

It's amazing how those two little words came to define Crean from the very beginning. But that simple line resonated in the hearts of Indiana basketball fans everywhere.

Since Bob Knight was dismissed from the university in September 2000, Indiana basketball fans had longed for a coach they could wrap their arms around. They felt as if the hiring of Mike Davis had been shoved down their throats. And though no fault of Davis', his six-year tenure at IU was never a perfect fit. With a coach who lacked prior head coaching experience leading a program like Indiana, fans were always waiting for the bottom to drop out, the other shoe to fall. Davis was a good man but simply in a little bit over his head.

When Sampson was hired, there was a large segment who believed this coach had been dumped on them, as well. This was President Adam Herbert's man. Rick Greenspan played the role of good soldier to the very end and took the ultimate responsibility for the hiring of Sampson but this had Herbert's hand and fingerprints all over it. The basic message Indiana fans received here was simple: No matter how much baggage Sampson brought with him to Indiana, this was going to be the man to bring IU basketball back to prominence again.

All of those experiences simply served as a backdrop for the importance of the next Indiana basketball hire. When Rick Greenspan appointed a 10-person search committee headed by Harry Gonso to find IU's next basketball coach, the pressure was clearly on to find someone whom Indiana fans could call their own.

Of course, the fans wanted someone like Steve Alford, Randy Wittman or Mike Woodson to take over the program. What could be a better way to reunite Indiana fans everywhere than to bring back one of their own? But it was never that easy. Indiana needed someone who could handle a reclamation project like few, if any, in college basketball history had experienced. In many ways, Indiana was about to begin anew.

In Crean, Indiana wasn't getting a guy with Indiana ties, but they were clearly getting a person who loved Indiana and all that the university and basketball program stood for.

And if Hoosier fans weren't sure about that before Crean's initial press conference, they certainly realized it when that day was done.

Reggie Hayes, the longtime columnist for the *Fort Wayne News-Sentinel*, captured the essence of Crean's hiring completely. His column on April 3, 2008 started this way:

Now we see the difference between a coach who intellectually understands Indiana University basketball and someone who feels it in his gut.

There's no way Tom Crean could fake the passion he displayed Wednesday when he was introduced as the Hoosiers' new coach. His unfiltered fervor is exactly what the program needs, too.

Kelvin Sampson understood the "idea" of IU basketball. Crean breathes the air.

"This was a heart decision," Crean said, "not a business decision."

Crean had a picture of Kent Benson on his wall as a kid, for crying out loud. He talked about the 1976 national championship game being a defining moment for him. He reminisced about attending a Bob Knight clinic. He rattled off a number of IU names through the years, from Wayne Radford to Damon Bailey. He didn't need to read those names from a list, either. They were ripe in his brain for the picking.

"It's Indiana," Crean said, as if he were stating the obvious in explaining why he left a place he loved at Marquette.

He said it like a true believer would say, "It's the Celtics," or "It's the Yankees," or "Ladies and gentlemen, the Rolling Stones."

If there is such a thing as the perfect news conference, Crean delivered.

He told the "Hoosier Nation," as he kept calling the IU fan base, exactly what it wanted to hear. Namely, the school finally found a coach who believes Indiana is the summit of college basketball. I don't know if fans are ready to forgive athletic director Rick Greenspan for the Sampson Error, but Crean seems determined to make them forget.

Crean's passion was too strong and too continuous to fake. When he held up the t-shirt reading "Crean & Crimson," he looked like a guy who had signed an $18 million deal but would take the job for free.

I remember Sampson saying at his introductory news conference that he had come to Indiana to win championships. Thanks to the NCAA violations that never went away, his promises were overshadowed that day by a cloud over his head.

Crean seemed illuminated by Bloomington sunshine.

I have no doubt he can talk Devin Ebanks and Terrell Holloway into giving IU another look. I have no doubt he can convince future big-time recruits into building something great with him. If Crean brings half the energy to his new program that he brought to the news conference, he'll take Assembly Hall to new levels of noise.

The more I listened to Crean's almost evangelic zeal about IU's play in college basketball, the more I wondered if he couldn't even do the impossible and earn the blessing of Knight and heal those always festering wounds.

"There's no way I would have left what I had (at Marquette) unless it was for what is the pinnacle, the absolute pinnacle of college basketball — to be the head coach at Indiana University," Crean said.

Crean cautioned, in one of his few nonrapturous moments, that rebuilding the program would take some time. Indiana fans understand that. A lot of damage has been done. There's still the matter of what additional sanctions the NCAA will deliver.

But there's no way an Indiana fan could watch and list to Crean's first appearance as Indiana coach and not feel like the good times will soon roll again.

Keep preaching, Brother Tom, keep preaching.

You have the congregation's full attention.

⁐   ⁃

In the days leading up to Crean's hiring, a long list of names had been bandied about as possible candidates to become the next Indiana head coach. One of the hottest was that of then-Washington State coach Tony Bennett.

A Fox Sports report on March 29 claimed that Bennett had been offered the Indiana job. Later an ESPN report quoted Bennett as saying he hadn't had any conversations with Indiana and therefore had not been offered the job. Washington State athletic director Jim Sterk also said IU had not asked permission to speak to his coach.

The ESPN report did have a source with firsthand knowledge of the search process confirming that, among others, IU was looking at Bennett as well as former Stanford and Golden State Warriors coach Mike Montgomery.

Later, Washington State beat reporter Vince Grippi wrote in his blog at the *Spokane (Wash.) Spokesman-Review* that he had spoken with Tony Bennett, and the Cougar head coach had decided against pursuing the Indiana head coaching opening.

Mike Pegram, the editor and owner of the wildly popular website peegs.com, had this post the day prior to Crean's hiring.

Sources indicate to peegs.com/Inside Indiana that a top three are emerging as we head into the homestretch in the search for the next Indiana basketball coach. The search is still very fluid but word is Sean Miller of Xavier, Anthony Grant of Virginia Commonwealth (VCU) and Brad Brownell of Wright State are the trio now standing out through Monday discussions. Meetings with all three coaches or their representatives are expected over the next day or so per our source.

Also gaining ground per sources in the search is Dan Dakich, your current interim coach. Dakich's reported decision yesterday to dismiss Armon Bassett and Jamarcus Ellis from the team has created a firestorm of debate on our peegs.com message boards.

The Indiana search is expected to reach a conclusion by Thursday or Friday at the latest.

An *Associated Press* report out of Indianapolis written by Mike Marot used a quote from IU Board of Trustees President Stephen Ferguson saying that there was a lot of speculation out there, but most of it was just that: speculation.

"The speculation that's going on is amazing, and there's a lot of speculation that's not based on fact," Ferguson said.

Attempting to clear up some of the reports, Marot wrote this in his *AP* report:

Washington State's Tony Bennett, long considered a front-runner, issued a statement Sunday saying he had talked with Indiana athletic director Rick Greenspan but would not pursue the job.

Xavier's Sean Miller, another candidate believed to be on Indiana's short list, emphatically denied having any interest in the job after Saturday's regional final loss to UCLA.

"I will be at Xavier," Miller said. "I'm looking forward to coaching at Xavier and continuing on with what we've done for years behind me and what we've done this year. You know, we have the bar set high and we're anxious to recruit the very best we can – to have the opportunity to get back here."

Still there's no shortage of names to stoke message boards and blogs.

Familiar names such as Louisville's Rick Pitino and Michigan State's Tom Izzo, who have both won national championships, have made the rounds, as well as those of up-and-comers such as Butler's Brad Stevens and Wright State's Brad Brownell. Even ex-NBA coaches Mike Montgomery, Scott Skiles and Lon Kruger, now at UNLV, have been mentioned.

Mentioned? Mentioned by whom? That was the problem with this coaching search from the beginning. In past searches (and there had been a number of them for new basketball, football and athletic directors in recent years) there had always been plenty of leaks within the IU athletic department or president's office. Someone was always talking and plenty were listening, too. Getting the story in the paper first before the press conference confirmed the selection was never difficult within Indiana circles.

That changed with Rick Greenspan's watch. The athletic director kept everything very close to the vest and expected his people to do the same. That's why from the very beginning it was difficult to know any of the names on Greenspan's short list. I remember being asked by my newspaper to come up with a list of possible candidates and throwing together a list that we then ran in the paper. The problem was they were just guesses. Educated guesses? Sure. But no one on the inside had actually confirmed any of them. They were just the usual suspects.

But the leaks from within were harder and harder to come by. There was one suspected leak in Bryan Hall (the president's office) who many believed had a direct pipeline to ESPN, but that was never confirmed. Beyond that, a lot of media outlets were resorting to the "a person with knowledge of the coaching search at Indiana" kind of source. And that could have been anyone. Heck, that could have been a reporter talking to another reporter. That's exactly why unnamed sources are a dangerous animal.

At Crean's introductory press conference, I found it interesting that Harry Gonso, the head of the search committee, wanted to take one final shot at those who had rumored different candidates and specifically anyone who had reportedly been offered the job.

"Good morning," Gonso began the press conference. "We started this process about two weeks ago, and we are here today with a good result. President McRobbie delivered to us a charge and we, I think, satisfied every requirement that he asked we achieve in our search."

Gonso went on to thank the various committee members who were in attendance as well as Eddie Fogler, who served as a consultant for the committee.

"I want to make it clear that we offered this position to only one person, notwithstanding press reports, and this morning, today and hereafter we will only talk about Tom Crean, and we will not talk about anybody we considered, did not consider, or anybody that we talked with."

Rick Greenspan took it from there. He welcomed the Crean family to Bloomington and thanked Gonso for his service. He then talked about what the search was really all about.

And also what it was not about.

"This process of hiring a coach is not about gamesmanship, it is not about coaches leveraging their current institutions for more money or ego enhancement," Greenspan said. "The process is about identifying and hiring the best individual that can lead the IU basketball program to a level of academic and athletic success on par with the high expectations of our fans, our alumni and our campus leadership."

Then Greenspan took his own shot at the media.

"As Harry stated, the reports of many coaches, agents and others about their involvement, about their contacts, about their offerings, are both poor journalism and inaccurate," Greenspan said.

With that behind him, Greenspan focused at the moment at hand.

"It is my distinct pleasure to introduce our new men's basketball coach, Tom Crean," Greenspan said. "Tom understands our desire to build a partnership so that greater collaboration and appreciation between our constituents will occur. Through our most visible intercollegiate athletic program, our men's basketball program, we will positively exploit the success which will occur to introduce and re-familiarize many with this great institution that we call Indiana University.

"I am pleased to introduce to you Tom Crean."

॥ ॥

Jane Hoeppner, widow of IU football coach Terry Hoeppner, who had died of brain cancer the previous summer, listened to Crean's introductory press conference on the radio.

She said she closed her eyes and felt as if she could feel the same energy, enthusiasm and excitement for the task at hand with Crean as she had remembered with her husband when he was introduced as the new IU coach in December 2004.

"I thought I was hearing my husband speak all over again," Hoeppner said. "Tom had the same passion and the same excitement in his voice. You knew from the very beginning that he got it."

As he stood before members of the university hierarchy, athletic administration staff and the media for the first time, Crean was honest, sincere, and passionate about the task at hand. He may have been a little humbled, too. Crean was clearly a person who embraced tradition, and he was now in a place where that tradition sprung from every corner of Assembly Hall.

"It has been a whirlwind of feelings, emotions, some incredible sadness with the people I am leaving, but at the same time incredible joy with what I am doing," Crean said as he began.

It was then that he held up the Crean & Crimson shirt. As an aside, by the end of the week, it seemed like everyone in the Hoosier Nation had picked up one of their own.

"I was handed this about an hour ago," Crean said, holding up the shirt. "I guess that puts a little in perspective of where I'm at. I have so many feelings, so many emotions that are swirling around in me, and I am going to try and tie them up in the right way."

He introduced his family one by one and asked them all to stand. "There is no chance for me to have any success whatsoever without the love and support and the joy that my family brings me," Crean said.

He talked about his extended family: His wife Joani's brothers, the football Harbaughs John and Jim, and father Jack. "I have to start with family because that is what I just walked into," Crean said. "And I want you to understand how important family is to me."

Crean then began to talk about what it meant to be at Indiana.

"I walked into a tradition I've understood and had great feelings for since I was really young," Crean said. "I'll never forget the '76 championship game. I was 10 years of age. When I went to Marquette nine years ago yesterday, I'll never forget the '77 game when Marquette played North Carolina. Those were the defining moments in a little boy's life, in my mind as I go back and look at it, of what basketball turned out to mean to me.

"Even though I lived in the state of Michigan and I was too young to be a fan, I loved watching Indiana. I loved it. Later that summer, Special Olympics was really big at Central Michigan and they were one of the forerunners of getting celebrities in. And I would go and get autographs from the different actors and actresses and different things like that. There was never a bigger celebrity in my mind that walked in to Central Michigan University than Kent Benson. And I kept a picture in my mother's house back in Michigan for many, many years. I'm not sure, it's probably so old and broken up right now because it was a picture of Kent Benson standing there in his Indiana uniform. Those are things that I remember. I remember so much of growing up in the state of Michigan and becoming a Big Ten basketball fan. I remember so much watching Indiana play."

Crean said the first coaching clinic he attended out of Mount Pleasant, Michigan, was with Bob Knight.

"I had a chance to come with my two high school coaches to a Bob Knight coaches academy for two days," Crean said. "It was one of the most mesmerizing things I had ever seen in my life. Those are the things that shaped my feelings about Indiana at a young age."

It was then that Crean began to try to put into words how difficult it was to leave Marquette, a place he had once believed was his dream job.

"I haven't had the right words when I've been asked whether it was yesterday when I tried to explain why I was coming here and leaving what I felt for the last nine years at Marquette was the greatest job," Crean said. "I have told some friends (at Marquette) that have covered us that I feel like I have the greatest job in the world. I did not know that when I first started. The people that I worked with, the players that I coached, the 23 out of 23 people that used their eligibility at Marquette that all graduated. I felt like I had the best."

But that was before he received a call from Eddie Fogler, who was a consultant for the IU search committee. Fogler played at North Carolina and then spent 15 seasons as the head coach at Wichita State, Vanderbilt and South Carolina from 1986-2001.

"For those of you that don't know, if Eddie Fogler calls you, you pick it up," Crean said in the press conference. "Because when he calls, you are going to be a lot better off when you are off the conversation. Now I had no idea how much better off I was going to be. But I listened, and I thought, and I listened and I thought. And I'd still come back to what I thought at the very beginning if anybody asked me why: It's Indiana. It's Indiana."

Again, those two little words that when uttered, sent chills down the spine of Indiana basketball fans everywhere. They were words that trumpeted home a single message: He gets it.

Crean followed up on those words with more talk about tradition.

"That is the bottom line," he said, "and that is the premise that we are going to work under here. That is the premise that we are going to undertake the challenge. Because the incredible tradition that is at this university and in the state of Indiana, and I grew up in Michigan and I've spent the last nine years in Wisconsin, I know what the state of Indiana holds. I know what the values are because in coming in to recruit, in coming in to compete and in being part of the Midwest fabric for all these years, I know the fabric of this state.

"I don't know it like I am going to know it tomorrow. I don't know it like I am going to know it in a week. I don't know it how I am going to know it in the next five to 10 years. Well, I tell you, I guess I have an eight-year contact, I better say 10. Hint, hint. But I am going to learn more and more what the state of Indiana is all about. I am going to learn what Indiana is all about. I am going to learn what IU stands for. But I am going to have no trouble whatsoever embracing the tradition of what this university has stood for in the side of men's basketball. Because I have been a fan for a long, long time. It's Indiana."

Crean said one thing you realize very quickly is that Indiana basketball is bigger than any one person.

"As we go through this process, as we embrace the tradition, we take over a very challenging situation, which I hope all of you realize it is, and I realize that," Crean said. "And more than anything else, I think that has lit something in my heart that I couldn't explain. That I have incredible passion and desire to come in and help build on this tradition. Because Indiana basketball is probably much like the state of Indiana. It's been bigger than any one person.

"Household names have coached here, like Branch McCracken and Bob Knight, obviously. Household names have played here. Some of the most successful businessmen and businesswomen, leaders in education, leaders in the political world, leaders in the law field, you name it, have come through this University. When I learned there were 500,000 alumni and 250,000 are in the state of Indiana, that hit home to me. Because this is Indiana. It's Indiana."

Back to that Indiana thing again. The more Crean talked, the more you could feel the energy, enthusiasm and excitement that Jane Hoeppner said reminded her of her husband.

"I don't have a lot of eloquent things to tell you in the sense of why I am so excited, I just know how I feel," Crean said. "It's an honor. It's a humbling honor. And just as it was nine years ago to take over the Marquette program and to build on the tradition that was there and to work with people that aren't household names to you but are in the fabric of our lives. Father Robert A. Wild, our president. Greg Kliebhan, our senior vice president, Bill Cords, the athletic director that hired me; Steve Cottingham, the athletic director that I left yesterday, and all the other administrators, faculty and athletic personnel, student-athletes, academic support, strength coach, trainer, but most importantly, those young men.

"I've had a chance to meet with my team today and without getting into details of everything we talked about, I told them the same thing I told my team last night. Which was as painful as anything I think I have ever done in my adult life. I won't say I said goodbye, but to tell them how I felt about them. I had their heart, and they had mine. And that is exactly what I am looking for at this university. That is exactly what I am looking for."

From that he transitioned into his thoughts of what he's looking for in an Indiana basketball player.

"I am looking for people that are going to understand why we wear the candy-striped pants," Crean said, clearly scoring points with the IU traditionalists everywhere. "I am going to look for people who understand what that uniform stands for, why it says 'Indiana' on the front. I want people to understand what I feel from being at Michigan State. When I was at Michigan State working for Tom Izzo, there was never, ever a louder place or more challenging place to play than Assembly Hall.

"One of the three greatest locker rooms I have ever been in, in my life, was at Michigan State when we had an opportunity to beat Indiana here. Because when you beat Indiana, it was something. It was absolutely something. And that hit me and it hit me as I flew in here last night. We are going to have that. We are going to have a presence in here. We're going to have a standard that when people come to Indiana, they know they're here. They know they're here. The opponent will know that they are smack-dab in the middle of Hoosier Nation, which I am absolutely emphatic and excited about getting a chance to meet and get to know."

Crean talked about the first group of people who met him the night before at the Monroe County Airport. They had found a way into a restricted area and wanted to welcome their new coach.

"I had a chance to meet about seven or eight of them last night that snuck into the hangar in their big red wigs hair and their sweatshirts," Crean said. "And I signed every shirt I could sign of those seven or eight. I got the fight song sung for me out in front of the Hilton Garden Inn last night. And they were right on cue, and I don't know if they knew the words or not because I don't know it yet, but I'm going to trust them.

"That, I guess to me, is what Hoosier Nation is all about. And the Crean family cannot wait to be a part of that. Because for the last nine years, we've been as blessed and as fortunate as anybody who does this job in America, to work with the people that we worked with, to be in the environment that we were in."

Which again took him to trying to explain how he could leave a situation like that. A place where he had advanced a team to the Final Four in 2003. A place where in his final seven seasons, Marquette had a record of 160-68.

"There is absolutely no way, for what it's worth to you, from the bottom of my heart, there is absolutely no way that I would have left what we had there and what we were building if it wasn't for what I feel is the pinnacle, the absolute pinnacle of all of college basketball," Crean said. "And that is to be the head basketball coach at Indiana University.

"And I am extremely proud, I am incredibly grateful. There is no question that we are humbled. And I cannot wait, I cannot wait to represent these young men, to represent this University, to represent the faculty, to represent the student body, to represent the state of Indiana as the head basketball coach here."

He concluded his opening remarks by thanking Greenspan, Gonso and President McRobbie.

"I thank you very much for giving us this opportunity," Crean said. "Thank you to everybody up here. Your president, our president, I am a big fan of right now. In a short period of time, I've had a chance to visit with him. Just as I held up this shirt at the beginning and talked about the people at the hangar, our eyes are wide open right now for the greatness that is Indiana basketball, Indiana University and the state of Indiana.

"And we cannot wait to get started. Thank you."

Chapter 9

Next on tap at Crean's introductory press conference was to field questions from the Indiana media.

The first person asked Crean to address the challenges that were ahead for the university, which was currently under a dark cloud with the NCAA investigation.

"This place, this university, this basketball program, for as long as I can remember, as long I've paid attention, as I said a little while ago, has been bigger than any one person," Crean said. "There are household names that have coached it. There are household names that have played in it, but all along the way it has stood for class. It has stood for integrity. It has stood for doing the right thing. It has stood for being the right way. It has stood for treating people with respect. It has stood for giving people respect, and the only way that you can get respect is to have self-respect.

"If you do those things, and right now we are not going to be overwhelmed by the challenges. We're going to have to embrace them because there is no other way to look at it. I'm going to say this. The sanctions that were imposed in-house on Indiana by Indiana, they are very, very strong. They are very strong. I have to say I was shocked when I looked at them because Indiana grabbed a situation, and they handled it."

He said he didn't really have many personal feelings on what happened before he arrived.

"That is not on my watch," Crean said. "My watch started when I got in town last night, and it really started at 10 o'clock when I met our players. We're going to deal with this head-on. We're going to deal with it with everybody that is a part of my life inside of this program, that is a part of this staff, that is a part of this team. We're going to deal with it with our eyes wide open. We're going to deal with a connection of trying to make what is best for each other happen. We're not going to let it detour us. Is it going to be a challenge? It is probably going to be a greater challenge than even I realize, and I've thought a lot about it."

And again Crean leaned on tradition and how that tradition would help carry Indiana through.

"We have an incredible tradition during a very challenging time at Indiana," Crean said. "We're going to build on the tradition, and the only way to do that is to go full boar, and that is what we're going to do. As far as the young men, I've paid attention, I've read, I've listened, but now it starts and I don't have an answer for you. We're going to take it, I'd like to say day-by-day but we'll get a lot more things done than a couple of things in a day, so I guess we're going to take it hour-by-hour and we'll just see how it all shapes out. I don't have an answer that I could give you that would be correct right now on that part."

An obvious question on the minds of many had to do with recruiting. A few days before, Dan Dakich had dismissed Armon Bassett and Jamarcus Ellis from the team. The numbers were dwindling within the program, and Crean and his staff were going to have to put together a group that could represent IU on the court in a very short period of time.

"We're going to get into that process quickly," Crean said. "I don't want to comment on recruiting as much right now except that we're going to do everything we can to study and to get to know the four young men that have committed or signed to this university, and also to continue to recruit. We're going to need the Hoosier Nation's help, in a good way, and this is what I mean by that. We need everyone to understand that this is going to take some time. We need everyone to understand that we're here for the long haul; we're here to build.

"I walked away from a very long contract, and I got one that I'm very proud of right here. The years to me and the security of the years is important for the family, but it also shows values of what you want in recruiting. I want the people looking at this university, including those four young men, to understand that we are here for the long haul, we are here to build it in a way that is going to be outstanding."

Crean said he didn't have a quick master plan in place but rather he planned to do things the right away. After what Indiana basketball had been through the previous two seasons with Sampson, that was another breath of fresh air.

"I have no timetable, no promises to make," Crean said. "I have no numerical goals to hit right now, but that we're going to build it the right way and I want those people to feel a part of that, and I want to make sure that they understand where we're coming from. With that being said, with the four signees and what else we do with recruiting, the way the Hoosier Nation can help so much is to make sure that you keep showing that passion and you keep being excited about the tradition and trust that we're going to do everything that we can do to build on that tradition and have that excitement.

"I don't need people to be making phone calls. We don't need any of that. What I need people to do is wear the shirts, if they're selling these (he held up the Crean & Crimson shirt again), go buy a couple. Wear your shirts, wear your sweatshirts, wear your hats, because the more that that is shown throughout this state, the more people are going to understand again how important this program is to everybody, and I think that is going to help as much as anything."

Crean was asked how quickly he made the decision to take the Indiana job.

"I would say that it has been so quick," Crean said. "There is no good time to leave. There is no good time to say goodbye. It happened so fast. I would say at some point in time between the first two conversations and feeling that there was a genuine interest from this university, and that really brought the fan out in me.

"If you are a college basketball fan you realize that this is, maybe somebody is going to rank it in the top three, maybe someone is going to rank it in the top five, maybe someone is going to rank it in the top 10. I'm going to rank it number one."

Crean said it was simply a feeling in his heart.

"When my heart felt that, my wife and I were able to talk about that," Crean said. "I was able to go back to being the fan that I was of this program. It was hard because I knew what I was leaving, but in my heart I just felt like this was the right thing for me and for us, because I'm incredibly excited about the challenge. So, it happened very fast."

Crean was asked to talk about his style of basketball, both offensively and defensively.

"That is a good question because I think it is constantly on-going," Crean said. "I think the one thing that I've always tried to be and surround myself with is people that have questions and not just answers. I think every time you can tweak your system to make it better, every time you can take a part of it and add to your personnel, I think that is a big deal.

"What we're going to try to do first off is we're going to have to be in incredible condition. Incredible condition. Coming from the Big East and certainly having awareness of the Big Ten, if you are not in great shape and you don't have outstanding physical strength, it is going to be tough, but more important than the conditioning and the physical strength is going to be the mindset, the mental toughness that you have to have to win in this league, to win at home, to win on the road."

Crean said he believed the character development, the player development would be an ongoing thing.

"I felt that always at Marquette I was the player development coach, and I worked with our players," Crean said. "I rarely ever missed an individual instruction, and during the offseason, I missed probably two in the last four years. I believe wholeheartedly in the individual development of the players, and I believe in it as an on-going process throughout the offseason in the time allowed by the NCAA and certainly the time inside the season.

"Then, I think your style develops from there. I would like to see us be able to have an outstanding fast break, a team that runs not only on misses, but on makes. That is something I got from Tom Izzo from the years at Michigan State. That is something that they obviously do an outstanding job of and that's something I took from him."

Crean said he wasn't a coach that runs the motion offense. He said he doesn't run the Georgetown offense, either, or what some may call the Princeton offense.

"We're a team that is going to get up and down the floor, drive in space," Crean said. "We're going to do our best to get the ball inside out. We want to score points in the lane. Some of our best post-up players at Marquette have obviously been our guards. Dwyane Wade was obviously one of the best, but young men I'm leaving behind, Jerel McNeal and Wesley Matthews, were outstanding. Dominic James from Richmond, Indiana, was as good as anybody we've had from the post —and he's 5-10—because he can create for so many people.

"I think our offense is going to be based on drive and kick, quick hitters, mismatches, matchups and pushing the ball at every turn. Having a team that wants to learn how to play inside of that allows them some real creativity and freedom."

Crean said the Hoosiers will also be a team that plays in-your-face defense.

"On the defensive end, we're going to guard the three," Crean said. "We were one of the best teams in the country this past year of guarding the three. I want to have an outstanding half-court defense. I think there is room to mix defenses. I think there is room to pickup full court, but most importantly inside of the game is you've got to have guys that are going to make great decisions, guys that can execute under pressure, and the constant is going to be the rebounding."

Crean said it was still early. He said there was a lot of film left to evaluate, too.

"With all that being said, I don't know our team yet," Crean said. "I haven't studied the film. Some coaches walk into a situation and they don't want to watch any film. I want to watch every film I can because I know they've been successful. I want to watch how they were coached, I want to watch how they responded, I want to watch how they played, I want to watch their competitive level. I'm really looking to see how I can help them within these next few weeks before school is out in their individual development."

A natural question for Crean was going to be what it would be like to be in the same conference with his close friend and mentor Tom Izzo at Michigan State.

"We've talked quite a bit and I'll say this, the Big Ten has an incredible friend in Tom Izzo, and Indiana has a big fan in Tom Izzo, because he is as good a friend as I have," Crean said. "That isn't going to change. Our friendship is so far above anything that would happen competitively, which it has got to be. With the same thing in mind, we want to kick his tail. Make no mistake, the last time I matched up with him, we didn't play so well in the NCAA tournament.

"But, he thought this was a great move for me. He has been the one constant outside of my family and a few others that I turn to. He has been a mentor through so many situations. He gave me outstanding advice, and like I said, he is a big fan of this university and of the league, and he was very high on me coming in here."

Crean was asked about the importance of recruiting within the state of Indiana, a hotbed of basketball recruits in recent years. Crean said recruiting begins inside out.

"I've learned that from every coach that I've ever worked for," Crean said. "If you start inside out, then you can branch from there. It is going to be so important right now that the state of Indiana understands that this is the state university. This is the university that has been on people's lips and people's minds for decade after decade after decade. And I'm sure that there are many people that have grown up in this state and they've understood that since birth, and I want to make sure that we find those people. I want to make sure that they understand that we're here for the same reasons that they grew up that way."

Crean talked about quotes that he had read in the newspaper that day with a few former IU players weighing in on the projected hiring of Crean by the Hoosiers. One of those quotes was from Isiah Thomas. Thomas had been quoted earlier in the process about believing that the Hoosiers should hire interim coach Dan Dakich for the full-time position.

"(Tom) has a brilliant basketball mind and it's definitely a good hire for Indiana," Thomas said. "I was very vocal about Dan (Dakich) getting the job, but Tom is definitely qualified and will do an excellent job at Indiana. Any way that I can help him, I definitely will."

Jared Jeffries, a former IU All-American and then a player for the New York Knicks, agreed with Thomas' assessment.

"I think it's a very good move," Jeffries said. "He's proven himself to be a successful college coach at this level, a very good recruiter, recognize talent. That's who we need at Indiana, we need somebody who is going to be stable, a foundation for our future."

Reading those words struck a chord with Crean, too.

"I understand the tradition. I understand the great players," Crean said. "I saw Isiah Thomas' quote in the *Associated Press* article and Jared Jeffries quote. I wanted to cry. That to me was awesome. That is the sign of where we've got to be. I want people to understand Wayne Radford, Chris Reynolds, Ted Kitchel, Kent Benson, Scott May, Quinn Buckner, Damon Bailey, Calbert Cheaney.

"When I came to that Bob Knight clinic, Pat Graham was on an unofficial visit, I believe. I've got to go on and on and I'm not trying to miss anybody because I'm going to try to make sure that I touch everybody. But this base of alumni is just so strong that somebody growing up in Indiana should want to follow in that. It is our job to help them understand that. It's our job to keep giving the education as to why this is."

Back on point, Crean said IU's recruiting will begin with Indiana first.

"The inside out starts with Indiana, it branches throughout the Midwest, but there is absolutely no reason that the state of Indiana can't be a great opportunity with Indiana basketball in the forefront for any young man in any state in the country," Crean said. "We will recruit programs as much as we will recruit players, because when you can find great programs that develop talented, character-driven, work ethic, energy-filled people, you're going to win, and that is what we're really going to start looking for real quick."

Crean continued on in his question-and-answer session. He fielded a question about how he would assemble his staff, and another on whether it's important to have an a assistant with Indiana ties.

"No matter if you played here, no matter if you've never been here, you've got to continue to sharpen that knife every day where it comes to understanding the passion that you need to coach at a place like Indiana," Crean said. "Right now, with that said, I don't have anything ruled or etched in stone right now."

He was asked about convincing Holloway and Ebanks to stay with Indiana or let them move on.

"I think the biggest thing I'm going to try to do is explain why I'm here and what Indiana means to me," Crean said. "Every person that chooses a university, a job, a spouse—you name it—there is a reason. Every one of those young men chose this university for different reasons and it is probably more than one. Certainly the coach and the coaching staff is a big part of that. There have got to be things that drove them to make that decision, just like there were things that drove me to make my decision.

"I'm going to try to get that across to them. I'm going to try to let them know what I feel about Indiana. I'm also going to let them know what I feel about winning and what I feel about work ethic, what I feel about what it is going to take to be successful here and do my absolute best to convey that."

Crean said it might not work out, but it was too early to tell.

"If it is not good enough, or I don't think it is the right fit, then we're going to have to make that decision," Crean said. "It is like the players I met with today. We're all going to start, we're going to get to know each other and see where it can go. I plan to meet with those people quickly, very quickly. It is not going to just be me talking to them about what I see. I want to know what they see and what they want.

"I've only been here for a few hours, but I don't know what there is not to want or what there is to get that you can't get at Indiana. I know that we don't have the arena full for a game for them to come in and see right now, but I know we'll find some video. I can't wait for people to be on this campus. I can't wait to start the unofficial visits, which are absolutely going to be paramount to whatever success we have in recruiting. I can't wait for them to see what this arena is like when it is filled, but in the meantime, there are going to be a lot of other things that have to go on before that. We're going to work at that starting today."

Crean was asked if there was anything Marquette could have done to keep him after he had decided to leave Indiana. He said the answer was 'No.' Apparently the question had been asked by a student reporter from Marquette.

"I tried to explain this to our president and our senior vice president last night," Crean said. "I can't be thankful enough for my time at Marquette. Steve is a reporter for our student newspaper. When I arrived at Marquette nine years ago, we probably weren't selling six hundred season tickets to the students. Every year the student ticket seating has gone up.

"The students at Marquette, it has been a love affair. When I first got there, we had an event called 'Coffee, Crean and Donuts' that 17 people showed up for. I wasn't sure we were going to have the fan base then, but the 22 largest crowds in the state of Wisconsin later, our fans and our students really bought in and I'm proud of that.

"There is absolutely nothing that could've happened once I got the feeling, because Marquette has done more for me than I ever could have imagined. They did more for me in every area, and this was a heart decision. It was not a business decision, it was not a legacy decision. This was a heart decision. There had been other chances to leave, and it never felt like that because I felt like I had the greatest job in the world. I walked away from an incredible job to take another one. It just so happens that this one has been at the pinnacle of this business of college basketball for a long time. I'm going to miss those people there a lot. I really am. I'm excited to learn this environment. I learned so much at Marquette. I learned about appreciating fans, appreciating students, appreciating young children for what they mean, and I'm going to do what I can do to bring my lessons there to here."

Finally, Crean was asked about what he hoped to experience with Indiana's students.

"Get them set up right now, we'll find out. Let's meet them right now," Crean said. "I've probably met twelve so far. Four in front of the Hilton and seven or eight last night. I can't wait. I can't wait. Roy Williams said something the first summer I was at Marquette when we had that 'Coffee, Crean and Donuts' event that 17 people showed up for. He said that when he got to Kansas, the first clinic they had had 18 people. The first camp he ran had 117 people.

"That put everything in perspective for me that you have to build it up. We worked incredibly hard to build it up. I have no doubt that I've walked into the Cadillac area of students, fans, alums, supports, and I've got to say that when I was at Michigan State with Tom (Izzo), there was never a tougher place to be than Assembly Hall. I doubt it has changed much. I doubt it has changed. We're going to do everything we can do as a family of the Crean's, as a coaching staff, as a support staff, and as a player group to make sure that every one of the students knows that we appreciate them and respect them, and I can't wait to start meeting more of them."

On the day that Crean was hired, Bob Kravitz wrote a simple column in the *Indianapolis Star* that set the stage for what was to come. His basic premise: Indiana got the right guy.

They got it right. Whether it was the 10-person committee or embattled Athletic Director Rick Greenspan, or maybe a much-needed stroke of dumb luck, Indiana University's basketball coaching search unearthed a very good man for the Hoosiers job.

Tom Crean.

He isn't the biggest name out there, or the sexiest, and I continue to be confused why Greenspan and his minions didn't even contact Michigan State's Tom Izzo, who actually helped groom Crean during four years in East Lansing.

But this is a solid choice.

A smart choice.

A choice that should, at least for the moment, quiet those of us who have ripped the school's administration for its amateurish bungling of all things Kelvin Sampson.

Here are a few reasons to like the hiring, which will be announced today in Bloomington:

He's clean. At least he hasn't been called on the carpet for his ethics or suspected NCAA rules violations. Crean has been at Marquette for nine years, and there's never been a whiff of impropriety. We're going to assume the 10-person committee spent some quality time perusing his phone records. I wonder, what cellular service does he use?

He has Big Ten/Midwest ties. In some ways, he's Izzo Light, having worked as Izzo's right-hand man. He was a big–time recruiter at Michigan State, helping land Mateen Cleaves and Morris Peterson. At Marquette, he brought in Dwyane Wade and Richmond's Dominic James. He won't need a GPS to navigate the state.

He's a winner. The won-loss numbers (190-96) aren't gaudy, but understand he went 30-28 in his first two seasons. Since then, he has been a consistent producer of 20-plus win seasons, reaching one Sweet Sixteen and, of course, the Final Four in 2003, led by Wade and current Pacers guard Travis Diener. Marquette's success continued even after the school moved from Conference USA to the beastly Big East in 2005.

He makes sure his players graduate.

This time around, the new coach won't have to deal with uncomfortable questions about his brutal graduation rate at his previous school.

In a study of graduation rates for teams in the 2008 NCAA Tournament, Marquette finished in the top 10, alongside Butler, Purdue and Notre Dame.

In the latest Graduate Success Rate chart, Marquette's basketball team had an 89 percent graduation rate, including 86 percent for black student-athletes, who historically graduate at a far lower rate than white players.

Those numbers are important to the people around here. And, apparently, they're important to Crean as well. Another reason this is a good, smart fit.

Crean is here because Crean wanted to be here, desperately wanted to be here, despite a lucrative contract at Marquette that stretched until 2016-17.

While IU has not played or acted much like a top five — or even top 10 — program in recent years, Crean and most others understand that this is a sleeping giant, that despite the turmoil this decade, IU basketball still means something. With the right man and the right decisions, IU can be one of those top-five programs once again.

But it's going to take some work. A lot of work. Crean should know this going in: He's taking over a giant mess.

He will have to deal with the sanctions IU self-imposed during Sampson's reign. The Kelvin era is the gift that keeps on giving. There will be limits on recruiting this summer, which is bad news any year, but especially now, with IU's roster down to bare bones.

He will have to deal with whatever sanctions the NCAA might impose after this summer's hearing. It's unlikely the Hoosiers will get blasted since they got rid of Sampson, but that's no guarantee.

He will have to deal with a rebuilding situation. D.J. White is leaving. Lance Stemler is leaving. Eric Gordon will surely announce for the NBA draft.

Then there's the sad, strange case of Jamarcus Ellis and Armon Bassett, who were dismissed from the team by interim coach Dan Dakich.

Now the question becomes: Is that dismissal still in force, or will the players be given an opportunity to somehow work their way back into the program's good graces? It seems to me Dakich did the right thing and the tough thing, and if Greenspan signed off on the decision, then it should be binding. Either Bassett and Ellis disgraced IU basketball or they didn't. That shouldn't change because a new coach is in charge.

That said, Greenspan and Crean know how badly they will need Bassett and Ellis, who would be the only two starters returning.

Do they make the basketball decision? Or the right decision? We will learn a lot about Crean by the way he handles a very awkward and explosive situation.

So welcome to Bloomington, Tom. Just business as (un)usual around these parts. Fix a broken program. And do it within a year. Maybe two.

Sure you still want this gig?

Fans have high hopes that Tom Crean can be the coach who restores Indiana basketball to prominence and will one day lead IU to its first national championship banner since 1987.

Chapter 10

Before Tom Crean was even officially introduced at a press conference on April 2, 2008, he had his first meeting with the potential returning members of his team. There were six players in attendance: Jordan Crawford, Eli Holman, Brandon McGee, DeAndre Thomas, Kyle Taber and Brett Finkelmeier. Eric Gordon, though still technically a member of the team, had all but officially decided to head to the NBA and wasn't at the meeting. The following week, Gordon made his NBA intentions known in a press conference in Indianapolis.

The future of two other players was still in question, too.

Two days before Crean was hired, interim coach Dan Dakich had dismissed two of IU's starters from the previous season: Jamarcus Ellis and Armon Bassett. Dakich was tired of the attitude he was getting from the two players on their academics and on issues both on and off the court. He scheduled an appointment to meet with them, but they skipped it. Because of that, he told them they were going to have to run laps for their punishment. When they also skipped out on that, Dakich informed them he had kicked them off the team. He placed all of their gear in trash bags and left them in the basketball offices with their names on them to be picked up.

The night before Crean was officially introduced as IU's coach, Dakich stood in the entryway to the basketball offices and talked candidly with a reporter about what had happened. And leaning against the office walls were the trash bags of gear still unclaimed.

It was initially unclear whether Crean would uphold that decision or allow the two to come back. If he did the latter, he would at least be returning two starters. Bassett averaged 11.4 points and Ellis 6.8 the year before.

But truthfully, Dakich's move, though it may have been the right one, put Crean between a rock and a hard place. If he allowed the pair to come back, was that really the message Crean wanted to convey in his first month on the job? All eyes would be on him until he ultimately made a decision.

As Crean looked around the room in that first meeting, he at least still had some warm bodies in the program. Five players in the room were on scholarship (everyone except Finkelmeier).

The first thing Crean did when he walked in the room was he look at Eli Holman and smile. He told everyone in the room that he had recruited Holman for Marquette but added that he apparently hadn't done a very good job. The six players in the room, including Holman, smiled. The ice was broken. He then added that he hoped he would have a chance to coach Holman with the Hoosiers.

A few days later, Holman returned to California to talk things over with his family. But his first impression of Crean that day was favorable. He said Crean was passionate, confident and straight forward with what he said to the players.

"He didn't beat around the bush about anything," Holman said. "He came out straightforward and said what he had to say whether people liked it or not."

Part of Crean's message that day had to do with attending class. That was one of Dakich's biggest beefs with this group, and Crean was pounding that point home. If they didn't do anything else, they needed to complete their academic requirements.

Overall, Holman said he thought Crean made a good first impression with all six players in the room.

Crawford, who admitted that first day that he had yet to decide if he would return to IU in the fall, said he thought Crean was committed to making the Hoosiers better.

"He told us how he was going to get us ready and how he was going to get on the recruiting scene," Crawford said. "He said he's ready to have a good season next year rather than just holding off and trying to build up, year by year."

A big question on the minds of several of the players in that room had to do with the status of Bassett and Ellis. Neither of the two were at the meeting, but Athletic Director Rick Greenspan said he didn't think either were invited.

When Crean was asked about it after his press conference, he said he hadn't decided the longterm status of the pair.

Crawford said at the time that he hoped the players would be allowed to return. He said Ellis, in particular, never said he wanted to transfer, contrary to some media reports. He said both players were excited when they first heard the news that Crean had been named the Indiana coach.

"I think it was all a big misunderstanding," Crawford said that day. "Jamarcus had no intentions of leaving at all, and Armon, he loves playing with everybody on the team. I think they're both excited and want to come back."

Rick Greenspan, on the other hand, made it clear that he supported Dakich's decision to dismiss the two players.

"Dan and I had a lot of communications about expectations for right and wrong, and how kids should be in the right place at the right time and be respectful," Greenspan said. "The actions that Dan took were supported completely by me. People can criticize that. But when I asked Dan to be the interim coach, I told him that I wanted him to run this team like it was his team until it wasn't his team anymore."

Greenspan said both Bassett and Ellis had tried to meet with him earlier in the week, but he had been out of the office with the coaching search. He felt that what needed to happen was for both players to speak with Crean.

"I believe they need to talk with Tom because he's the basketball coach," Greenspan said. "What Tom does moving forward, whether he wants to talk to those players or whatever, has not been determined. We have not taken a formal step of scholarship revocation. But I thought it was a very significant and important message that Dan sent about what I think this university stands for."

If Crean was to uphold the dismissal of Ellis and Bassett, his returning nucleus would have looked like this:

- Jordan Crawford, a 6-2 sophomore shooting guard, had been the fourth-leading scorer from the year before. He averaged 9.7 points.

- DeAndre Thomas, a 6-8, 303-pound power forward, averaged 3.6 points. The problem with Thomas is that he and Ellis had always been a package deal, both in high school in Chicago and then in junior college at Chipola in Florida.

- Eli Holman, a 6-10, four-star recruit out of Richmond (Calif.) High School. He had suffered a left wrist injury after six games as a freshman but had a good chance of receiving a medical redshirt.

- Brandon McGee, a 6-7 power forward from Crane High School in Chicago. McGee played in 17 games and averaged 1.5 points per game as a freshman.

- Kyle Taber, a 6-7 forward, had played in 22 games and averaged 1.3 points the year before. Taber was a walk-on his first two seasons at IU but was put on scholarship by Kelvin Sampson as a junior.

- Brett Finkelmeier, a 6-foot guard, played in seven games as a walk-on the year before and scored a total of two points.

One of the things the players learned in that first meeting was how Crean hoped to conduct individual workouts with those six players he had on hand.

The first week he held two one-hour workouts. The first one was on Tuesday, April 8, and four players were in attendance: Crawford, McGee, Taber and Finkelmeier. Thomas was sick and Holman was still in California.

The second week he had three 40-minute workouts, and all players were in attendance. Crean said players were working three in a group, and the staff was trying to maximize that time as much as possible.

೫೦   ೮೪

At the same time that he was watching film of his current team and getting acquainted with those who could potentially be on his roster in the fall, Crean had plenty of other things on his plate.

He had to assemble his coaching staff and support personnel. He needed to figure out where he was with the four players who had signed letters of intent the previous November to play for Kelvin Sampson. And he also needed to figure out with the compliance people just what he was and was not able to do from a recruiting standpoint. Because of IU's self-imposed sanctions, Crean and his staff were behind the eight-ball in terms of the off-campus recruiting they were able to do in the first few months.

As for filling his coaching vacancies, the first two assistants to be added to the staff were no-brainers. Tim Buckley and Bennie Seltzer had been with Crean at Marquette, and he wanted them to join him at IU.

Buckley had come right away, and in fact he and Crean had been scouring recruiting literature at a hotel room at the Hilton Garden Inn the first night Crean was on the job. With recruiting being a round-the-clock operation anyway, the process had been made that much more difficult with the Hoosiers basically having to form a team in the spring that would compete in the fall. The talent pool of players who chose not to sign in November simply was not at the highest levels and made Indiana's initial recruiting efforts that much more difficult.

"As soon as Coach took the job, we started to compile a list of potential prospects," Buckley said in a 2012 interview. "In the spring there are still some players that had not yet signed. One of the first people we got in touch with was Verdell Jones III. He is someone that we recruited when I was at Iowa, and then when I went to Marquette we stayed in touch even though we did not have a need for a guard like Verdell. Fortunately, he was still available when we got to Indiana."

Buckley said not only were he and Crean making phone calls, but there were people calling in with the names of prospects and sending video. He said they had three boxes that were full of DVDs of prospects.

"At the same time, as each day passed and we lost players from the current Indiana roster, we were also trying to recruit the freshmen, sophomore and junior classes like they were seniors," Buckley said. "We knew we had a lot of work to do to get the program up and running and then to one day keep it going."

How crazy was that first year in terms of recruiting for Crean and his staff? Buckley estimated that they had more than 325 unofficial visits from the time they took the job in April until the first season came to an end.

"We started every day before 7 a.m. and finished well after midnight and sometimes past 2 a.m.," Buckley said. "It was a daunting task, but at the same time it made the fruits of the 2011-12 season that much greater."

Crean said in an interview with Mike Pegram of peegs.com that familiarity with his staff was that much more important at IU because of the self-imposed recruiting restrictions that had been placed on IU basketball because of the NCAA investigation.

"Right now with the way the restrictions are, the way the sanctions are, I think it is incredibly important for me to have people that I have had a working relationship with," Crean said. "We have had a lot of very good applicants and people that I have even reached out to talk to, and I know there was a good staff here. But the bottom line going into this is I have to have people that I have a working knowledge of. They are going to have to be the eyes and ears for so much of what is going on with the evaluation process.

"I feel like a football coach, in a sense, because I'm watching a lot of tape. We have to work within the rules and have (Seltzer and Buckley) representing us. We had a home visit the other night and I have never missed home visits. But Bennie and Tim went into the home visit, and I am sure they did a great job. But that is different, that is a very awkward feeling for me. But it is not awkward in a sense that I don't feel comfortable with them."

In addition to hiring Buckley and Seltzer, Crean plucked two more familiar members of his Marquette staff to take administrative positions at IU. Brian Barone, son of former Texas A&M coach Tony Barone, was hired as IU's video coordinator. He had served in the same position the year before at Marquette and prior to that had been an assistant coach at Illinois State.

The other hire was Jayd Grossman as the assistant athletic director for men's basketball administration. Grossman was Crean's coordinator of student-athlete performance at Marquette. There he supervised sports medicine, strength and conditioning and academic services.

"It was important for me to fill open positions with individuals who are familiar with how I like to do things," Crean said. "Both are two of the best at what they do."

While Crean had plenty of oars in the water with putting together his current team as well as recruiting for the future, he also knew all of the foundation elements were important, too.

"Rick Greenspan said it best," Crean said. "He knows I'm concerned about recruiting, but he said 'Build your foundation.' That's the way I'm looking to build my staff. Get that built, then build everything else around it."

Crean also talked in an early interview with Mike Pegram about three major jobs in every program that have to be filled with the highest level of personnel.

"The three major jobs in your program that have so much guidance with your team, 12 months a year, are your trainer, your strength coach and your academic advisors," Crean said. "We all just have to build our team. Right now with Ian Rickerby we are really working close with him on compliance. So that builds the team up that much more. Just spending a lot of time making sure our foundation is right."

Because of all the struggles that Indiana had been through with the NCAA investigation into recruiting practices, and the reality that Crean and his staff would now be living in a glass house, the new IU coach and his staff were paying extra close attention to compliance issues. That's not to say they didn't before, but they certainly had their arms around it with the Hoosiers.

"When we have meetings (with compliance) they are so detailed, they are so organized, you learn something," Crean said in his interview with Pegram. "Every Indiana question we have had, they are getting an answer for. I have oodles of sheets already. Like I told our coaches, we are going to have a couple of different files or books, and our operations spot will really be a spearhead of that. Every coach has to be totally locked into it. I'm enjoying learning that part of it."

Crean didn't describe it as overwhelming, but it was clear that it was a taxing process nonetheless.

"We have to learn what we have to deal with here," Crean said. "At the same time, the rules are always changing for all of us in coaching and we have to continue to learn those. Then we have to see how we can learn to work inside of those rules. It has really been good. If we are not on the same page in this one area, it really doesn't matter what else happens. We can be on the same page in every area, we know what each other is thinking, but if we are not on the same page in compliance, it won't matter. So we are going to be on the same page."

Another major task for Crean in his first few weeks on the job was looking at the four-man class that had signed in November to play for Indiana and Kelvin Sampson.

The jewel of the class was Devin Ebanks, an athletic 6-8 power forward ranked No. 13 in his class. When he initially signed his letter, he did so with foresight. He had an escape clause in his letter that allowed him to get out of his commitment if something changed with the head coach.

A few days after Crean took the IU job, Ebanks announced that he had formally reopened his recruiting. His summer coach told rivals.com that Ebanks would visit Texas, Rutgers, Memphis and West Virginia. He would eventually choose West Virginia and play for Bob Huggins.

Holloway gave it a little more thought but eventually chose to stay closer to home in Cincinnati and attend Xavier. He also had an escape clause in his letter of intent that gave him an out if there was a coaching change.

That left two members of the class. Fortunately for Crean, both opted to stay at Indiana. Tom Pritchard visited Crean the weekend of April 18-19, and when he got home announced that he was staying put. The other one was Matt Roth, the 3-point specialist from Washington, Illinois, and the all-time 3-point scorer from the state of Illinois. After a little thought, Roth announced he would be staying, too.

With the five players currently in the program on scholarship (Crawford, Holman, McGee, Taber and Thomas) along with Pritchard and Roth, Crean had seven players on scholarship. If he chose not to keep Bassett and Ellis, Crean would have five scholarships to give, as the Hoosiers had taken one away as part of their self-imposed penalties. If Bassett and Ellis were allowed to return, Crean would only have three scholarships to give.

The late signing period went from April 16-May 21, meaning that two weeks after Crean took the job, he potentially would begin bringing players to Indiana.

Because of IU-imposed restrictions, Crean was not supposed to be allowed to recruit off campus or bring players in for official visits until August 1. The university, however, lightened that sanction and gave Crean 10 recruiting days so that he would have a chance to see some of the prospective talent.

"I'm appreciative that the administration was able to look at this and deem that it was appropriate that we could get out and do some things and lift some of these sanctions," Crean said at the time. "I'm excited to be able to do it."

He also didn't waste any time. The next day he was at Ben Davis High School in Indianapolis, where he saw several of the top in-state recruits in the 2009, 2010 and 2011 classes. He even got a good look at Derek Elston, the Tipton (Indiana) standout who had committed to the IU program on September 10, 2007 and was part of IU's class of 2009.

There were coaches from all the major programs in the state in attendance, including Purdue's Matt Painter and Butler's Brad Stevens.

"We're all here doing the same job," Crean said. "I'm behind a little bit more because I am seeing some guys for the first time."

While he wasn't able to bring in players for official visits because of the restrictions, Crean could host any number of unofficial visits and planned to do so that first weekend after getting the job.

"I'm looking forward to getting some recruits on campus and talking to them about what we're hoping to do here," Crean said at the time. "I don't think we'll have a difficult time getting people to come. I think that people who are interested will come and give us a look. At least I hope so."

The Monday after Crean took the Indiana job he made the trip to Indianapolis to be on hand when Eric Gordon made his announcement that he would be heading for the NBA.

After the press conference, Crean talked to reporters. One of the topics that came up was a report that there were some serious academic issues with the players still in the fold. Because of student privacy laws, Crean had to walk gingerly around the question. But he didn't back away from it completely, either.

"I can't elaborate on it, but it's not good," Crean said. "We have a lot of work to do. I think you're going to get sick of hearing me say that, but I have no other way to put it. It's a situation that has to be addressed immediately. But I had no opinions before I got into town and I'm trying to keep it that way. I'm just trying to work every day as we go forward."

Crean's first month on the job was a piece of cake compared to his first few days of May. In a 48-hour period, all hell broke loose within the Indiana basketball program.

It started with an incident in the men's basketball coaching offices involving Eli Holman when he came in to tell Crean of his decision to not return to Indiana. That news was not the news that Crean, in rebuild mode, wanted to hear. So he tried to get Holman to talk about it a little bit more. Holman had probably expected to do a quick in and out, tell Crean he was transferring and be on his way. Instead, the conversation was going on much longer than he anticipated.

The more Holman talked, the angrier he got. By the time he was done, he had thrown a tantrum in the office that led to a flower pot on a secretary's desk getting knocked over and eventually a call to campus police to settle Holman down.

"His behavior took me, along with the other people in the office, by surprise," Crean said in a statement released by the university. "We saw him as a danger to himself and wanted to take precautionary measures to help him. We felt bad for Eli and, hopefully, were able to help him."

According to an *Associated Press* report of the incident, Captain Jerry Minger of the IU Police Department said police were called as more of a precaution and that no one felt threatened. Police did not arrest Holman but took a statement from Crean and others who had been in the office.

Later, Greenspan took Holman into his office for about an hour as officers waited outside. Eventually Holman emerged from the office and left calmly without speaking to police.

The entire situation took Crean by surprise. He had been led to believe that Holman had planned to stay, but then after he talked with "his people" in California, he did an about-face with his decision.

Earlier that day he had met with Buckley and Seltzer, and that's when Crean first heard that Holman was wavering.

"He had a good meeting with our assistant coaches earlier in the day," Crean said in a story with the *Bloomington Herald-Times*. "I felt like he still was not sure whether or not he wanted to be here, which surprised me, because everything we have seen from him had been very positive, in terms of staying at Indiana and moving forward. I have no idea what made him change his mind."

As it would turn out, the Holman decision would just be the tip of the iceberg.

The next day, on May 2, IU announced some sweeping changes within the men's basketball program. In a press release from the university, Crean announced that junior DeAndre Thomas had been dismissed from the program and would not have his scholarship renewed. In addition, Crean announced that sophomore Armon Bassett would not be reinstated for failing to comply with university and athletic department guidelines. Junior Jamarcus Ellis also would not be reinstated to the active roster. The final announcement, an expected one given the first three, was that freshman Eli Holman had decided he would not return to the Indiana program.

"Before you build a team, you need to develop a family," Crean said in the release. "We will go through the learning process, feel some growing pains, and experience some bumps in the road along the way. We need the Hoosier Nation to rally around this program as we go through these stages."

Crean went on to make clear his expectations for the IU program.

"Our staff is going to ensure that anyone who attends this university and wears the Indiana uniform will make this privilege among their highest priorities and not treat the opportunity as an entitlement," Crean added. "We fully expect our student-athletes to accept the responsibilities academically, athletically and socially that come with representing one of the top programs in college basketball history."

With one fell swoop, Indiana basketball had been brought to its knees. Suddenly, only four remained in the program from the year before: Jordan Crawford, Brandon McGee, Kyle Taber and Brett Finkelmeier.

Three weeks later, the number was down to three. On May 22, Crean announced that Brandon McGee had also been dismissed from the team.

Crean cited academic and team guideline negligence for his decision.

"Our coaching and support staff tried to make this work out, but we felt that there were some basic standard operating procedures that were not being met," Crean said in a statement. "I feel badly for his family and Coach (Anthony) Longstreet (Crane head coach) who were helping us to try and make this work, but in the end it just was not possible to continue in the current direction."

The final piece in IU's defection puzzle occurred June 11 when Jordan Crawford informed the IU staff that he would be leaving, too.

In a one sentence statement from IU, the chapter reached a conclusion.

"Jordan Crawford and his family informed us today that he will not return to Indiana University," Crean said.

The mass exodus was finally complete, and only two players who had been on the roster the year before remained. It was down to Kyle Taber and Brett Finkelmeier, two players who would ultimately stick it out and be part of Crean's first IU team in the 2008-09 season.

When the 2007-08 season began at Indiana, the Hoosiers had 14 players on their roster. Twelve of them were now gone. Lance Stemler, D.J. White, Mike White and Adam Ahlfeld all went the conventional route as they used up their eligibility. Eric Gordon headed for the NBA. A.J. Ratliff quit the IU team for personal reasons in January. Armon Bassett, Jamarcus Ellis, DeAndre Thomas and Brandon McGee were all dismissed from the team for various violations of team rules. Jordan Crawford and Eli Holman simply decided to transfer.

ESPN college basketball analyst Jay Bilas said he couldn't recall a mass exodus from an NCAA Division I program like the one Indiana had experienced. But Bilas added that IU was fortunate to have Tom Crean as the coach to turn the Hoosiers' fortunes in the right direction.

"Tom could start out with 10 players, five players or none, and he'll do really well because he's the real thing," Bilas said. "He'll build the foundation the right way, and whoever wants to get in on the ground floor with him will be happy that they did."

Chapter 11

A common sports phrase when a team gets better by losing players rather than adding them is addition by subtraction.

In the first three months after Tom Crean took over at Indiana there was plenty of subtraction. The easier route clearly would have been to massage a few egos, look past a few disciplinary issues that occurred before Crean arrived at IU, and keep at least a semblance of the previous team intact.

But Crean was never about the easier way. He was about the right way. And the right way, in this case, was to show the knuckleheads the door and get on with the task at hand, which was rebuilding Indiana basketball from the ground up.

When the dust had settled and Jordan Crawford had announced he was not returning (and eventually heading to Xavier), Crean was left with the task of assembling a squad that wouldn't get completely obliterated in his first season with the Hoosiers.

Along with all of the defections that Crean experienced in those first three months, he had his share of additions, too.

The first player to come on board wouldn't impact Crean's first team but rather his second. Bobby Capobianco, whom Crean had recruited at Marquette, announced April 17 that he would play for Indiana. Capobianco became the second member of the 2009 class as Derek Elston was still in the fold after committing in September 2007.

Capobianco was familiar with the Indiana program and a lot of its players because he had played for the Indiana Elite AAU program. He hailed from Loveland, Ohio, where he had averaged 21 points and 12 rebounds as a junior.

In an interview with Mike Pegram of peegs.com, Capobianco said the reason he wanted to play at IU was Crean.

"He is one of the most personable guys I have known, I can sit and listen to him for hours," Capobianco said. "I went to a couple practices up at Marquette and a couple games and the way he talks in the locker room, the way he runs his practice—it is very positive. He is not the kind who yells and gets into guys' faces a lot. He will if he needs to, but he is mostly positive and high energy."

After playing for Crean for a few seasons, Capobianco may have had a different take, but that's a story for a different time.

For now, Crean had his first recruit of his own in the class of 2009, and within a couple of days his 2008-09 roster would begin to take shape.

℘ ℭ

His first addition was junior college transfer Devan Dumes, a 6-2 shooting guard from Vincennes, who committed on April 20. Dumes had played his high school basketball in Indianapolis at Decatur Central, where he was twice named to the *Indianapolis Star*'s Super Team. He averaged 24.4 points as a senior and was named Marion County player of the year.

In his first year of college he played at Eastern Michigan, where he averaged 8.1 points and got Crean's attention when he scored 16 points in a game against Marquette.

But things didn't work out for Dumes at EMU, and he transferred before his sophomore season to Vincennes University, an Indiana junior college. There he averaged 16.9 points and set a school record with 109 3-pointers.

"I just did not feel like that (EMU) was the best fit or best situation for me," Dumes said. "When I was handed my release, Vincennes called me, which was ironic because I was already trying to figure out how to get in contact with them."

Crean didn't know it at the time (though he probably suspected it), but in Dumes he would have a player who would start 25 games for him in the 2008-09 season.

Dumes had several scholarship offers coming out of Vincennes and had actually planned a visit to Ohio State. But when IU got involved, Dumes couldn't say no. He cancelled his visit to Columbus and instead took an unofficial visit to Indiana. A few days later, he told Crean he wanted to be a Hoosier.

"I just think the whole thing turned out to be a blessing, really," Dumes said the day after he committed. "Right after Coach Crean got the job, some people that I knew got in touch with him, and we got him some tape, and things just progressed very quickly from there.

"I just really liked his approach. He's someone who is a very straightforward person, someone who is going to make you work hard, and someone who will help make you the best player you can be."

Among the other schools that Dumes had been considering before signing with the Hoosiers were Ohio State, University of Texas-El Paso, Colorado, Arkansas and Alabama.

Prior to Crean's interest, Dumes had never been recruited by IU. He said when Crean showed interest, he knew he wanted to play for the Hoosiers.

"I think every kid who grows up in this area thinks about what it would be like to play at Indiana," Dumes said. "I can't wait."

Crean didn't have to wait long for his next commitment in his first recruiting class, as Nick Williams announced the next day, on April 21, that he would sign with Indiana, too. It was technically the second time that Williams had signed to play for Crean. The previous November, Williams had signed a letter of intent to play at Marquette, but when Crean moved on to Indiana, Williams was granted his release.

Williams committed to play at Indiana despite never having stepped onto the Bloomington campus. The Mobile, Alabama, native wanted to play for Crean, and he had a lot of respect for Assistant Bennie Seltzer, who was from Birmingham, Alabama, and had been the lead recruiter in bringing him to Marquette. Oh, and there was also the phone call that Williams received the day before he committed from D.J. White, another former standout from the state of Alabama, who tried to ease any apprehension Williams might have about coming to Indiana sight unseen.

"When D.J. called me, he told me about the fans at Indiana and how crazy they are about their basketball," Williams said the day he committed. "He told me there really couldn't be anyplace else that I would want to play than Indiana."

So Williams signed on April 21, the first day of the signing period, and then two weeks later made his unofficial visit to IU. A 6-4 guard, Williams chose Indiana over Alabama, Arkansas, Georgia Tech, West Virginia, Kansas State and Mississippi State.

As a senior in high school, Williams averaged 21 points per game and was Alabama's equivalent of Mr. Basketball.

"Nick really addresses a need for us and gives us a big, strong presence in the backcourt," Crean said when the ink was barely dry on Williams' letter of intent. "He is a winner who is tough and physical, and he boasts a work ethic that has helped him improve his game in a variety of ways each year. He has done a wonderful job at making the transition as a perimeter player after beginning his career as an inside performer. He comes from an outstanding high school program and has been well coached throughout his career."

Williams said he hoped to have a chance to start right away as a freshman, but he said Crean made no promises in that regard.

"Coach Crean has said that any coach who tells you that you're going to come in right away and start is not telling you the truth,"

Williams said at the time. "He just told me he knows what kind of player I am, and he knows how hard I'm going to work, and if I do those kind of things, then I'll have a great chance to start."

With Dumes and Williams on board, IU's roster numbers were up to six. Kyle Taber and Brett Finkelmeier were the two players coming back, and Matt Roth and Tom Pritchard were the two incoming freshmen who had agreed to honor their commitments.

A few weeks later, Crean was asked how he planned to fill out the remainder of the roster. He was quick to point out that he and his staff were not impulse shoppers in the recruiting game.

"We cannot rush any decisions with scholarships," Crean said. "There can be no knee-jerk reactions. There can be no 'Let's reach on a guy.' There can be none of any of that. We've got to build it right. We're going to have young guys. We just have to move forward with it and stay with the plan for what kind of players we want to have. Is it easy? No. But it's the way we have to do things right now."

Looking ahead, it was clear Crean would like to bring in another frontcourt player or two to complement Taber and Pritchard. He also needed a true point guard.

But he reiterated that he wasn't going to reach to fill the remaining spots.

"I think we're in a position right now where we have to look at this more than ever with a longterm mind-set," Crean said. "Certainly next year is most immediate, but the longterm over the long haul has to be important, too. We're not looking to do any quick fixing.

"I'm looking to talk to Norman Dale (the fictional character from the movie *Hoosiers*) to see if that preacher's kid still has any eligibility. I'm sure Jimmy Chitwood used all of his, but I'm guessing the preacher's kid may still have some. And those are the kinds of guys we need right now."

ॐ ॐ

The fifth member of IU's basketball class of 2008, and one who would eventually play a key role in Indiana's four-year hoops turnaround, was point guard Verdell Jones III.

Jones, the No. 127-ranked player in the nation by rivals.com, had been the highest-rated point guard available in the spring signing period. Hailing from Champaign, Illinois, Jones had felt a little snubbed by the hometown Illini, and his final choices of schools to attend had come down to a pair of Big Ten suitors: Indiana and Minnesota. He made an unofficial visit to IU in late April and then visited Minnesota the week before he made his decision.

What the Hoosiers could offer that perhaps others could not was immediate playing time. Crean had never been one to promise players starting roles, as he had told Williams just a few weeks before, but this case was a little different.

To put it simply, IU didn't have a point guard on its roster. Sign with the Hoosiers and Jones was going to get instant playing time. And a lot of it.

Jones, who averaged 17.6 points and 6.5 assists his senior season at Champaign Central, said the respect he had for Crean played a big role in why he chose Indiana. He said Crean had come to one of his high school games, while still at Marquette, and then had talked to him later about the kinds of things and areas of Jones' game that he thought could improve.

"He talked about certain areas of my game where he felt he could help me," Jones said in a question-and-answer session with Mike Pegram of peegs.com. "Anytime a coach takes the time to do that, it means he has a lot of interest and is dedicated to improving me as a player. His enthusiasm was a main selling point. I feel like he can push me."

Jones waited until the spring signing period simply because he wanted to let colleges take a look at him based on his senior season, too. That decision paid off as Arizona, Kentucky, Indiana and Minnesota all entered the picture late.

"When I first started off, I had some big schools looking at me, but the whole time we all felt we were going to wait until the end to see what opens up," Jones said. "Coaches leave, players leave, different situations happen. I felt it was the best thing for us. At first there were some good schools like Tennessee, Virginia Tech, schools like that. But at the same time, Kentucky, Arizona, Texas and Indiana opened up for me by waiting."

Crean was equally happy that Jones had waited until the spring, because it allowed him to pick up a key component in the class.

"Verdell is an excellent addition to our recruiting class," Crean said the day Jones signed his letter of intent. "He is a great floor leader with a tremendous ability to direct an offense, and he also has the ability to make plays on his own. His wingspan will make him a tough defender, and we like the fact that he has played in so many big-game environments in high school and AAU ball that he will be able to compete for our program right away. We are very excited about his upside."

With Jones, IU now had five members of the 2008 class.

In addition, the 2009 class was growing as well. On May 4, the day before Jones signed, IU picked up its third commit in the '09 class when Maurice Creek gave his commitment to play at Indiana. Creek, a 6-5 shooting guard from Oxen Hill, Maryland, was someone to get excited about. At the time he committed, he was the No. 63-ranked player in the rivals.com top 150. That clearly made him IU's highest-ranked recruit.

He chose Indiana over Maryland, Miami, Pittsburgh, Texas and Marquette.

Much like Williams, Creek chose Indiana without ever seeing the campus. Call it blind faith, but the top priority for Creek was that he wanted to play for Crean.

"The day that Coach (Bennie) Seltzer left Marquette to join Coach Crean in Indiana, I spoke with him and he told me nothing had changed in terms of their interest in me," Creek said. "That's really all I needed to hear. I wanted to play for Coach Crean, and I didn't see any reason to wait any longer before I committed."

Maurice Creek drives for a shot against Kentucky in his freshman season in 2009.

The day he committed, Creek said he hoped to see the Indiana campus for the first time soon. He also was very matter-of-fact in his thoughts moving forward.

"I'm just looking forward to showing Indiana fans what I can do," Creek said.

Two weeks later, Indiana had two more pieces of its puzzle in place.

One was a commitment who would go on to have a major impact in IU's turnaround. Jordan Hulls, the 6-0 foot guard who would go to become the *Indianapolis Star* Mr. Basketball his senior season from Bloomington South, told Tom Crean on May 20 that he wanted to spend four more years in Bloomington.

Hulls' stock had improved dramatically after he helped lead his Indiana Elite travel team to a major tournament victory that spring in

Pittsburgh. Along with Indiana interest, Hulls had also gotten some looks from Purdue and Duke. He had planned to visit both in June.

But after sitting down with his family and drawing up a list of pros and cons, Hulls kept coming back to Indiana, said his father, J.C. Hulls. On May 20, the young Hulls stopped by Assembly Hall and informed Crean of his decision.

"He liked Coach Crean's energy, and he loved the excitement of what Crean is trying to build there," J.C. Hulls said in an interview with the *Indianapolis Star*. "I asked him if he was sure he didn't want to visit Duke or make another trip to Purdue and talk to Coach (Matt) Painter, and he finally just said that his gut was telling him he wanted to play for Crean. He said he wanted to be part of something special and he was convinced that coach Crean is going to bring that to Indiana."

Along with Hulls, Indiana also picked up its sixth player in the class of 2008 that day. Even though Crean had insisted that the Hoosiers would not reach for any players, the signing of 7-foot junior college center Tijan Jobe felt different.

The previous season Jobe averaged 4.3 points, 3.9 rebounds and 1.5 blocks in 13 minutes per game for Olney (Illinois) College and was clearly a work in progress. But he had the one thing that former IU football coach Terry Hoeppner once said you can't coach when referring to his talented wide receiver James Hardy — size.

"You can coach players to be quicker, stronger and better in many, many areas," Hep said. "But the one thing you can't control is height. You either have it or you don't."

Jobe had it. Originally from Gambia, he was 7-foot, 245 pounds and had a 7-5 wingspan.

His junior college coach, Jeff Burris, told Jeff Rabjohns, then of the *Indianapolis Star*, that Jobe had only been in the United States for four years.

"He's very, very physical, which led to some foul trouble, but he plays extremely hard," Burris said. "Offensively he's still a little raw, but he's developing his skills. He gets better every day. He runs the floor well. He's a great kid, goes to class every day. He's a high-character kid, which I know Indiana is making a priority."

Burris said Jobe would be better suited to the Big Ten than junior college, which often is a run-and-gun style with few true post players.

"The two things I think will be his initial impact are a post presence and a physical presence," Burris said. "I have not seen a better body this year. He has an NBA body up top."

Jobe chose the Hoosiers over University of Alabama-Birmingham, Auburn and Nebraska.

There was no question that Jobe looked good getting off the bus and running on the court for warm-ups, but unfortunately his contributions beyond that wouldn't be major for the Hoosiers.

Still, at the time, Crean was happy to have picked up another frontcourt player to help a light interior for the Hoosiers that was limited to just Tom Pritchard and Kyle Taber.

"We are excited to be able to sign a player with the defensive ability and rebounding presence that Tijan has," Crean said the day that Jobe signed. "We feel he has a lot of room for growth in the sense of improving on both the defensive and offensive end, and we love the fact that he plays extremely hard. His height and wingspan are something that our team was in great need of."

IU now had 10 scholarship players on its roster. Because of a self-imposed scholarship reduction of one, IU was allowed to offer 12 instead of 13. But again, Crean had said he wasn't just going to extend an offer for the sake of doing so. He would save the scholarships for future seasons, if need be.

℘   ℘

Crean was almost done assembling his first team, but not entirely.

There were still two players—one who would come and the other who would not—that remained to be resolved.

First, Crean picked up his first transfer to the program on May 28 when Jeremiah Rivers announced he was leaving Georgetown and would play at IU. Rivers played two seasons with the Hoyas. He would sit out the upcoming season and have two years of eligibility beginning with the 2009-10 season.

"I have been a fan of Jeremiah since early in his high school career," Crean said. "I admire his all-around abilities and the way he approaches the game. He will be an asset both offensively and defensively and is a fierce competitor who knows how to win. Having our teams go head to head these past two years has given me even more of an appreciation for what he is capable of bringing to this program."

Rivers was expected to bring both toughness and leadership to Indiana. At Georgetown, he had played in 68 career games, and had averaged 18.6 minutes per contest. He wasn't called on much as a scorer but instead was considered a standout defender.

"In our opinion, he was one of the best defensive players in the Big East this past season," Crean said. "When you look at the experience that he has gathered in being in the Georgetown program and having the opportunity to win championships and be in the Final Four, his presence will be exactly what this program needs moving forward."

Crean got to know Rivers while at Marquette. Jeremiah's father, Glenn "Doc" Rivers, was the head coach of the Boston Celtics. He had played 13 seasons in the NBA and prior to that had an outstanding college career at Marquette.

"We feel Jeremiah's best days are ahead of him as he continues to build his game on both sides of the ball," said Crean. "He has great size and length, court awareness and potential, and his basketball IQ is outstanding."

About this time, the name of another potential transfer, one who could play right away in the fall, began to emerge with Indiana as a potential suitor.

Emmanuel Negedu, a 6-7, 225-pound power forward from Nigeria, had been given his release at the University of Arizona and had re-opened his recruitment. Negedu was ranked No. 40 in the rivals.com top 150 in the class of 2008. He had gotten out of his commitment to Arizona because Josh Pastner, the coach who recruited him to the Wildcats, had left and taken a job as an assistant at Memphis. Along with IU, Negedu said he was also looking at Tennesee, Georgia Tech and Memphis.

Negedu was familiar with Bloomington and the Hoosiers, in particular because he had played summer basketball for Bloomington-based Indiana Elite. Negedu had said he wanted to visit all four schools. His first visit came on June 3 to IU. Eventually, after making all his visits, Negedu decided on June 9 to attend Tennessee.

Jerry Meyer, a college basketball analyst for rivals.com, told the *Indianapolis Star* that playing for the Hoosiers was ultimately too tough of a sell for someone who wasn't expected to play more than a year or two of college.

"He would have been the most talented player on the team," Meyer said. "But also, getting a big recruit when your program is down like Indiana's is, can jumpstart some momentum and get some positive energy going. I think that's more important than anything. It looks like next year's season is a lost cause for Indiana. It looks like the battle is to get things back on track for the future."

A few weeks later, Indiana picked up its final player in what would be a seven-player recruiting class for 2008.

Malik Story, a 6-5, 220-pound guard from Los Angeles, had initially committed to play as a sophomore for the University of Southern

California. Just after his senior year of high school, however, he changed his mind and opened up his recruitment.

Other schools that had given him a look included Kentucky, Oregon, Marquette, Arizona and Georgetown.

In a story by Jeff Rabjohns in the *Indianapolis Star*, Story said he was familiar with Bloomington from playing at the Adidas May Classic, a travel team event, in the past.

"I always liked Indiana from the two tournaments I played there, but I didn't know much about Coach Crean, expect for what he did at Marquette," Story said. "Coach Crean and the whole coaching staff, the way they are, they want to develop players and help me out as a person. They seem like they really like their players."

According to Rabjohns, Story was "a recruiting coup this late in the process."

Story was considered to have a good 3-point shooting range and the size to defend frontcourt players. He won two state championships in California's largest class at Artesia High School, and last year played on a summer national championship team with UCLA's Kevin Love, Arizona's Chase Buddinger and Brandon Jennings, one of the top incoming freshmen this fall.

As for his visit to IU, Story said he got a chance to play with his future teammates and spent most of his off-court time talking with Crean.

"He's down to earth," Story said. "I laugh when I talk to him. He wasn't so serious all the time. He was serious but wasn't overly serious. He was talking to me like I'm a regular person. There was a bond between us, I could tell."

With Story in the fold, not counting the walk-ons, he became the 10th new player to join IU for the coming season. IU lost a total of 81 points per game when players either graduated, went to the NBA, were dismissed from the team, or transferred.

"Everybody there is going to have to get used to everybody and a new offense. We're all new," he said. "I think it's going to be better than what people think it's going to be."

Along with all of the scholarship players, Indiana had already settled on a pair of preferred walk-ons to play beginning with the 2008-09 season, as well. Daniel Moore, a point guard from Carmel, Indiana, and Kory Barnett, a 6-5 wing from Rochester, Indiana, had both decided prior to Crean's arrival that they wanted to walk on at Indiana. After Crean got the job, both players told the new coach they would like be a part of his first team, and both were given the OK to join the squad.

Barnett said at the time that he had mixed feelings at first but in the end thought staying with IU was the right move.

"I had gotten close to (Kelvin) Sampson there at the end," Barnett said. "But the player situation, other than (Eric Gordon), I didn't really know many of the players. Adam Ahlfeld hosted me on my visit, so really both of the players I knew well were leaving anyway. From a basketball standpoint, I would have loved to see many of those guys stay but a different part of me thought maybe it is better if Coach Crean can get his own guys in there, guys who want to do it the right way, and I think he is doing that."

PART 4:
Growing Pains and a BIG Program-Changing Recruit

Chapter 12

On July 3, almost three months to the day that Tom Crean took the Indiana job, he sat down with members of the media in Bloomington to reflect on all that had transpired.

Crean began by talking about how he has had to help people understand that there is the perception, and then there is the reality to everything that is going on at Indiana.

"Certainly we get a strong feel for it because of the recruiting and the negative recruiting and the comments made and things of that nature that we have to deal with," Crean said. "At the same time, we keep looking at what it really is. It is a great place. There are so many great things happening here. There are so many good feelings."

Crean said the perception has been created because of all the issues facing the program. But he felt he needed to remind people sometimes that the IU program has never completely lost its luster.

"And I hope it never does on our watch, either, because it is very strong," Crean said. "In three months, we've had a lot of opportunities to try to get that across, even as many different circumstances have come up to try to show that it is not. That would probably be the biggest thing to me.

"The second thing is, we've tried to recruit people that had some courage, that were competitive and had an understanding. That we could try to get across that understanding of what it means to play at Indiana. The responsibility that comes with that, the standards that go into that, and even though they've been verbal, we haven't had a real opportunity to coach that yet, even though the young men are here. I'm excited about that."

Crean talked about the team that he had been able to assemble, looking at it as a group and not as individuals.

He also said that the dynamic in terms of the players who were thought to be returning versus those who actually did, made the program building much more different.

"We tried to address needs," he said. "We came in with an idea that we were going to have to recruit some people to play in the program. We certainly didn't come in with the idea that we were going to have to build basically a whole new team, but that is exactly what's happened, so with that being said, we tried to fill the needs.

"I maybe would've liked to have signed someone that was a little bit bigger and had a little bit more scoring ability. They just weren't there. We took a shot at some guys. It didn't work out for one reason or another."

Crean believed he had recruited what could be a competitive team.

"It has got to the point with the recruiting that we have to have a competitive team, a team that we can build with, a team that we can build and move forward with," Crean said. "That is what we've really been serious about trying to find...We don't have anyone that is above and beyond the system or what we are trying to get done right now. It's going to have to be a very balanced unit."

Crean also said the Hoosiers will have to find ways to overcome their lack of size.

"We know that we're going to have to play bigger than our size," Crean said. "We know that we're going to have to play smarter than our experience. There is no doubt about that. Those are all things that are going to have to come out if we're going to have a chance to compete, but I know we've signed guys that want to compete."

Crean talked about the decision not to fill every scholarship that was available.

"We've tried to fill the positions, and we're trying to work with the premise that we're going to have 10 scholarships this year and that is what we're under now," Crean said. "We have eight new players and we have Kyle (Taber). We'll see what happens. If anything comes about this summer, there would probably still be a few situations that we would look at, but the last thing that we wanted to do was reach on size or reach on potential if there really wasn't some concrete chances there.

"I would rather hold the scholarship and go into next year because with the young people that we have committed, we know that we have to get somebody that is of bigger size that can score and rebound. That has to happen. If we had one scholarship next year, that's what we would look at. We'll certainly see what happens with the rest of the scholarships."

Crean said one of the most difficult things with the players that he recruited was the simple notion he had to have players who could play right away rather than recruit some with the idea they could blossom at some point down the road. He said the fact that in a few months time the Hoosiers would be knee deep into a competitive schedule has been an eye-opener.

"They're not canceling the season," Crean said. "It is not like we're going to get a reprieve, where all of a sudden they're like, 'We won't send you here, we won't send you there. You don't have to go to Maui now.' We do. We have to play a season. We have to build for the future, not just for the season. That is the balancing act.

"How do you get a group of guys who have the courage and competitiveness and the character to come in here and be excited about doing it now and at the same time have the talent and the potential? We're not shying away from potential, but you don't want to reach if it is too big of a risk. If we were going to sign anybody right now, it would certainly have to be somebody bigger. If not, we'll wait until next year."

Crean said it was important to lay his foundation with a group of young players, as will be the case with this IU team.

"I look at it this way," Crean said. "We don't want to start over twice. We're starting over now. That is understandable. That is where we are at. We don't want to get down the road with these players we're recruiting and find we're not ready for the hit if any of them leave early or graduate and their eligibility is up.

"It started where we knew we had to get a class for now, and then we were trying to focus hard on the rising (high school) seniors, but we really tried to dive hard into the rising juniors, rising sophomores, and even paying attention to who the freshmen are going to be. You have to know. You don't have to all out go crazy and recruit them as eighth-graders, but you should know who they are. We've tried to do that. We've got a lot of focus on finishing this rising senior class the right way, and then locking into the young guys."

The white elephant in the back of the room continued to be the upcoming NCAA ruling. Crean was asked what he tells recruits regarding that.

"I tell them what I know, and it hasn't changed a whole lot," Crean said. "I was surprised the other day with the failure to monitor because I've sat in on all the meetings and obviously sat in in Seattle. From my vantage point and what I'm listening to and for the people that I'm working with and for the things that I heard, I can't share with you what I really think of the way it went inside of there and some of the things that were said, but I don't share that opinion.

"I have no qualms going to work with these people every day. There is a very strong team of people that work at Indiana inside the athletic department. I tell people that. I keep going back to this. We are under such hard penalties that were imposed inside of Indiana."

Crean said people need to understand just how much IU lost based on its self-imposed sanctions.

"The phone calls are one thing, but with people being able to call you and the ability to email and write letters, you can work through that," Crean said. "You're not in a position, especially when we first got here, where you're anywhere close to what everyone else has got, but when you lose the recruiting days that we've lost, when you're down to 10 scholarships like we are, that is the competitive disadvantage.

"The fact that I've got to figure out how to work seven days in, the fact that we're only going to have two coaches on the road while everyone else has got three on the road, that is really there. I have to live that every day."

Crean stopped himself at the point because he didn't want to give the impression he was frustrated.

"I'm not trying to whine," Crean said. "It is what it is. I knew that when we took the job. It caused a lot of pause in the short period of time when I took the job. Now we're smack dab in the middle of this. April, to me, is more important than July. Every coach might not agree, but to me it is. Because you're not going to leave your team a lot during the winter, so you're not going to be all over the place in the winter, seeing recruits instead of coaching your team, so April becomes that time period. Well, we lost that. I had three days inside of that. Now July becomes that important, and now we're going to lose that.

"At the end of the day, it is not the story, but it is sure there in the first paragraph. It really is. These are severe penalties that Indiana imposed on itself. Like President McRobbie said, these are harsh penalties, and so we're dealing with those. I'm going to be there as much as I can. I'm trying to prioritize as much as we can. I'm trying to be in as many places as we possibly can."

And Crean once again asked Indiana fans to be patient.

"At the same time, bear with us because we're going to get through this," Crean said. "We're going to get through it hopefully in a short period of time. I keep stressing to people that so much has been done to Indiana at this point that it is hard to believe that a lot more could be done."

૪૦ ૦૩

One of Crean's main themes since taking the Indiana job on April 2 was how much he wanted to involve former IU players in the program. He wanted them to realize that this is still their program even if the coach they played for was no longer at the school. For the majority of them, it was a refreshing approach.

Pat Graham needed just three words early in the 2008 season to describe how Crean had been able to win back former players and re-energize Indiana basketball's hurting fan base so quickly.

"He gets it," said Graham, who played at IU from 1989-94.

What Crean gets, numerous former players said, is how important tradition is to the program. He gets the impact of having former players on a united front.

He gets Bob Knight and all he built.

"I don't know if we've tried to do that so much the last six to eight years," Graham said. "I don't think that was even a thought. It was more about 'win, win, win,' and less about the former players.

"And I think more than anything else, he has tried to get the message out there that he's going to bring Indiana basketball back, and he's going to do it the right way. And I've got to tell you, that's a message we've all been waiting to hear."

Talking to former players, it was clear that they believed Crean had won over a fan base before winning his first game.

One major supporter was none other than a member of the IU basketball program's first family. No, it wasn't Bob Knight. But it was close.

"I think he was a great hire," former IU player and assistant coach Pat Knight told WNDE 1260-AM in an interview in the fall of 2008. "I wish him nothing but the best. He knows that. I've talked to him and I've told him if there's anyone that I can call for him — like past players who may not be buying into what he's doing — that I'll vouch for him. I just hope people are patient because he inherited a brutal situation.... But since he took it, you couldn't find a better guy. I think he's going to get it done, and I hope he gets it done.

"I'll admit when we first got fired (in September 2000), I didn't root for Indiana at all. It took several years. But now that Tom's there, it's kind of nice to be able to root for my alma mater."

Crean gained approval from the time he was hired in April through the fall of 2008 by touring the state, turning speaking engagements into revival meetings. And he reached out to former players.

"I told them I wanted them to be part of the program, because this is their program," Crean said. "There's nothing more important in Indiana basketball than the tradition, and all of the players that have come before that are part of the fabric of that tradition."

The Gospel according to Tom says players will attend class, graduate, and represent the university the right way. His perfect graduation record at Marquette pounded that point home.

He wasn't promising instant success but rather was pleading for patience.

Expectations were low for Indiana in the 2008-09 season. IU would have nine freshmen and only eight scholarship players, only one of whom played the previous year. Several publications picked them to finish last in the Big Ten.

But hopes were high for the future.

Graham said at the time that Crean had delivered a team fans could be proud of and enjoy watching. He said the past two years weren't enjoyable. Talented players but not a team. A lot of those players didn't care and didn't want to be in Bloomington, Graham said.

They didn't play Indiana basketball.

Joe Hillman, not surprisingly by the way, was more succinct.

"He came in and he cleaned house," said Hillman, who played on the 1987 championship team, in an *Indianapolis Star* story in the fall of '08. "He got rid of all those punks and bad guys and just said, 'Hey, this is the way we're going to do it. We're going to take some lumps, but we're going to do it the right way.'

"You can say what you want about Bob Knight, but we didn't have many bad guys. Mike Davis didn't bring in many bad guys. But Kelvin Sampson brought in a whole rack of bad guys. Crean basically said we're going to get rid of these guys, and I don't care if we go 0-28, but we're going to do it the right way and get it back to where it was."

Todd Meier, one of three seniors on the 1987 championship team, lives in Wisconsin and became a Crean fan when the coach was at Marquette. Shortly after Crean got the IU job, Meier sent him a congratulatory e-mail. A few days later, Crean called. He thanked Meier and invited him to get back involved.

"It's so nice to go back to Bloomington now and feel like they're glad to see you and want you to be there," Meier said. "It's been very refreshing and very energizing. It's going to be a rough year at IU this year, but I think they'll win a lot more games than a lot of people seem to think."

Hillman, like many former players, never liked the Sampson hire. Sampson, he said, avoided IU's past.

"Coach Crean has embraced the past and wants to use every bit of our tradition to help turn the program back around," Hillman said.

So much so that Crean hosted a two-day IU basketball reunion in West Baden, Indiana, in August. Bloomington businessman Bill Cook paid for the party. More than 180 former players and managers, dating to the 1940s, attended. More than 300 guests attended a dinner and golf outing the next day.

Archie Dees, a two-time IU All-American in 1957 and 1958, said Crean told former players he wanted them involved in the program, in whatever way they could. He wanted them at games and practices. An IU season-ticket holder since 1962 and a Bloomington resident, Dees said Crean is the right man at the right time.

"I think he's the communicator of all communicators," Dees said. "I feel sorry for Coach Crean that he has inherited the problems he has, because none of this is his fault. But if anyone could get this turned back around, there's no doubt in my mind that it's Tom Crean."

Bryant Mosbey, an IU manager from 2003-06, attended the event in French Lick, too.

"From the very beginning, Coach Crean wanted to make sure that all former players and managers knew that they were all an important part of what he was trying to add on to," Mosbey said. "Our reunion in French Lick provided us with an opportunity to witness Coach Crean's passion and enthusiasm firsthand.

"I walked away feeling very confident that it was not *if* but *when* IU would return to the place where I had always remembered it being."

Dane Fife, then the head coach at Indiana-Purdue-Fort Wayne, played for both Knight and Davis at IU. He said wherever he went that summer and fall of 2008, people were discussing IU basketball again.

"There's a real buzz right now about Indiana basketball again, and about Coach Crean," Fife said in an interview with the *Indianapolis Star* in 2008. "And the nice thing is, it's a positive buzz again."

ꙮ   ꙮ

Also in mid-August, Tom Crean completed his coaching staff at Indiana when he hired former NBA player Roshown McLeod. McLeod, who also played collegiately at both Duke and St. Johns, was brought on board to work specifically with IU's inside players.

"Not only was Roshown an outstanding player, but he is a very good coach who has been a student of the game for a long time," Crean said. "His ability to teach the game, adjust quickly on his feet to different circumstances, and make players better were very apparent in the process of getting to know him. He will be a tremendous mentor to our team, but especially to our inside players."

At the same time Crean was completing his staff, the university was announcing the final details of his contract that had been slightly redone since he signed a letter of understanding on April 2.

When he originally agreed to the deal, Crean had signed on for eight years. The new contract was for 10 years for an average total of $2.3 million per season. The contract pays Crean $600,000 per season in base salary with an additional $17.6 million in outside marketing and promotional income during the life of the deal. The contract was signed through June 30, 2018.

"I appreciate the confidence that President McRobbie and the university have shown in me by offering the two additional years to the agreement," Crean said. "It is a great responsibility to lead this program, and I look forward to the challenge of bringing the program the respect it deserves. The process of restoring this great program is going to take a lot of time, more than probably any of us anticipated."

The contract offered several incentives for Crean and his coaching staff based on things such as winning either the regular season or Big Ten Tournament titles and advancing through the NCAA Tournament.

It also had an interesting clause stating that Crean would owe the university a significant sum of money if he chose to leave IU before the end of the 10 years. If Crean left within the first three years, he would owe IU $3 million. If he left after years four or five the total was $2 million, and if he were to leave anytime after that, prior to June 30, 2018, he would owe Indiana $1 million.

"It is very easy to sell the tradition that is Indiana basketball knowing that we are committed to IU for a long time and that the university believes in what we are trying to accomplish," added Crean. "I'm especially grateful for the way Rick Greenspan, former players, supporters and the entire Hoosier Nation have made my family feel welcome and helped us during this transition."

With his final coach in place and his contract resolved, Crean was able to focus specifically on the basketball issues.

His first one, however, was on the injury front.

On August 26, IU announced that senior forward Kyle Taber had suffered a knee injury the previous week in practice that would require surgery. He was expected to be out 10 weeks but would be back in time for the majority of the season.

"This is very unfortunate for Kyle," Crean said. "He has been a strong presence and has done things the right way for us since we arrived here. We will move forward and help him through his rehabilitation and look to him to provide us with the leadership that is expected from a fifth-year senior at Indiana."

℘   ℘

Crean's first season at Indiana was about a month away from the mid-October Hoosier Hysteria event, where more than 10,000 fans annually descend upon IU's Assembly Hall at midnight on the official first day of practice. At about this time, the Hoosiers started getting some more positive press. This didn't have anything to do with the 2008-09 squad but rather with another big commitment to the next class.

When a kid named Christian Watford, a 6-8 forward from Birmingham, Alabama, announced September 9 that he would attend Indiana, people around the country began to really take notice.

Before Watford signed, there were many recruiting analysts that put the class in the top 10 in the nation. With Watford coming as well, the analysts were saying that the Hoosiers were challenging for one of the top spots in the country in 2009 recruiting classes.

Bob Gibbons, a national recruiting analyst for All-Star Sports and ESPN.com, said IU's class was on par with North Carolina as the best for 2009. Justin Young, a basketball recruiting senior writer for rivals.com, said Watford's addition vaulted IU five spots to No. 4 in its rankings.

Why all the fuss with Watford? He came to IU ranked No. 34 in the nation by rivals.com. ESPN.com had him ranked No. 26, and All-Star Sports listed him at No. 12 in the country.

Much like Purdue was able to do with its 2007 class, IU had assembled a team with its five players. Watford was a small forward. Maurice Creek was a 6-5 shooting guard. Jordan Hulls was a 6-foot point guard, and Derek Elston and Bobby Capobianco were 6-8 post players. On September 26, the Hoosiers added the center when 7-foot Bawa Muniru from Durham, North Carolina, gave his commitment.

"It was already a great class, and now you get a substantial upgrade with Watford," Young said. "At 6-8, Watford just creates a lot of matchup problems at the small forward spot. He is very versatile and can be used in a lot of different ways.

"What I like about Indiana's class is they now have a lot more versatility on their front line. They addressed the guard position in the Class of 2008, but they've taken care of the frontcourt in '09."

Watford said the 2009 class already was forming a relationship after competing in AAU events and attending IU's recent Elite Camp.

"I just think we have what it takes to get IU basketball back to where people expect it to be," he said.

Chapter 13

The least productive season in terms of wins in Indiana University basketball history ended at 6:52 p.m. Thursday night on March 12, 2009 in the first round of the Big Ten Tournament.

Why would I begin the recap of Tom Crean's first season at Indiana with the last game? Well, it was simply one of those seasons that had a lot more memories that Indiana fans would much rather forget than savor.

Indiana's first season under Crean concluded almost mercifully with a 66-51 loss to Penn State. It was IU's 10th loss in a row and 21st in 22 games.

Since beating Texas Christian on December 10, IU only experienced one more victory. That was a 68-60 victory over Iowa on February 4. Take that away, and IU would have gone an imperfect 0-18 in Big Ten play. As it was, IU lost as many games in conference play (17) as any team in Indiana history had ever lost for an entire season. Yes, IU's worst previous season on record came in 1969-70 when the Hoosiers finished 7-17. This Indiana team not only became the first in IU history to lose 20 games or more, but the Hoosiers finished 6-25. That's eight more losses than any team in Indiana history had ever experienced.

Gene Wojciechowski, a national college basketball columnist for ESPN.com, summed up Indiana's season this way after watching the Hoosiers bow to Penn State in the first round of the conference tournament.

> INDIANAPOLIS – *Other than a few family and friends, there won't be anybody waiting to welcome the Indiana team bus back to Bloomington on Friday morning. The losingest Hoosiers team in Indiana history returned to the IU campus under the cover of basketball infamy.*
>
> *But if ever a team deserved a standing O and maybe even a ticker-tape shower, it was this season's Hoosiers. They lost 25 games, including their one-and-mercifully-done appearance in the Big Ten tournament Thursday evening, but they won hearts. They finished with the fewest IU wins in 93 years, but also with the most life lessons.*

Afterward, there were tears, lots of them, shed in the cinder-block locker room used by the Hoosiers at Conseco Fieldhouse. When first-year Indiana coach Tom Crean finally emerged from the room after his postgame speech to his team, his eyes were as red as IU's jerseys.

Standing just outside the metal door, you could hear almost every word he spoke. You could hear the emotion that comes with surviving basketball hell.

"None of us — none of us! — signed up for what we had to deal with," said Crean to his players, his voice crackling with intensity. "But I'm glad I went through it with you. I'm glad I came through it with this staff. We've got a long way to go to get better, but you've come a long, long way."

There was a pause, a long pause, before Crean continued. When he did, you could hear him remind his team of the support given to it by IU fans during this brutal season. You could hear him say how much he respected his players for never phoning it in.

"The last thing is ..."

Then Crean flashed back to spring 2008 and the final day of individual workouts with the few players left on his team. By then, after the vast crater left by disgraced Kelvin Sampson, there had been mass defections, dismissals and transfers. One of the remaining players on the decimated roster was former walk-on Kyle Taber, a 6-8 senior forward from Evansville who had exactly zero Division I scholarship offers coming out of high school.

"You were so pathetic that day," Crean said. "You were so awful that I walked out of there saying, 'What have we done? What have we done?' I want to tell you: I was dead wrong. Because you got better. You got a lot better."

Once again, you could hear Crean's voice break. Silence, then ...

"I saw an article today that had a lot of quotes from (Taber's) mom in the Evansville paper," Crean said. "He wanted to be at Indiana. And his mom said if he got to play two minutes as a senior [pause] it would be worth it.

"You did a lot more than that, man. You did a lot more than that. ... Everybody was going to push you to a place where you could be. And you did it. You did it. You did it, OK? You did it. You have earned your way into history. And nobody can ever take that away from you."

Penn State officially ended IU's season with its 66-51 victory in the opening round of the Big Ten tournament. How the Hoosiers won even six games this season (they were 1-18 against conference opponents if you count Thursday's loss) is beyond me.

Yet how can you not have a soft spot for a team with a desperation roster that includes one senior, five true freshmen and six walk-ons, including a 5-8, 150-pound student manager named Michael Santa? Santa actually played in the waning moments of Thursday night's loss. Afterward, he sat in front of his locker and tugged at his size 46 jersey.

"I'm going to leave it on as long as I can," said Santa, who returns to full-time student manager duty next year.

"It mattered to Taber and Santa, and the rest of them, to wear the IU uniform. But guess what Santa, the emergency guard, did after the media eventually cleared out of the locker room? He helped the other managers pack the equipment bags.

"It was fun while it lasted," he said.

Fun? Finishing 6-25? Winning just one Big Ten game? Fun?

"I think when people look back at this season, they'll say 'This is where it all started,'" Santa said. "From here on out, we're just going to keep going forward."

Crean undoubtedly will coach more talented Indiana teams, but it's doubtful he'll coach one with more dignity. Regardless of the grotesque (for proud IU) record, this is a team worth celebrating.

"What would I tell my kid one day?" said IU guard Jeremiah Rivers, the son of Boston Celtics coach Doc Rivers. "I'd probably tell him it was the toughest, most rewarding year of my life."

And Rivers is a transfer from Georgetown, so he didn't even play this season. But after a practice earlier this week in Bloomington, he told his teammates, "Man, no matter what happens, I think we need to take some pictures and sign autographs because a few years from now, when we're all out of college, in the NBA, overseas, in businesses, however you want to put it, we're going to remember this year. It's been special. Yeah, the losing's been tough. But it has been an honor just to be around this team we have."

Years from now, he said, "We're going to look at our team picture and smile."

Taber played for four different head coaches in five years. IU played without injured starting guard Devan Dumes at season's end. Freshman guard Verdell Jones III played more than half the game against Penn State with a thick wrap around his right calf. Smile?

Crean half-jokingly said that if he had known then what he knows now, "I would have gotten more (contract) years at the very beginning." (He began with eight; IU later extended it to 10.) Indiana entered the season with two returning players who had a grand total of just 19 combined points and 185 minutes of experience.

But it was Crean, the eternal optimist, who brought a framed photograph from his house and had it hung in the IU locker room back at Assembly Hall.

The photograph: Two guys are strapped to the wings of a flying airplane as they play tennis. At the bottom of the picture, it reads, "Who says it can't be done?"

It couldn't be done this season, but not for a lack of trying. Indiana was overmatched and sometimes overwhelmed, but never outworked.

"We ain't going through this again," Crean said Thursday night behind that door at Conseco. "We're not going through this again."

A few moments later, you could hear Crean call his team together. Then came the chant, "1-2-3 ... Hoosiers."

Together at the beginning. Together at the end.

∵ ∴

The first season in the Tom Crean era of Indiana basketball began the same way that every IU season has kicked off in recent memory: Hoosier Hysteria, formerly known as Midnight Madness, is a big event in Hoosierland. Usually on the third Friday in October every season, basketball kicks off its season in Assembly Hall. At Indiana, generally the football team has faded into the sunset by now, and fans are ready to focus on their beloved basketball team.

At midnight, when IU can officially begin practice for the upcoming season, the Hoosiers are introduced to their adoring fans. In recent years there is usually a 3-point shooting contest, a spot shot competition, a dunk contest and then a short scrimmage. Admission is a canned food item that is donated to the Hoosier Hills Food Bank, and there's usually 10,000 or more fans on hand. The women's basketball team has also taken part in recent years and even engages in some friendly battle-of-the-sexes-type competitions in the shooting events.

The Crean and Crimson era of Indiana University basketball had a little bit of everything on Friday night, October 17 at Assembly Hall.

Former players. Future players. Hula girls. Yes, even hula girls were on hand to get the crowd in the mood for a November trip to the EA Sports Maui Invitational.

All of it played to the approval of a crowd estimated at more than 8,000 that turned out for the annual Hoosier Hysteria festivities to kick off the 2008-09 season.

The players had a 12-minute scrimmage at the end of the night that gave IU fans their first chance to see what is basically a group of relative unknowns who will suit up for the Hoosiers this season. Kyle Taber is the lone returning scholarship player, but as the evening progressed, several fan favorites began to develop. Whether it was 7-foot junior center Tijan Jobe dunking during the scrimmage, Devan Dumes knocking down a 3 or freshman point guard Verdell Jones III splitting defenders on his way to a driving basket, IU fans seemed to like what they were seeing.

"We're definitely going to be undersized, but I think we're going to be scrappy, too," said Troy Gonzalez, an IU fan from Carmel who had a front-row seat. "I thought it was a good night. It just seemed like there was a family atmosphere both with the families of the coaches being introduced and all of the former players who were on hand."

Hoosier Hysteria '08 had a little bit of the past, present.

The past was represented by 23 former players spanning seven decades of Hoosier basketball. They were introduced to the crowd and shook hands with this year's players. Later, six joined current players in a series of shooting competitions.

The future was present in the form of more than 30 recruits, including the Class of 2009's Bobby Capobianco, Derek Elston and Christian Watford, and 2011's Matt Carlino.

Crean addressed the crowd for about 10 minutes. He talked about how the fans' reaction to the former players' introduction told him everything he needed to know about Indiana basketball.

"What you said about the former players said a lot about you," Crean said.

He talked about the tradition.

"This is the greatest tradition of any sport, any place in the country!" Crean shouted into the microphone.

Next, a video was shown on the scoreboard overhead that was titled "The Rebuilding Begins."

It showed the Hoosiers in offseason conditioning workouts, doing everything from karate to rolling semi-truck tires on the football practice field to lifting weights and doing a variety of running drills.

Crean concluded by saying, "Like Norman Dale said, 'Our team is on the floor.'"

He then brought all of the current players and former players to the middle of the court, where they huddled and chanted "Hoosiers."

At the end of the evening when the scrimmage was concluded, Crean took the microphone one last time and thanked the crowd for coming.

"We've had a great night and this has been an absolute honor," Crean said. "We're just so glad to be part of the Hoosier Nation. We're looking forward to making you proud."

∓ ∔

Indiana held another scrimmage that was open to the public on October 25. At the end of it, Crean said he was pleased with how hard his team was competing.

"This is something for us to build on," Crean said. "Now we have some tangible tape for them to look at."

The IU coach said he is starting to see things in this Indiana team that he hopes will be there all season.

"Right now I'm looking for a spirit, I'm looking for an energy," Crean said. "I'm looking for us to excite our fans. I'm looking for our fans to understand that they have a huge, huge job for us this year. But I'm also looking for us to understand what we need to do for them.

"If there was ever a time to be in it together, this is the one. It's not the fans' fault, it's not my fault, it's not the players' fault. It is the way that it is. But the only way we're going to get through it is together."

After a couple of exhibition games, Indiana opened the 2008-09 season at home November 15 with an 83-65 victory over Northwestern State. Junior Devan Dumes led the Hoosiers with 21, and freshman Verdell Jones III added 18.

But IU had some early telling signs. The Hoosiers committed 23 turnovers, gave up 27 offensive rebounds and missed 13 free throws. Any one of those statistics could cost you a game against quality competition. The only thing going for Indiana in the opener was that Northwestern State was not exactly a formidable foe.

The second game was against IUPUI and the Jaguars gave Indiana everything it could handle before IU's Daniel Moore hit a pair of free throws with 1.2 seconds to play to help lift the Hoosiers to a 60-57 victory.

IUPUI's Alex Young had a good look at a 3-point shot with five seconds remaining and the Jags only trailing by one point.

Still, a win was a win, and the Hoosiers had opened the season 2-0. Little did they know that from that point on they would go 4-25 the rest of the season.

It didn't take IU long to experience reality. At least if the Hoosiers were going to get pounded, they chose a nice tropical paradise in which to do it. In the EA Sports Maui Invitational, IU lost by 38 to No. 8 Notre Dame, by 26 to St. Joseph's and then had to rally to beat Division II Chaminade, 81-79. The Maui experience had the necessary effect on the Hoosiers. They left the islands humbled.

"I think this was a humbling experience for myself and my teammates in a lot of ways," said freshman point guard Verdell Jones III. "But it was humbling in a good way. When you play against a top-10 team, you find out pretty quickly that they're top 10 for a reason. "I think this experience made us more hungry, and more enthusiastic to go back and practice and work hard and come out with more energy every time we play."

Crean said that playing three games in three days would help his team immeasurably as the season goes on, especially when it has quick turnarounds. But Crean said perhaps the biggest thing IU got from the trip came Tuesday night when the Hoosiers were in the stands. Crean and the team watched the North Carolina-Oregon game just to watch a No. 1 team.

"As I said to our players, for 30 or 40 years Indiana has been in the same sentence with North Carolina and we will be again, but until we get there, we've got to learn what that looks like," Crean said. "And I think being in that gym and seeing the way that Carolina played was a great teaching experience for our team."

One of the themes that emerged from IU's trip was that Daniel Moore, a walk-on guard from Carmel, Indiana, was getting as much playing time as anyone. In Maui, Moore played 81 minutes. With Moore, Crean said IU basketball is simply at a place where it's not about scholarship players or nonscholarship players but more about putting the best group of players on the floor.

"Walk-on, scholarship, it doesn't make any difference right now," Crean said. "Someday it won't be that way, when we have a full gamut of scholarships, but I never want to lose the ability to have guys like Daniel Moore in the program."

℘   ℭ

Perhaps the biggest news for Indiana during the trip to Maui was that the NCAA Committee on Infractions finally ruled on Indiana's recruiting violations investigation. The timing of the announcement came just after IU had dropped an 80-54 loss to St. Joseph's in the second game of the tournament.

For the previous few months, Tom Crean had been on record as saying the Hoosiers had penalized themselves enough for the violations committed by former coach Kelvin Sampson and two of his assistants, in particular. The NCAA Committee on Infractions confirmed Crean's belief when it announced IU would be placed on probation for three years but suffer no additional penalties.

Reaction from Indiana and its fans was consistent, including those attending the EA Sports Maui Invitational.

"This is just a huge relief for everyone concerned," said IU basketball fan Lee Ann Borden of Brownstown, Indiana "I really thought it was going to be worse. I'm sure Indiana basketball fans are feeling a lot better today. And it's not just the fans but players and coaches and everybody. I think this is a big monkey off our backs."

Crean said he believed the NCAA's decision proved the system works.

"(IU) implicated themselves in the sense of creating internal sanctions, and the NCAA looked at that and they respected that," Crean said. "Because the sanctions imposed obviously were very, very hard. But we just have to deal with the aftermath for so long. This is what gutting a program and starting over looks like right now. We can't break down. We can't lose faith. We just have to keep moving forward. And that's exactly what we'll do, and we'll do it in the long term with this program."

Incoming IU athletic director Fred Glass, who was hired to replace Rick Greenspan and would begin his duties January 2, said the announcement means IU can finally move forward in a positive way.

"To paraphrase a political figure (President Gerald Ford), the long national nightmare is over," Glass said. "We'll take seriously the terms that the probation turns out to be, but we can finally put this in our rearview mirror and move forward. And hopefully we can do great things, not just with the basketball program but with the entire athletic department moving forward."

Crean said one of the biggest positives with the ruling is that it may finally signal the end of negative recruiting by other schools.

"We dealt with so many innuendos and false rumors and other schools telling recruits what was going to happen, and they had no idea," Crean said. "Now all our recruits can feel good about it, our future class recruits can feel good about it, and our current players can feel good about it."

℘ ℘

Following that victory over Chaminade, Indiana would win just three more games the entire season.

Somehow the Hoosiers knocked off a good Cornell team 72-57 at Assembly Hall. The following season, pretty much that same Cornell team made it to the Sweet Sixteen.

Indiana lost its final three games heading into Big Ten play. One of the losses was respectable, as it was to Kentucky. The other two— Northeastern and Lipscomb.

The Hoosiers would then lose the first eight games of the Big Ten season, beat Iowa at home, and then lose the final nine conference games heading into the Big Ten Tournament.

When the finality of the loss to Penn State had sunk in, Tom Crean stood at the podium at Conseco Fieldhouse and tried to put his first year into perspective.

"I think it's hard to put—we haven't coached this season with perspective. I don't think they played it with perspective," Crean said. "I think we played it every day to try to get better, to improve them, to give them an opportunity to have a game plan to win in games. So I don't look at it like that. But I have great respect. I think what I've learned the most is there really is no substitute for improvement. I mean, it doesn't matter what your talent level is. There's so many things you can get better at if you're willing to do that.

"If you have the desire to improve, really nothing can stop you. Maybe you'll get to a certain level, because maybe your talent can't overcome this or that. Maybe your height can't overcome this or that, but there's no limit on how hard you can work to improve."

Then Crean changed the direction of the press conference over to talk about one of his favorite topics: Indiana fans.

"This team over time, the memories begin with how people supported it," Crean said. "I mean, when there wasn't winning streaks to bring them to the gym, there wasn't 30-point scorers. I mean, there wasn't high wire dunks. We didn't run an alley-oop play all year. We had many dunks, but we didn't run an alley-oop play all year. But yet everybody supported it. And to me that's where the memories will be.

"We had a lot of great speakers. Tony Dungy, probably a month ago now, when he came in and talked to guys, he was up for his book signing in Bloomington, and he said you will always be remembered for building the foundation if you continue to do it the right way day in, day out. And I think that makes a lot of sense. I know they've talked about that at times. And I think it makes a lot of sense."

So where would Indiana go from here? Crean was asked what the next step for the program would be.

"We haven't thought that far," Crean said. "Certainly recruiting, because that's paramount. And spring break starts. So I think give it a little time. But we're not going to take much time off. We've got to continue to build our athleticism, we've certainly got to build our strength, and I've never liked the eight hours where only two of them are oriented for basketball.

"I still think that's one of the most ridiculous rules put out there. If you're on campus, you should be able to work with your players as close to year-round as possible. Somebody's going to. It should be the coaches they signed up to play for. But we'll maximize our eight hours. We'll maximize everything we can to help them have a great spring and at the same time keep them on the great track that they're on academically right now."

Crean said he was looking forward to the incoming class and the fact that his current team would move forward with a lot of experience under its belt.

"I want the guys that come in here to become a part of the foundation-building of this program, not have anybody look at it like, well, now these guys are here, now we can go," Crean said. "No, we have to come together. We've had a lot of guys get better this year. And hopefully we'll get ourselves to a point we have that consistent depth. I think that's a big part of winning. And there's so much improvement to be made. And I'm looking forward to doing it. I think our coaching staff is, as well."

Chapter 14

Between Tom Crean's first and second seasons at Indiana, the Hoosiers experienced a little roster movement.

Nick Williams and Malik Story, who both had been contributors for Indiana as true freshmen, both decided they preferred to continue their careers elsewhere.

Story was at least somewhat explainable. He was a California kid living in the Midwest for the first time, something to which I can personally relate. When I moved to Indiana in the spring of 1986, I had only been east of Tempe, Arizona, one time in my life and that had been a few months before when I visited at Christmas. Going from the Midwest to the left coast is quite a bit different than vice versa.

So with Story I could see it from that standpoint. But it wasn't like he hadn't been a significant contributor for the Hoosiers, either. He was sixth on the team in scoring and was primarily the team's sixth man. He averaged 5.9 points in 17.9 minutes of action per game. He played in all 31 games but only had three starts.

And you certainly can't argue with how his story would ultimately play out beyond Indiana. The kid who was born in Pasadena and went to Artesia (California) High School transferred west to play at the University of Nevada. At the time of this writing, he will be a senior in college in the 2012-13 season. Since becoming eligible for the Wolfpack, Story has started all 67 games in which he has played. As a sophomore he led the team in scoring with a 14.5 average. As a junior, he was second at 14.1 points.

So it was simply a better fit.

In Williams, though, the decision to transfer was more of a stunning development. As a freshman at IU, Williams started 29 games and averaged nearly 27 minutes of playing time. He was fourth on the team in scoring at 8.9 points and also averaged 4.5 rebounds. Still, he wasn't happy and transferred to Mississippi.

After sitting out a season at Ole Miss, Williams started 26 games his sophomore year. He averaged 24.5 minutes per game. He averaged 6.2 points and 2.8 rebounds. His junior season he played in 34 games, averaged 31.7 minutes and 10.1 points. But he also missed out on IU's magical 2011-12 season which, had he stayed, would have been his senior year.

Williams said he left IU for his own reasons.

"I just felt like with the team we had, I should have been playing more," Williams said. "But stuff like that happens all the time between coaches and players. We just disagreed. I felt like I should have played more and I should have got the ball more, but everything happens for a reason and I'm very happy where I am now."

While Williams and Story were gone, Indiana got significantly better with the players that came in, both in terms of transfers and members of the 2009 freshman class. There was the transfer of Jeremiah Rivers, son of Celtics coach Doc Rivers, who had grown up a big fan of Crean's at Marquette. Rivers played two seasons at Georgetown, sat out Crean's first season at IU, then would play the next two years for the Hoosiers. Then there was the freshman class, one of the best in the nation. The six players included Maurice Creek, Christian Watford, Jordan Hulls, Derek Elston, Bobby Capobianco and Bawa Muniru.

Right from the start, that group was a serious contributor to Indiana's cause. That first season, those six players combined to average 43.5 points. That was 65.2 percent of Indiana's season average total of 66 points per game.

The first two games of the 2009-10 season were about what you would expect. The Hoosiers played a couple of cupcakes in Howard and USC Upstate at Assembly Hall and came away with two victories. The Howard win was by 23, while the Hoosiers beat USC Upstate by eight. A few days later, IU headed to Puerto Rico to play in its annual exempt event.

The first season under Crean ,the Hoosiers were humbled in Maui, having to rally for that 81-79 victory over Division II Chaminade in the final game.

The second season, in Puerto Rico, was another tough trip for the Hoosiers. Off the court, Matt Roth broke his foot in a practice and would wind up being lost for the season. On it, the Hoosiers struggled in each of the three games. IU lost to Mississippi by 18 in the opener, then fell to a pair of beatable opponents in Boston University and George Mason. Against George Mason, IU missed layup after layup but appeared to put forth some of its most inspired effort of the season in a 69-66 loss.

Tom Crean said in the postgame that he thought IU looked the best it had as a team "in the sense of trying to do the right things and trying to play harder for longer periods of time."

"Now we made some mistakes and we have some guys who do not sell out, defensively, the way that they have to," Crean said. "Our communication is still not as good as it needs to be. But today we had some guys come in off the bench that provided real energy and that's what we are looking for.

"But we lost this game in the first half. I know they (George Mason) were aggressive and physical and all of that, but they didn't have anything to do with us missing 13 or 14 layups because we didn't use the backboard. Three of our first four shots were shots in the paint that we should have used the backboard or dunked the ball."

The lack of fundamentals was clearly something that Crean was not going to put up with.

"I know you haven't seen a lot of our practices, but one thing I can promise you we spend a lot of time on is rebounding, and another thing we spend a lot of time on is layups and making them with contact," Crean said. "Obviously I'm not doing a good enough job there, because I either don't have strong enough guys hitting them or strong enough pads. And that's going to change, because we are not buying in to how important that glass is.

"As I told our guys, I have a guy that is going to make $100 million next year (Dwyane Wade), and he didn't have any trouble listening to me and figuring out how to get to the glass, and I sure am not going to tolerate anyone not listening now. I know it's not that they don't want to, a lot of it is that they just don't realize how important it is. It just isn't engrained into their minds yet."

Overall, Crean thought it was a performance his team could learn from.

"We should not have had a close game in the second half," Crean said. "We are going to take the learning parts from it, and there was a ton to learn from this tournament. There is some disappointment, but I hope the fans and the university stays with me on this, that there is no way to be discouraged.

"I learned things about this team and I thought the team would learn a lot about each other, but I'm not sure. I know I did, and I'm looking forward to getting on that plane and studying the films and then getting home and getting right back to practice."

In the first five games, Indiana had gone six or seven deep off the bench. Looking at the five games as a whole, Crean felt like that might be an area that would require change.

"We have a lot of determinations to make, like 'How do we really want to play?'" Crean said. "I am trying to play too many guys right now, but we are trying to get out and run. Are we going to all-out get after it and press more and shrink the bench? It is all about these guys really understanding the foundation we are building."

A few games later, Indiana put forth arguably its most impressive game of the Tom Crean era to that point at the Jimmy V Classic at Madison Square Garden. IU took on a Pittsburgh team that came in with a 7-1 record. The Hoosiers were 3-4.

Verdell Jones III scored 20 points and Christian Watford added 18 as IU knocked off Pitt 74-64. It was Crean's 200th win of his head coaching career.

"The bottom line is that they (the players) really earned it," Crean said. "It gnaws at you as a coach, as a leader or as a parental figure when your guys are working so hard and you want them to have success. I called my wife after the game and that's the first thing she said, 'It's so great for them, they earned it.'

"That's what we all feel like. These guys are working so hard and they needed a reason to see why they practiced twice on Thanksgiving Day and why we do individual workouts in the morning. But this was great, at a great venue and it was fantastic."

The next game was a 90-73 loss to No. 4 Kentucky at Assembly Hall that had some positive signs for Indiana on a couple of fronts. For one, the game was not as bad as the scored indicated. IU actually led 48-47 with 17:42 to play. But the Wildcats flexed their collective muscles and went on an 18-0 run and put the game way.

But the game was encouraging in another way for the Hoosiers, in that it was kind of Maurice Creek's coming-out party. The freshman guard poured in a career-high 31 points, hitting nine of 14 shots from the field and five of eight from 3-point range. That was 12 more than his previous career best of 19 against Maryland in the Big Ten/ACC Challenge.

He was the first IU freshman since frosh became eligible in 1973 to score more than 30 points against Kentucky. Bracey Wright, who was a junior, was the only other IU player to score more than 30 points against UK since the 1971-72 season. IU Hall of Famer Steve Downing had 47 points against the Wildcats on December 11, 1971.

When the two teams played in Crean's first year at Rupp Arena in Lexington, Kentucky had scored the game's first 14 points and the Hoosiers were never in it. This time they were hanging around before the Cats exploited them with the 18-0 run.

Still, Crean believed he had witnessed progress.

"A year ago, we played at Kentucky and it was a stunned locker room," Crean said. "This year we play Kentucky and it's a hurt locker room. That's progress to me."

Kentucky coach John Calipari complimented Creek's performance following the game.

"How about this Creek kid?" Calipari said. "We've played a lot of good teams, and he's as good as any player we've played. That's how you start to build a program. You get guys like him and Christian (Watford)."

Three games later, however, in the nonconference finale against Bryant, the focus was on Creek for a very different reason. In a freak noncontact accident, Creek fractured his left knee cap while driving to the basket for a layup in a 90-42 victory over Bryant.

Immediately, his teammates, who had come to his aid, had to look away. His knee cap had split down the middle. Someone close to the program told me later that it was so pronounced, you literally could have put your finger in between the two pieces of the kneecap.

Creek had come into the game as the nation's leading freshman scorer, with a 17.6 points-per-game average. He left it on a cart as he was wheeled off to a standing ovation. The reality for the Hoosiers, however, was that any hopes they had for being competitive in the Big Ten went down with their star.

This is what I wrote the next day in the *Indianapolis Star*.

BLOOMINGTON, Ind. – Indiana University won a basketball game Monday night at Assembly Hall but lost its best player for the season.

High-scoring freshman shooting guard Maurice Creek, who came into the game averaging 17.6 points per game, fractured his left knee on a drive to the basket early in the second half and will have surgery today, IU Coach Tom Crean confirmed following the game. Dr. Steve Ahlfeld will perform the operation.

Creek went down hard underneath the basket with 15:26 remaining in IU's 90-42 victory over winless Bryant and was wheeled off the floor on a stretcher.

After laying on the baseline for several minutes while being attended to by team physician Larry Rink and athletic trainer Tim Garl, Creek tried to get to his feet with the help of teammates but was in too much pain. Crean called for a stretcher to make it easier for Creek to get to the locker room.

Crean said he didn't have a good view of Creek's move and landing. He said the players who were near Creek as he tumbled, including Verdell Jones III, Derek Elston and Tom Pritchard, all had a bad feeling after seeing their teammate.

"My initial hope before I spoke with Dr. Rink was that it would be a dislocation, but I knew that would be the best-case scenario," Crean said. "But that wasn't the case. It turned out to be the worst case scenario."

Crean said the team gathered around Creek in the locker room after the game to offer prayers and best wishes.

"Our players are stunned," Crean said on his postgame radio show. "They're going to need some help to get through this one. They're going to need help from our crowd in the next game. Our guys are going to fight through this and play hard, but they're going to need some help.

"Maurice is one of those players who just brings so much confidence to the court, and everyone in the game feeds off of that confidence."

Somehow, three days later, Indiana opened Big Ten play with a 71-65 victory over Michigan. Jordan Hulls hit six free throws in the final 23.8 seconds to allow IU to open conference play 1-0.

It was a significant victory on more than one front. Considering IU was coming off a 1-17 Big Ten season in Crean's first year with the Hoosiers, already equaling that conference win total in one game was an accomplishment.

But winning that conference opener against a decent Michigan team without leading scorer Maurice Creek was big as well.

"You can't replace someone like Maurice, but I knew we were going to be all right," said freshman forward Christian Watford, who scored a career-high 19 points on seven-of-12 shooting. "We rallied around each other and did what we had to do. The one thing about this group of guys is that we're really a team."

The Hoosiers also got a spark from an unexpected source before the game. Pam Morgan, Creek's mother, delivered an emotional pregame speech and assured the Hoosiers that her son would be OK and urged them to fight on without him this season.

"To have her come and speak from the heart to our team, not only about Maurice's situation but how she felt about Maurice being with us, you could have heard a pin drop," Crean said. "I'm surprised I didn't have bloodshot eyes when I came out of there."

Creek returned to Bloomington early Thursday after being in Indianapolis for his surgery to repair a fractured kneecap. He wasn't able to attend the Michigan game, but his Hoosier teammates had him on their minds.

"It was great to have his mom come and talk to us, because I know he was in all of our thoughts," Verdell Jones III said. "She told us he was thinking about us, that he can't wait to get back with us, and that he was feeling better (Thursday) than (Wednesday). We're looking forward to having him back around us."

ಶಿ   ೞ

Six games into the Big Ten season, IU was a respectable 3-3.

The previous two games had been an 81-78 overtime victory over Minnesota at Assembly Hall and a huge 67-61 win over Penn State in Happy Valley. Think using the words "huge" and "win" and "Penn State" in the same sentence is an exaggeration? Maybe, but in the future, after the first three seasons of the Tom Crean era, that win over Penn State would represent IU's only true Big Ten road victory in those three years. After three seasons, IU had a 1-26 record in conference road games.

So that Penn State game was indeed big. And with a 1-5 Iowa team coming to Assembly Hall three days later on January 24, IU's road to respectability appeared to be on the upswing.

Then Iowa happened.

The Hoosiers scored the game's first basket 39 seconds in on a short jumper by Christian Watford. Iowa's Jarryd Cole made a three-point play at the other end, and the Hawkeyes never trailed again.

Iowa led by as many as 16 points and cruised to a 58-43 victory over the Hoosiers. Indiana missed all nine of its 3-point shots and hit just 35.6 percent from the field for the game.

The Hawkeyes had lost their previous 15 consecutive road games including their last 11 in Big Ten play. IU, though, made them look like road warriors.

This is what I wrote the next day in the *Indianapolis Star*:

BLOOMINGTON, Ind. — Just when it appeared the Indiana basketball team might be turning the corner, it reverted Sunday evening against Iowa.

The statistics were ugly.

Sixteen turnovers. Three assists. No 3-point field goals. Outrebounded by 16. A 34-16 deficit in points in the paint. All against an Iowa team that hadn't won on the road in 15 games.

When IU coach Tom Crean assessed Indiana's 58-43 loss to Iowa, he narrowed the problems to one specific area.

"We just did not have a toughness about us today where we would have beat anybody," Crean said. "This all came down to our lack of being willing to be in a fight today. I can't explain it. We just did not come to be in a fight today."

Crean wasn't happy. Check that. Crean was furious with IU's play, especially inside and on the glass, and took out his frustrations on his team both in his postgame radio show and in his press conference with the media.

Chris Korman, of the *Herald-Times* in Bloomington, had this to say in his story the next day.

Perhaps sensing how drastically the rebuilding effort was hurt by Indiana's galling lack of effort on the basketball court Sunday, Head Coach Tom Crean made a decision many had been waiting for.

He blamed the players for the Hoosiers 58-43 loss to Iowa at Assembly Hall instead of the circumstances — mostly.

"This all came down to our lack of willingness to be in a fight today," he said early in his postgame press conference.

Minutes earlier he'd been blunt on the radio.

"That was one of the softest low-post performances I've ever been a part of," he said. "I apologize to our fans...That's not who we're going to be."

Crean did then mention that he had players who needed to get stronger over time, and that future recruits would bring toughness. He's not going to give up on that talking point. He believes it.

Sunday clearly represented something of a shift for Crean, though. He has steadfastly accredited a majority of his team's struggles to this point to youth and inexperience. He finally pushed past those viable but tired explanations, possibly endearing himself to a faction of the fan base unhappy with how unrugged the Hoosiers have been at times.

"You put it on yourself and you say maybe you aren't being demanding enough," he said. "I think I am, but then you see a team go out there and you see the lack of fight in that game, and I'm not putting this on youth. I am putting this on fight. We just did not have a toughness about us today that would allow us to beat anyone."

Perhaps more than any job in the country, being the head coach at Indiana ensures that no move can go without being interpreted.

Figuring out the head coach's moods and signals is as much a part of being an Indiana fan as adoring the site of flags being jogged around center court.

Crean has been criticized for, of all things, clapping too much on the court. What's probably nothing more than a way to expend and perhaps spread energy has come to symbolize his lack of sternness with his players. His willingness to repeatedly mention the ruin he found the program in is — according to one narrative currently running through Hoosier nation — both evidence of coddling and a ploy to shuck responsibility.

Of course, it is difficult to tell how Crean actually deals with his players, as practices are closed to the media. Culpability is something he certainly thinks about — there are few coaches more dedicated to speaking with fans — but that 10-year, $23 million contract he signed pushes off any real thought of his job being in jeopardy any time soon.

But Crean's shift in tone Sunday was the right thing to do. He often says that he can't speed up the development process, can't help his players gain 10 pounds or add 25 pounds to their bench press in a week. But he certainly can at least partially dictate expectations.

That doesn't mean he should come out and declare Indiana even a middle-of-the-pack Big Ten team. He needs to continue to be clear that the Hoosiers have far to go, as he was Sunday.

"I told (the players) after the game I would be shocked if we had anyone who was ridiculous enough to overlook Iowa," he said. "Based on where we are at with this program right now, I would have a real hard time accepting that.

"If that were to play itself out over a period of time, obviously a person like that couldn't make it here."

ᛒ   𝒞ᵌ

The Iowa loss turned out to be a sign of things to come.

The Hoosiers would go on to lose 11 games in a row and had a 9-20 record going into Senior Night against Northwestern. There, the Hoosiers posted an 88-80 victory to wrap up Big Ten play.

Five days later, the No. 11-seeded Hoosiers drew that same Northwestern team in the Big Ten Tournament. This time it wasn't close. The Wildcats posted an easy 73-58 victory over Indiana, a loss that brought IU's season to a close.

Indiana's second season under Crean wrapped up at 10-21 overall and 4-14 in Big Ten play.

Here's how *Indianapolis Star* columnist Bob Kravitz wrapped up the season the day after IU bowed out of the Big Ten Tournament with the loss to Northwestern.

There are no fast-forward buttons in Indiana basketball Coach Tom Crean's Bloomington office, although I'm pretty sure IU Athletic Director Fred Glass has looked far and wide for one. There is no way to suddenly make it 2012, no way to put a running clock on IU's massive and painful rebuilding program.

It was miserable last year, it was slightly less miserable this year, and it's only going to be marginally better next year.

Shortcuts? Shoot, that's how IU got into this mess in the first place, because a brain-dead administration hired a serial cheater named Kelvin Sampson, and Sampson – surprise, surprise – acted like the rules didn't quite apply to him.

For now, the Hoosiers are going to have to accept incremental progress, from 6-25 to 10-21 and maybe a shot at .500 next season. There are no savior recruits out there right now, no Mike Davis-esque rallying cries of "Help is on the way!"

"We have a lot of needs, and I think we've got to develop the bigs that we have," Crean said after IU's 73-58 loss to Northwestern in the Big Ten Tournament. "We've got a very tough situation right now.... We had to get a team on the floor before we could build a program. OK, that was last year. Then we were able to recruit guys that we wanted, that we had a chance to develop relationships with. We're very bottom heavy.

"We have to have a balancing act right now between what do we need to do in the short term versus how are we not going to have to start over again when these guys get older."

Next year?

Yes, there are two nice-looking freshmen on the way, Victor Oladipo and Will Sheehey. Both, though, are wing players, which is why Crean is beating the junior college bushes for a big man.

There are no quick fixes, however. If IU is going to be better next season, it's because Verdell Jones III and Christian Watford got into the weight room this summer.

If IU is going to be better next season, it's because Jeremiah Rivers got his head straight and became the play-making point guard Crean hoped he would be this season.

If IU is going to be better next season, it's because Derek Elston, Jordan Hulls and Bobby Capobianco got one year older and wiser and tougher. (Not so sure about Tom Pritchard, who took about 10 steps backward his sophomore season.)

If IU is going to be better next season, it's because their best player, Maurice Creek, returns, and Matt Roth comes back with his perimeter game intact.

"They've all got to get stronger, bigger, better, more athletic than what we have in the program," Crean said. "But we also need somebody that's better at getting in the lane. We need somebody that can create havoc, that can get into that paint and make decisions to get the ball to shooters.

"Our team will look different when you add the spacing element into it that Matt Roth and Maurice Creek bring.... But we're not anywhere close to being done recruiting."

By midway through the second half, you could see the belief drain from the players' faces. Once Northwestern extended its 1-3-1 trapping defense, once the Wildcats started challenging every pass and forcing turnovers, the accumulated weight of all that losing left the Hoosiers punch-drunk and reeling.

Crean talks about it after almost every game: His team's collective will, its toughness, is lacking. But a lot of that is perfectly understandable. This is a team whose four seniors (Tijan Jobe, Devan Dumes, Steven Gambles and Brett Finkelmeier) made minimal contributions. This is a team that has had to rely on freshmen and sophomores to accomplish the little they've accomplished.

A little perspective on the issue of rebuilding: Michigan's John Beilein, in his third year, stands at 15-16. Iowa's Todd Lickliter, who is dealing with rumors he will be fired after his third season ended Thursday, just went 10-22. And neither began his first year with an empty cupboard.

I'm sure it gets tiring to read it — and really, it gets tiring to write it over and over again — but this is going to take time, a lot of time, and it's going to try the Hoosier Nation's patience. So far, they've stuck with the program, consistently showing up at Assembly Hall in generous numbers. There is the occasional leather-lunged fan and the message boards are always filled with the addled ramblings of fans with short memories. But by and large, IU fans have remained loyal.

The players know what must happen this offseason. We asked Watford, who talked about living in the weight room. We asked Jones, who talked about putting on pounds. We asked Elston, who talked about working this summer to improve every facet of his game.

There is no fast-forward button in Crean's office.

Believe me, he has looked.

Chapter 15

When people talk about the three dates that had the biggest impact on the return of Indiana basketball, they would likely say something like this:

April 2, 2008

November 11, 2010

December 10, 2011

The first one was the day Tom Crean was hired as Indiana's coach to rebuild a program from the ground floor.

That's a no-brainer.

The last one, obviously, was the day IU beat No. 1 Kentucky on Christian Watford's 3-pointer at the buzzer. Again, an easy event to look at and say that was the day IU basketball came of age. That one shot probably added five or six wins (or more) to IU's victory total that season because of the confidence that came with knocking off the No. 1 team in the land.

But what about November 11, 2010?

It was the day before Indiana would open its third season under Tom Crean, and the news that day exploded like a sonic boom all across Hoosierland. One simple statement at a press conference in Washington, Indiana, had the IU Nation feeling as if it could see a light at the end of the tunnel. Hoosier fans believed they could be whole again. Some will say it was the first day the sun had shined brightly on the Indiana program in years.

November 11, 2010 was national signing day and the day that Cody Zeller chose the Hoosiers over a final three that also included North Carolina and Butler.

The Hallelujah Chorus can generally be heard in the background by Indiana fans when retelling this moment. It can't be understated or undervalued. The biggest fish — both literally and figuratively — had decided to stay home in the state of Indiana and play for the Hoosiers.

Jeff Rabjohns wrote this story the next day in the *Indianapolis Star* to which I contributed. The message was simple: Indiana basketball was on the verge of becoming relevant again.

WASHINGTON, Ind. — A few hours after announcing he would play basketball for Indiana University, Cody Zeller donned his black high school jersey Thursday for team photos at center court of the Hatchet House.

It was an appropriate moment. The 6-10 Washington High School senior is now the picture of IU's resurgence.

Landing Zeller after a long recruiting battle with North Carolina and Butler – and others who were weaned out earlier in the process – is a watershed moment for a program with five national titles battling back from NCAA sanctions related to a previous coaching staff.

Zeller's decision to attend IU after his two highly sought brothers went elsewhere is evidence third-year coach Tom Crean can attract the state's ultra-elite talent to Bloomington, something that hasn't happened consistently for nearly a decade.

"Tom Crean was hired to padlock the borders to the state. This is an amazing step in doing that," ESPN recruiting analyst Dave Telep said. "Cody Zeller is the statement guy."

Ranked No. 20 in the senior class by Rivals, Zeller is important because of his skill, but there is a bigger context.

His recruitment was, in a way, a referendum on whether a new staff at IU could beat marquee programs around the country for the state's elite players. After a decade of many key players going elsewhere, that was the question hanging during the process.

Zeller's commitment was an answer, and one with national implications.

"Cody Zeller is the kind of guy that Indiana University would love to have as their model," said Gene Miiller, Zeller's coach at Washington. "This is a young man with great skills, works hard, a great student, great character.

"He's everything you want for a college athlete. I think he's going to be that poster-boy kind of kid you can have for Indiana University to show everyone, 'This is the way we're going to do things.' "

Zeller's oldest brother, Luke, played at Notre Dame. Tyler, who also had IU among his finalists, is a junior at North Carolina.

Now the youngest of Steve and Lorri Zeller's three boys becomes the face of the rebuilding for an IU program coming off consecutive losing seasons for the first time in history, a result of serious sanctions spawning from former coach Kelvin Sampson.

Crean said before their first meeting that "Cody Zeller was going to be a major priority" for IU. Thursday's decision left Crean searching for words.

"What Cody did today was he validated the level of where Indiana is today with everybody else out there," Crean said. "And for that, I can't thank him enough. Like I told him today, I won't be stunned and speechless very often like I was with him today."

Zeller understands the significance of his commitment to IU and embraced it.

"Representing the state of Indiana will be pretty special to me," he said. "Growing up in Indiana, I think it'll mean a lot to me playing for this state."

That was precisely what Crean wanted to hear.

"I don't blame others for coming into this state," Crean said about non-Indiana schools raiding the state for top talent. "But we're trying to do everything we can do to make it our state...like it was."

While Zeller is the face of what's happening at IU, he's not being asked to do it alone. In addition to young developing players already at IU, nationally ranked 7-0 center Peter Jurkin and top-10 ranked 6-8 forward Hanner Perea will join the Hoosiers in 2012.

Zeller might also become a pied piper of sorts, attracting players such as Park Tudor point guard Yogi Ferrell, his teammate in summer ball and the No. 17 player in the junior class.

"Growing up in this state, I wanted (IU) to be good, which is another reason I think I can help them out," Zeller said. "Hopefully we can get Yogi and a couple of those guys to follow in my footsteps.

"I'm not saying I'm going to turn it around 180 degrees, but I think I can help."

Steve Zeller said Cody was the calmest through the recruiting process, in part because he'd seen his older brothers go through it. The summer before sixth grade, Zeller went with Luke on official visits. "The coaches would joke around, 'We're recruiting Luke, but we're really recruiting you,' " Zeller said. "They were joking around, but they really ended up to start recruiting me."

IU didn't really have a chance at the two older Zellers. Former coach Mike Davis didn't heavily pursue Luke, and Sampson had questionable players on the roster when he tried to recruit Tyler.

Zeller knows the current players from visits to IU, and he has been summer basketball teammates with some. He has played summer ball with Perea, Jurkin and Hamilton Heights senior Austin Etherington, who signed with IU on Wednesday.

"Let's be honest: The situation at IU when the other two Zellers went through just wasn't right. You know it wasn't right," Miiller said. "This is a much improved situation. Coach Crean has done a great job of getting things turned around and getting things turned around the right way."

Part of the decision-making process stemmed from three days of debate-level discussions between Steve and Cody. They would pick a school, Steve would try to convince his son that it was the place for him and Cody would think through the pros and cons. At the end of the process, Steve still wasn't sure where Cody wanted to go. Cody didn't finalize his choice until a few days ago.

"There are a lot of things that go into it, but the players and coaches are the most important thing," he said. "And also the facilities. After talking to so many people close to me, I knew it was the right thing for me.

"I don't know if it was one thing, but you get a feeling that it's the right thing."

Todd Lancaster, a reporter for the Washington (Indiana) *Times-Herald*, filled in more of Zeller's decision-day comments in his story the following day. He said the thought of playing close to his hometown was important to him.

"That wasn't really a factor at first, but the more I thought about it, I realized it would be nice to see the Hatchet fans and people who have supported me since I was a kid," Zeller said.

Zeller has been at the top on all recruiting services. He is ranked No. 15 overall by ESPN and No. 20 (fourth overall among power forwards) by rivals.com. He is also a member of the nationally highly-regarded Indiana Elite AAU team.

Although the process has taken several years, Zeller said he enjoyed it.

"It was a tough process but I enjoyed it," said Zeller. "It is something you can only do once in a lifetime. I talked to my parents, my brothers and the few friends that I thought could give me good insight.

"I really didn't tell anyone until a few minutes ago. Even my high school coach didn't know until I walked in," added Zeller. "I'm glad to get this out of the way so I can start to focus on winning another state championship."

Before Cody made his announcement, his father, Steve Zeller, read a statement thanking the coaches from all three schools. The elder Zeller has been through the process three times now and feels this time was definitely the smoothest.

"It has gotten easier because we (as a family) are more relaxed," said Steve Zeller. "Instead of letting the process control us, we have tried to control the process. We feel like we have learned from some of the mistakes from the other ones."

Cody Zeller said he contacted North Carolina and Butler just before the announcement, and both coaches wished him luck.

"I wished them the best of luck as well. It is tough because they put all that time into me and I'm going to go to Indiana. I do appreciate all the time and effort they put into recruiting me."

考 考

People can say what they want, but the pressure that is on young people to make college decisions, especially those who are considered future NBA players, is off the charts. When that pressure is taken to another level because that player is an in-state kid whom the locals don't want to see get away, it just makes it that much more difficult.

With Cody Zeller, fans from the state of Indiana had a two-out-of-three chance as he had narrowed his choices to North Carolina and Butler.

North Carolina, based on recent success, would have been the safe choice. Sure, there would have been added pressure having to live up to the accomplishments of older brother Tyler, but the reality is that I think most people figured Cody would do just fine wherever he ended up. This was a talent who was destined to hold his own.

With Butler, which had just advanced to the NCAA title game where it lost to Duke in Indianapolis, there was probably more to lose from the standpoint of an Indiana fan. Choosing North Carolina over Indiana could have been accepted. But Butler? Even with the Bulldogs coming off a magical run to the title game, losing Zeller to Butler would have been a bitter pill for Hoosier Nation to swallow.

As for Indiana, considering the depths to which the IU program had slipped, Zeller would seriously have to have an eye toward the future if he considered signing on with Tom Crean and the Hoosiers. Most people thought that if Zeller went to IU, the Hoosiers would be much closer to respectability in his freshman season, but they also thought it would be the year after, when Yogi Ferrell and company arrived, that Indiana would have its best chance to return to the NCAA Tournament.

Zeller had been saying for some time that he liked what Crean was doing at IU, but liking it and pulling the trigger to attend Indiana were two completely different animals.

When the day arrived for Cody to make his decision, the majority of fans weren't completely sure what to think. Dan Dakich on his daily radio show on 1070-The Fan had been saying for months that it was a slam dunk that Zeller would go to Indiana. I'm not sure who his sources were, but if the Zeller family is to be believed, the decision really went down to the 11th hour.

There were early reports that day that Zeller had decided to attend North Carolina, then reports later that it was Butler. Basically nobody knew for sure.

Dustin Dopirak, the IU beat writer for the *Herald-Times* in Bloomington, had this to allow on the day Zeller was to make his announcement.

> *Zeller and his family long ago walled themselves off from media inquiries, and on Wednesday it was virtually impossible to find anyone with real knowledge of what his decision might be.*
>
> *"I don't know of anybody that knows," said Mark Adams, Zeller's well-connected AAU coach in the Indiana Elite program. "I don't know if he knows."*
>
> *Perhaps he doesn't. The only thing anyone seems to know about Zeller's decision is that he's putting a lot of effort into making it. The brother of two high-level Division I basketball players — brother Luke played at Notre Dame and brother Tyler is currently playing at North Carolina — he played his entire recruitment close to the vest and took his time making his decision. All year, he said he would pare his choices down to five, take the NCAA allotted number of official visits and then make his decision. The only part of that promise he hasn't stuck to was the number of schools that would be involved. He ended up cutting it to three, taking his official visit first to Butler, then North Carolina, then Indiana in October.*

Throughout the process, he's kept quiet with the media and discussed little about where he might be leaning.

"It's the most important decision he's probably ever had to make," Adams said. "And he's gone about it the right way. It's just between him and his family. That's all that anyone really needs to know."

Also on Decision-Day 2010, I liked the column written by my colleague Bob Kravitz in the *Indianapolis Star*. One thing Kravitz does well is he provides perspective.

At this point, Cody Zeller needs more advice like Charlie Sheen needs a vodka martini.

For years now, he's had an entire state in his ear, telling him to stay home. And he's had the recruiters at North Carolina – and maybe a recruiter named Tyler Zeller, his brother – telling him to come east and set up shop on Tobacco Road.

So I'm not going to tell this young man from Washington, Ind., what he should do, because it's his life, his future, and the truth is, with his choices narrowed to IU, Butler and North Carolina, he can't make a bad decision this afternoon.

I would just tell him to listen to two guys who've gone through the process, who sat in roughly the same place he did six, seven years ago.

Tyler Hansbrough, who was a big-time recruit from Missouri but went to North Carolina: "This is a time in his life when he's got to be selfish. No one's going to go to college for him. So wherever you feel happy, that's where you have to go."

Josh McRoberts, who played at Carmel then committed to Duke before his junior year: "I'm sure everybody is telling him what he should do. I went through it. 'You're an Indiana kid; you have to stay home.' I'm sure he's got a lot of people in his ear. That's one of the reasons I committed so early. I'd just say, do what makes YOU happy."

It's vaguely amusing – "sad, really," McRoberts said – that so many grown and otherwise accomplished adults are so invested in the decision of a very tall, very talented 17-year-old. If Zeller picks any place other than IU, the Hoosier Nation will have to be talked off ledges.

It's the double-edged sword of hoops fanaticism in this state; people care deeply about their teams, but it makes them loopy when it's time for a teenager to decide where to play college basketball.

There are pros (and a couple of cons) in all three choices.

At IU, he gets one of the country's great business schools. He gets to stay close to home and establish an identity independent of his brother, Tyler. He gets to be at the center of IU basketball's renaissance, likely acting as a magnet for some of the state's other top recruits.

The cons? Just one — the pressure.

At Butler, he gets a phenomenal education. He gets a smaller campus, which may suit his personality. Again, he gets to stay close to home, gets to show up on Day 1 and be a marquee player for a unique program.

The cons? One, Butler lacks big-time facilities. Two, he would play in a lower-profile conference and would not get a whole lot of national TV time, assuming that's important.

At North Carolina, again, a great school. He gets to leave home; for some kids, the best way to grow up and become independent is to be a thousand or so miles away from home. He gets to play at one of the most storied programs in the country, gets to play with his brother, and he gets to take his time becoming an integral part of a program that is almost always loaded with talent.

The cons? Maybe he doesn't want to go away. Maybe he wants to be Cody Zeller, and not Tyler Zeller's Little Brother. Maybe he wants to play huge minutes the minute he arrives on campus.

As we all know by now, it's different for an Indiana kid. Top basketball recruits in New York and Colorado and Texas aren't expected to stay in-state or risk eternal derision.

"So much pressure to stay home," McRoberts said. "This state is so basketball-crazed, people want to see the guys they watched in high school stay in state. You hear it from everybody, before you commit, after you commit. I was always shocked how (former Duke teammate) J.J. Redick got so much attention because crowds were so bad to him, supposedly. I went to college, I said, 'This is nothing. High school kids are ruthless.' "

There was pressure on McRoberts to stay local, but he came of age at a bad time in local college basketball. When he graduated from

Carmel, Gene Keady was heading into his final year; two years earlier, when he committed, the job had not yet been given to Matt Painter. And IU? Mike Davis and his staff didn't show much interest.

That hasn't been the case with Zeller. Indiana coach Tom Crean, among others, has been on him for years now. So come this afternoon at 1, Zeller will sit at a table with three hats before him, and otherwise-sane adults will peer in like they're waiting for a white puff of smoke over the Vatican.

"I'm taking my talents to..."

By now, he's heard enough advice. So here's one or two more pieces to consider. Listen to Hansbrough and McRoberts. Be selfish. Follow your heart. And that will lead you to the place you're supposed to be.

⁞ ⁞

Many likened Zeller's decision to play for Indiana that day to a pied piper who would get all the minions to then follow him to Bloomington.

And that's exactly what happened.

Ten days after Zeller signed with the Hoosiers, IU picked up two big in-state commitments for the class of 2013.

Collin Hartman, a 6-6 wing from Indianapolis Cathedral and Devin Davis Jr., a 6-6 wing from Indianapolis Warren Central, gave their commitments to Crean. Both were on campus for IU's game with Evansville.

Hartman chose the Hoosiers over Butler, Purdue and Michigan State. Davis had offers from Illinois, Purdue and Xavier.

Davis' high school coach was former IU great Greg Graham. He said in a story in the *Indianapolis Star* the next day that it was big for Crean to keep landing in-state talent for the Hoosiers.

"He wants to be part of something special," Graham said. "What Coach Crean is doing there with Hoosier Nation is going to be something special. There's a lot of buzz right now, and getting these in-state kids is really going to have people talking."

Three days later, Crean and the IU staff landed another of its crown jewels. Kevin 'Yogi' Ferrell, a 5-11 difference-making point guard from Indianapolis Park Tudor, gave his commitment. At the time, Ferrell was ranked No. 17 in the nation by rivals.com. A past AAU teammate of Zeller, Ferrell would go on to become a McDonald's All-American.

The haul for Crean was continuing. And most of the players, much to the delight of the IU Nation, were from the state of Indiana.

As of late November 2010, Crean had solidified a presence in four recruiting classes. He had signed two in the class of 2011: Zeller and 6-6 wing Austin Etherington of Hamilton Heights in Cicero, Indiana. In the class of 2012, he now had four commitments with Ferrell being the most recent. The others included 6-8 power forward Hanner Perea, who was playing in prep school at La Lumiere in La Porte, Indiana, Ron Patterson a 6-3 guard from Indianapolis Broad Ripple, and Peter Jurkin, a 6-11 center from Charlotte, North Carolina.

Hartman and Davis had gotten things started in the class of 2013, and Crean had only picked up two commits to the class of 2014, who were about to begin their freshman seasons in high school. Those two were James Blackmon Jr., a 6-2 guard from Fort Wayne Luers, and Trey Lyles, a 6-9 forward from Indianapolis Tech.

Of all the committed recruits, Dustin Dopirak of the *Herald-Times* in Bloomington said you could make a case that Ferrell was the most important.

> *But in one way, Ferrell may be the most important addition. Perea is obviously higher rated and Zeller was the most symbolically valuable and influential of the group. But Ferrell gives the Hoosiers help in a major need position. The only true point guard on the roster is sophomore Jordan Hulls, and the Hoosiers don't have another in the pipeline until Ferrell.*

> *Ferrell said the most important reason he committed to Indiana was the other players Crean had coming, in particular Perea and Zeller. Both players were part of the Indiana Elite AAU program last summer along with Ferrell, who played up with Zeller and fellow Indiana signee Austin Etherington on the program's 17-and-under team.*

> *"The commitments of Cody Zeller and Hanner," Ferrell said when asked for his reason for committing. "Those two, I wanted to play with those guys at IU. Those were the two main factors. I told Coach Crean those were the two guys I wanted to play with in order for me to commit. So he got it done."*

> *Ferrell had been recruited heavily by the Hoosiers for some time, but his father, Kevin, said he probably wouldn't have gone to IU if he didn't know there was going to be other talent there.*

> *"You know that changed the process," Kevin said. "I'm not sure how much he would've looked at IU just to say 'I want to go to IU,' if nobody was there. After you've done what you've done all these years and work hard, you want to be a contender. I think he feels*

comfortable enough to say, 'We're gonna be a contender now.' When they committed, he was smiling every day. He was smiling every day. Then when Cody committed it was like, 'OK, Dad, let me talk to you.'"

Ferrell can certainly do a lot on his own to make them a contender. He's listed at just 5-foot-11, 165 pounds, but he's fast and skilled enough to overcome that. Ferrell led Park Tudor to the Class 2A state championship game last year, averaging 22.8 points and 4.3 assists per game.

"He's just got great speed," Park Tudor Coach Ed Schilling said. "His speed is at the highest level against the best. He's super fast against the guys that are the fastest. He's got that level of speed. He just goes by but he can change directions, he's got a great mid-range game. He can shoot 3s, but he can really create for others."

There was a lot of "creating for others" going on with the Indiana basketball program. Ferrell may have been able to do it on the court, but Zeller was obviously doing it off it, simply by signing on the dotted line and opening up the recruiting gates for in-state players to play for the Hoosiers.

Recruiting guru Jody Demling of the *Louisville Courier-Journal* wrote about the momentum that Crean and his staff was building, the day after Ferrell committed to play at IU.

Indiana University basketball coach Tom Crean is on an impressive run recruiting.

Crean has landed nine prospects in just more than 100 days, including the latest on Wednesday night when Indianapolis Park Tudor point guard Yogi Ferrell committed.

"Tom Crean needs a raise," Hoop Scoop analyst Clark Francis said. "What he is doing is totally amazing."

Ferrell is the third commitment in four days after Indianapolis Cathedral sophomore Collin Hartman and Indianapolis Warren Central sophomore Devin Davis gave the Hoosiers' coach their words on Sunday.

Ferrell, a 5-foot-11 point guard, ranks No. 17 nationally in the Class of 2012 by rivals.com. He announced his decision before his season-opening game with Park Tudor.

He also considered Butler, Florida, Virginia and Wake Forest and is close friends and an AAU teammate of Cody Zeller, who committed to the Hoosiers this month.

"I love guys that are pure point guards, and Yogi Ferrell runs the show," Francis said.

Indiana now has two players signed in the Class of 2011, four committed for 2012 and two apiece for '13 and '14.

"Guys have been on recruiting runs before, but this is such a different situation," scout.com analyst Evan Daniels said. "It was so thin when he got there, and it's probably taken longer than he wanted, but now he really has it rolling."

To make the run even more impressive, seven of the prospects have come from the Hoosier State and the other two are foreign big men from the Indiana Elite AAU program.

Seven of the prospects are ranked among the top 50 nationally, with the biggest coup being Washington (Indiana) center Zeller. The top-20 senior picked the Hoosiers over North Carolina and Butler.

"Last spring and summer, even a month ago, everyone said they have to get Cody Zeller," Francis said. "They did that, and now it's the case of Tom Crean recruiting like Bob Knight during the glory years."

Daniels said Ferrell is another sign that Crean's work in trying to restore the program's image is working.

"They are now reaping the rewards for the foundation they started building when they got the job," Daniels said. "(Crean) went in and not only recruited the players but the AAU coaches, the high school coaches and the parents.

"He has built great relationships with people in the state of Indiana, and it's paying off. They had a few dominoes, and then the big domino (Zeller), and now a few more."

Chapter 16

By mid-November of Tom Crean's third season at Indiana, he knew he had a big man he could covet when Cody Zeller signed to play for the Hoosiers. Six months before, however, in May of 2010, Crean thought he had another big player who would complement Zeller's talents.

Guy-Marc Michel, a 7-1, 265-pound center from North Idaho College, signed a letter of intent in May to play for the Hoosiers. He had played two years of junior college ball and would have two seasons of eligibility remaining with IU. He visited Indiana the week before and chose the Hoosiers over Boise State.

IU assistant coach Steve McClain had started recruiting Michel when he was an assistant the year before at Colorado. Michel, a native of the Caribbean island of Martinique, had originally planned to play at Gonzaga, but at the time of his initial recruitment, he did not have the qualifying SAT score. By August, Indiana's players were taking notice of how big and strong Michel played inside.

In a story in the *Indianapolis Star* written by Jeff Rabjohns, Bobby Capobianco said Michel was the center IU had been missing.

"Tom (Pritchard) and I have tried our best over the last two years to guard some of these guys, but it's a very big, strong league," Capobianco said. "Guy brings that presence in the paint. He is all of 7-feet, 7-1, and he's a legit 280. I look at myself as one of the stronger guys, and I cannot move that guy if I try my hardest.

"We're really looking forward to being able to have a guy that, where we come down in a half-court offense and throw the ball in the post, we know that he is going to bang and bang and get to the rim."

But by the time IU was set to open exhibition play against Franklin College in November, Michel had still not been cleared academically to play at Indiana. The night of that exhibition game, November 3, the IU media relations office put out a release updating the public on Michel's status.

"Prior to attending North Idaho Community College, Guy participated in club basketball in France, where he finished high school and enrolled in some college courses," Crean said in the release. "In three years with the French club, Guy participated as a member of an amateur team. In his third year, he was 'called up' for limited participation with a team that included professional players."

That was the sticking point. But at that point, Crean still believed that Michel might get penalized a few games but would eventually be able to suit up for the Hoosiers. As it turned out, that wouldn't be the case. On November 30, the NCAA ruled that Michel had no eligibility remaining with Indiana.

Because Michel played for a professional team in France, coupled with the fact that his five-year collegiate clock started in the fall of 2006, Michel was ineligible to play college basketball.

"We are disappointed by this decision, because everyone involved in this process agrees that Guy did not intentionally do anything that would have jeopardized his ability to play here or at any of the number of institutions that also recruited him," Crean said. "We will regroup, assess all our options, and do whatever we can for Guy, who demonstrated to us that he deserves to be part of the IU program."

IU announced Michel would be kept on scholarship for his two years and be allowed to complete his degree. His scholarship would count against IU's 13 for the 2010-11 season but would not count against the scholarship total the next year.

Anyway you sliced it, the decision was a blow to an IU team that had gotten off to a decent start.

૮૦   ૮૪

Three other major pieces were added to the IU puzzle during that offseason that had a major impact on Indiana basketball moving forward.

One was the hiring of assistant Steve McClain in April. McClain, who boasted 28 years of coaching experience at the collegiate level, was hired to take the place of Roshown McLeod.

McLeod had been hired for his ability to recruit, and his inability to close the deal with Kyrie Irving, who ended up going to Duke, may have proved to be his undoing.

As for McClain, Crean had nothing but good things to say about his new "McCoach."

"It means a lot to me to be able to bring in someone with the knowledge, experience and aggressiveness of Steve McClain," Crean said. "I have admired him for how hard he works and for how hard his teams, especially at Wyoming, played. He brings a toughness to our program that has shown in those who have played for him, and he carries that same mindset over into recruiting."

McClain came to IU after spending three seasons at Colorado, including the last two as associate head coach. Prior to his time in Boulder, the 1984 graduate of Chadron State College served as the 19th head coach at the University of Wyoming from 1998-2007. For nine seasons, McClain led the Cowboy program through one of its most successful periods in school history, posting the fifth-highest winning percentage in school history (57.7 percent) and achieving a 157-115 record, averaging 17 wins per season through his nine years.

"I'm really looking forward to being able to work with Tom and this staff," said McClain. "Our philosophies are exactly on the same page in terms of how you ought to play and the toughness it takes to win a championship. Whether it's what you do in the office or what you do on the court that day, how you go about things determines how quickly you can reach that goal, and Tom and I share the same beliefs."

Another key personnel addition for the Hoosiers was strength and conditioning coach Je'Ney Jackson. He had spent time on McClain's staff at Wyoming and later had worked with the football program at the University of Kanas and Southern Mississippi.

The final piece was the opening of Cook Hall, IU's multimillion dollar practice facility. The late Bill Cook and his wife, Gayle, donated $15 million to the "For The Glory of Old IU" campaign from the Cook Group to help fund the project. On the day it was dedicated, Crean talked about what it meant to the program to have such a facility.

"This facility, as you will see if you haven't already, is second to none in the United States of America," Crean said. "There's no doubt about it. We'll sweat in here and we'll work, but it's a monument for excellence, or as my sons Riley and Maceo Jack call it, the Chamber of Awesome. It's already been renamed by two 11-year-olds.

"For our present team and coaches, for our future recruits, for the people that get a chance to be a part of this on a daily basis, we are eternally grateful and thankful."

ꕥ

Looking at year three under Tom Crean before the season began, you figured that with the nonconference schedule IU had assembled, the Hoosiers should be able to get out of the gate quickly. Nine of the first 11 games were at Assembly Hall, and none of them were the types of opponents to which you thought IU would lose. But two years before, IU fans had said the same things about home games with Northeastern and Lipscomb. In 2009 it had been Loyola (Maryland). Still, as Crean's teams were beginning to progress, you felt like the Hoosiers would at least win the early games they were expected to win.

The other two games in that opening stretch were road games at Boston College in the Big Ten/ACC Challenge and against Kentucky in Lexington.

As it would turn out, Indiana would win all nine of its early home games and lose to both BC and Kentucky to take a 9-2 record into the final two games of the Las Vegas Classic at The Orleans in Vegas.

IU had buried the two campus opponents in the tournament, beating SIU Edwardsville 88-54 and South Carolina State 102-60. Indiana beat South Carolina State on Sunday afternoon, December 19, and then got on a plane that night and headed for Las Vegas where it would play December 22 and 23.

Crean and his staff had designed the nonconference slate for their young team with one purpose in mind. They wanted the Hoosiers to get some confidence.

In the first two seasons, IU had posted a 9-5 record at Assembly Hall in nonconference games. In year three that record was 9-0 as the Hoosiers headed West.

"This schedule, like I've said before so many times, was built to get these guys to a level of confidence where they felt they earned the right to win," Crean said. "Even though we haven't won on the road yet, we've had some really good, long stretches of basketball because of that confidence. Like (legendary football coach) Bill Parcells said in a book years ago, confidence comes from demonstrated ability. Well, before these guys were going to get confident, they had to demonstrate the ability to win, and that's what we're trying to do."

So it was a confident Indiana team that traveled to Las Vegas, where it would face Northern Iowa and the winner/loser of Colorado vs. New Mexico. A win over Northern Iowa, and the Hoosiers would be 10-2 going into what would be a fun game for IU fans against Steve Alford's Lobos.

South Carolina State coach Tim Carter gave Indiana the edge as it would play Northern Iowa in a few days. His team had lost to IU 102-60 a few days after falling to Northern Iowa 66-52.

"(Indiana) is very similar (to Northern Iowa) in that they are very patient in the half court," Carter said. "I think Indiana has better perimeter shooters than what Northern Iowa had. Northern Iowa had one guy that was an excellent perimeter shooter, while Indiana has two or three."

℘ ℭ

So much for confidence. So much for being on a roll. None of those things mattered in a 67-61 loss to Northern Iowa in a semifinal matchup in the Las Vegas Classic.

Crean wasn't happy with IU's defensive effort as the Panthers hit eight 3-pointers in the first half and nine for the game.

"Our defensive mindset just wasn't where it needed to be at the beginning of the game," Crean said. "We scored points, but we never guarded in the game the way it needed to be done from the beginning. Our defense was just never good enough to give us any kind of cushion."

So much for a possible date with Alford's New Mexico squad. IU now had to hope to salvage one game from the trip with a third place matchup with Colorado.

But that wasn't to be, either.

Christian Watford missed his first 11 shots of the game. Colorado led by 19 points with 12 minutes to play before Crean opted to go with a smaller, quicker lineup to shake things up.

It worked. Indiana rallied to cut the lead to three and had a chance to get it to one, but Verdell Jones III missed two free throws in a double bonus situation with 2:44 to play.

Colorado held on for a 78-69 victory over the Hoosiers, giving IU its first two-game losing streak of the season heading into the Big Ten opener the following week at home against Penn State.

If there was a positive to be garnered from the loss, it was the play of freshman guard Victor Oladipo. Oladipo scored a career-high 16 points, hitting seven of nine shots from the field. He also had seven rebounds in 21 minutes off the bench.

"I just had a will to get my team back in it, and I just had a mind-set that I was going to get every offensive rebound I could get," Oladipo said. "I need to continue to do that and be consistent in that area."

℘ ℭ

Indiana's hangover from Las Vegas continued into the Big Ten season. The Hoosiers dropped their first four Big Ten games, losing to Penn State and Ohio State at home, and then on the road at Minnesota and Northwestern.

Indiana's first Big Ten victory, an 80-61 home rout against Michigan, gave IU its 10th victory of the season. That matched the most wins by an Indiana team in the Crean era. Verdell Jones III scored 24 points and hit nine of 10 shots. Watford had a double-double with 17 points and 10 boards.

But it would turn out to be a costly victory, too.

With 1:41 to play, Maurice Creek got free ahead of the pack and scored on a driving layup. As he landed out of bounds, however, he came down hard on his right knee and was in obvious pain. The crowd at Assembly Hall held its collective breath until Creek was helped to his feet after team doctors had checked him out. He even went back in the game.

Two days later, though, Crean announced on his weekly radio show that Creek was out indefinitely after suffering a stress fracture in his right patella.

The sophomore guard missed the Big Ten season the year before after he suffered a fractured left kneecap. Creek had played in all 18 games this season with 13 starts. He was averaging 8.3 points per game with a high game of 19 against Evansville.

"You can't imagine how big a blow it is to him," Crean said on his weekly radio show. "It's a tough, tough situation, and I hope everyone will think about him and say a prayer for Mo and his family."

After the win over Michigan, IU would win two of its next five games and both were noteworthy accomplishments.

When IU faced No. 20 Illinois on January 27, the odds weren't good for the Hoosiers. In the Crean era, Indiana was 0-18 against ranked opponents. The Illini came in 14-6 overall and 4-3 in conference play. Add to that the fact that Indiana was without both Creek and Jones (who missed his second game in a road with inflammation in his right knee), and IU was a heavy underdog.

But after Brandon Paul's 3-pointer with 2:44 to play put the Illini on top 49-46, the Hoosiers scored the game's final six points to pull of the upset. A crowd of 16,297 stormed the court to celebrate IU's first win over a ranked opponent since Kelvin Sampson's final season at IU.

The unlikely hero for the Hoosiers in this one was Tom Pritchard. With IU trailing 49-48, Jordan Hulls missed a short jump shot, and Christian Watford crashed the boards hard and tipped the ball in the air, keeping it alive. Pritchard tipped it in to give IU the 50-49 lead with 44.2 seconds to play. Hulls hit two late free throws to provide the final margin.

Jeremiah Rivers watched Pritchard's tip unfold from the top of the key. He said he hoped IU's junior big man would not bring the ball down and go back up, but rather tip it in like he did.

Pritchard was three-for-12 from the foul line on the season.

"I was out at the 3-point watching it and all I was thinking was, 'Please, Tom, tip it in,'" Rivers said. "I was thinking, 'Please don't bring the ball down and get fouled. Just go and tip it in.' "

Pritchard finished with four points.

"For a guy that doesn't like to shoot, he picked a great time to break out of that funk," Crean said. "I never heard the crowd louder than when he got that tip."

Indiana was looking to make it two wins in a row the next game at the Breslin Center against Michigan State. Another improbable feat for the Hoosiers, but the reality is Indiana should have done just that.

The Hoosiers led 78-75 with 54.2 seconds remaining following a runner in the lane by Hulls to beat the shot clock. When Michigan State's Draymond Green missed an open 3 at the other end, Jeremiah Rivers got the rebound and was fouled.

An 88 percent free throw shooter, Rivers had a one-and-one opportunity with 43 seconds to play that could have been a nail in Michigan State's coffin. Instead, Rivers missed, Michigan State came back to tie the game and send it to overtime, and they eventually escaped with an 84-83 OT victory over the Hoosiers.

"It's just one of those things," said Rivers, who was 22 of 25 from the free throw line on the season. "When it left my hand, it looked good and it felt good. It just hit the back of the rim and kind of popped up. I think it was just kind of a fluke shot, to be honest with you."

Instead of gaining momentum with a second win in a row, IU now returned home to play No. 18 Minnesota at Assembly Hall.

And it would do so without another one of its top scorers.

First it was Creek, then Jones, who had missed the last three games with inflammation in his knee. Now came news that Watford suffered a broken left hand against Michigan State and was out indefinitely. Three of IU's top four scorers had gone down in a span of 17 days.

"I will never be one who subscribes to the bad-luck theory," Crean said the day of the Minnesota game. "These things just happen. I don't want to think about it like that, and I don't want our team thinking about it, either. We have to battle through it. That's all there is to it."

Creek, Jones and Watford had a combined scoring average of 38.2 points per game. The remaining eight scholarship players for the Hoosiers averaged a combined 39.2 per game.

While Creek's injury hurt the team, the sophomore guard hadn't completely recovered from fracturing his kneecap in December of his freshman season. Jones' injury was also significant, but he was expected back soon. Watford's injury may have been the most significant because of how he had played in recent games. Ten days earlier, he had a career-high 30 points against Iowa. Since then he scored 16 against Illinois and 21 against Michigan State. He had been playing the most spirited basketball in his two years at IU.

"We feel for him, because he's coming off his best week," Crean said. "He was absolutely relentless on Sunday. He was a huge part of why we had the game that we had. You take your leading scorer and your leading rebounder and a guy that can make shots and make plays the way he can, it's going to affect your team. But there's no choice (tonight). At 6:30, we have to be ready to go. But I'd be lying if I said it was going to be easy. And I'd be remiss if I didn't say we're going to need that fan base."

The fan base was another potential problem for the Hoosiers. With a winter storm creating havoc, it was difficult to estimate how many IU fans would brave the elements to attend the game. IU sent out a release the day before saying it would monitor the situation closely throughout the day and have updates at iuhoosiers.com.

Then Indiana knocked off the No. 18 Golden Gophers that night, 60-57.

Here's what I wrote the next day in the *Indianapolis Star*:

BLOOMINGTON, Ind. — *It wasn't clear how much Verdell Jones III would play Wednesday night, if at all.*

Little did anyone know he would be the hero.

Jones' 3-pointer from the right corner as the shot clock expired with 2:02 to play gave Indiana a six-point lead, and the Hoosiers held on for a 60-57 victory over No. 18 Minnesota at Assembly Hall.

"I thought that shot gave us great momentum, and it got the crowd back into it," Jones said. "I haven't been able to move too much (with my injury), so I've been working on my 3-point shot. I'm just glad the hard work paid off."

IU (12-11, 3-7 Big Ten) had to survive another wild finish. The Hoosiers led 60-57, and Minnesota had the ball out of bounds with 5.8 seconds to play. Blake Hoffarber got off an off-balance 3-pointer from the left corner with Daniel Moore in his face that fell short. Victor Oladipo grabbed the rebound as time expired.

It was a gutsy effort for Indiana after it learned Tuesday it had lost leading scorer Christian Watford indefinitely after he had surgery on his broken left hand. The Hoosiers were already without Maurice Creek for the season, and Jones hadn't played in three games with a knee injury.

Despite playing a Minnesota team that has the biggest front line in the Big Ten, the Hoosiers stayed even at 22 in points in the paint and lost the rebounding battle 36-35.

"This was all about team defense," IU coach Tom Crean said. "We weren't guarding these guys one on one. We were giving up size the whole game. But there were times tonight when we had Will (Sheehey) and Victor (Oladipo) on the bottom of our zone. That's just the way it is right now."

It was Indiana's second victory over a ranked opponent at Assembly Hall in six days. On Jan. 27, the Hoosiers knocked off No. 20 Illinois 52-49. IU lost its previous 19 games against ranked opponents.

ᛒᚩ   ᚲᚷ

Suddenly Indiana was 12-11 and had beaten two top-20-ranked teams in the past three games. In between, the Hoosiers should have beaten Michigan State, too. There were eight Big Ten games left, and IU was building momentum.

Next up was an Iowa team that limped into Assembly Hall with a 2-8 conference record.

An easy win, right?

Wrong.

In the last two seasons, Iowa had a record of 3-22 in the Big Ten against anyone other than Indiana.

Against the Hoosiers, Iowa was 4-0.

Indiana squandered a 10-point lead in the final eight minutes and was unable to convert on two potential game-winning shots in the closing seconds.

Jones, who was one of nine from the field in his second game back from a knee injury, missed a pull-up jumper from 15 feet. Oladipo tipped it toward the rim, but it bounced away as time expired.

"Any time at the end of the game, you want a chance to make the shot, a chance to get fouled and a chance to rebound it," Crean said. "We had all of those opportunities and it didn't happen. When we had a chance to keep momentum, we just didn't guard well enough down low."

Little did the Hoosiers know at the time, but the loss to Iowa would begin an eight-game losing streak to end the Big Ten season.

ಬಿ   ಌ

What once had been a 12-11 record slipped to 12-19 heading into the Big Ten Tournament in Indianapolis. Following a 3-15 Big Ten record, the No. 11 seeded Hoosiers would be matched against No. 6-seeded Penn State in the first round.

Penn State ended Crean's third season with a 61-55 victory at Conseco Fieldhouse.

When IU jumped out to a 9-2 start to the regular season, the Hoosiers did so because they were able to knock down open shots from the perimeter.

In their nine-game losing streak to end it, the opposite was true.

Inside the 3-point arc in the second half against Penn State, Indiana hit 11 of 14 shots (78.6 percent). But from beyond the 3-point line, with open looks, the Hoosiers were two for 10. In the final 12 minutes, they made just one of eight 3-point attempts.

"That's the hardest part," sophomore guard Jordan Hulls said. "If they were shots that we aren't capable of making, that would be one thing. But these are shots that we have made over and over during the season. But when we needed them the most, we just couldn't get them to fall, and that's very frustrating."

IU was four of 18 from 3-point range in the game (22.2 percent).

"What's hard to accept is that we all knock those shots down consistently in practice, but sometimes it just doesn't transfer to the games," said junior guard Matt Roth. "That's what leaves you shaking your head."

The nine-game losing streak marked the fourth streak of nine or more losses in Coach Tom Crean's three years at IU.

Fort Wayne *Journal-Gazette* columnist Ben Smith summed up IU's third season under Crean by saying that even in defeat the IU program was clearly headed in the right direction.

Sometime around 9:35 here Thursday night, March threw Tom Crean out of the car again.

It was Penn State vs. Crean's Indiana Hoosiers in the first round of the Big Ten Tournament, and when it was done, the scoreboard was too light for them again: Penn State 61, Indiana 55.

Too much length in the second half from the Nittany Lions, who led by one at the break and then figured out, brilliantly, that they could go inside on inside-deprived IU all night. Too little firepower from the Hoosiers, who scored all of 11 points in the last 10 minutes and, once again, had just enough to hang around but not quite enough close the deal.

And so they were done like dinner again, the final record standing at 12-20, a win short of even last year in the Big Ten, the conference mark standing at 3-15.

This does not feel much like progress, although Crean insists progress happened and there were moments Thursday when progress could be glimpsed. And it does not look or smell or sound anything remotely like triumph, not with just eight conference wins to show for the three seasons of the post-Kelvin Sampson purge, and zero W's this year after Groundhog Day.

But, hey. At least they're not Ohio State.

Where the football coach, Jim Tressel, just got off all but free and clear after violating certain express terms of his contract and then not being truthful about it.

Where the university president, Gordon Gee, made light of the situation, joking that not only did he never consider firing Tressel, he was just thankful Tressel didn't fire him.

Where everything that reeks like spoiled milk about big-time college sports — the lame excuses, the expedient "punishments," the betrayal of core values in deference to the bank balance — was laid bare this week in the most glaring way possible.

And so here is something to take away, as Crean and his boys thumb a ride home from another lost season: Indiana's basketball program might still be prostrate, but the school itself never stood taller. Faced with a similar situation — Sampson violating stipulations that he would never do at Indiana what he did at Oklahoma — Indiana never blinked. It showed Sampson the road, hired Crean, and then stood by without a peep as Crean purged the program of nearly all its talent, on grounds it was ethically tainted.

That might be cold solace for Hoosier Nation, having watched the fallout on full display Thursday. But it is solace of a sort, as the wait continues in Bloomington.

And over in Columbus?

Gee lays 'em in the aisles. Tressel draws his two-game punchline of a suspension. And when the hue and cry finally dies down, the titles and BCS berths and fat checks that come with them will keep right on rolling in.

Strange. Somehow I think IU will be richer in the end.

Indianapolis Star columnist Bob Kravitz said in his column after the season-ending loss to Penn State that the time had come for Indiana to right the ship.

There will be no more mulligans for Indiana University basketball. There will be no more talk about the unholy mess this coaching staff inherited from Kelvin Sampson, no more help-is-on-the-way refrains, no more deriving satisfaction from just showing up and being competitive.

Beginning next year, it's time for IU basketball to become IU basketball again, with visual, indisputable progress and growth on the floor and on the scoreboard.

The third mulligan season is finished now — did I hear a "hallelujah!"? — ending with the Hoosiers' 61-55 first-round Big Ten Tournament loss to Penn State at Conseco Fieldhouse. The final season numbers: a 12-20 record, just two victories more than last season; and 3-15 in the Big Ten, one victory fewer than last season.

Bleccch.

"We're still not on an even playing field," Crean said. "I wish we were."

At least there was life Thursday. At least there was pride. There was some question about how the Hoosiers might respond after a no-show loss at Illinois, but they got on the tournament stage at the fieldhouse and played hard, switching defenses, making life uncomfortable in the first half for Penn State's two leading scorers, Talor Battle and Jeff Brooks.

"I thought we played like warriors," IU sophomore guard Jordan Hulls said.

But every time the Hoosiers needed a late stop, the Nittany Lions threw it inside to Brooks, the 6-8 senior, who roughed up Will Sheehey, a 6-6 freshman. "That guy's a man," Crean said, shaking his head.

The bigger, older Lions used their size to take over the game, even as their top player, Battle, was struggling because of Jeremiah Rivers' good work and lots of changing, junk defenses. Penn State dominated the paint in the second half, killed IU on the boards, and took full advantage of the fact that IU's only big guys, Tom Pritchard and Derek Elston, were in foul trouble. (The other big guy, Bobby Capobianco, can't get off the bench these days. The speculation is he may not return to the program next year.)

You think Guy-Marc Michel, a 7-foot slice of humanity, might have made a difference in a game like this?

Next year, though, things start to change.

They have to, don't they?

Nobody is expecting 20 wins or an NCAA Tournament berth, but a .500 season, a chance to go to the NIT, a team that's genuinely competitive in the Big Ten, those are all well within the realm of possibility.

And Crean, who is poised to put these 20-loss seasons behind him forever, understands all of that. There will still be struggles, but it's nearing time for IU to put the bad, old days in the rearview mirror.

There are no reasons, short of major injuries, IU shouldn't be significantly improved next season. The much-ballyhooed recruiting class, led by Hulls, Christian Watford and the oft-injured Maurice Creek, will be juniors—it's time to grow up. The two freshmen, Victor Oladipo and Sheehey, showed lots of flashes this year and figure to take the next step in their progressions. And Cody Zeller, along with Austin Etherington, really ought to make a significant difference—especially for someone like Watford, who will be able to move to his more natural small forward position.

"There's a lot of room for improvement and there will be improvement," Crean said. "Obviously we've got to get more athletic. We've got to get better defensively. We were 2-15 this year when we got outrebounded. That was one of our biggest goals this season, so obviously we weren't good enough."

To put a bow on this lost season, let's just say this: It was disappointing. Even with the most minimal expectations, it was disappointing. The coaches may have seen individual and collective improvement, may have seen it in more subtle and nuanced ways, but progress wasn't quite as obvious when looking at it from the outside. Most of us can agree that Hulls came a long way and the freshmen showed glimpses, but who else got appreciably better?

Anybody?

Somebody?

That's the only criticism, the only concern here. Clearly, Crean has done a marvelous job recruiting talent for down the road, and we know how much smarter coaches are when they're surrounded by talent. But you have to look at Elston and Pritchard and others, guys who haven't taken that next step, and wonder what's happened.

I asked Hulls and Watford about the team's progress and both talked about how close the team became. That's important, but that's not enough. This isn't a social club or a fraternity. This is IU, and this is basketball.

Crean also pointed to the team's growing closeness but added, "Now the next thing is, will they hold each other accountable more? Will leadership rise to the top? Can we build more of a toughness and a warrior mindset where we can withstand lulls in games?"

Three full seasons in, this is still a work in progress, and that's understandable and to be expected. But it's time to take that next step, and not another baby step, but a huge step.

PART 5:
"We're Back."

Chapter 17

Everyone always wants to know the moment that turned things around for Indiana basketball. Was it Christian Watford's shot against Kentucky on that day in early December 2011? Was it the day that Cody Zeller decided he wanted to be part of something special and help restore a once-storied basketball tradition that had fallen on hard times? Or was it that day in late March 2008 that Tom Crean accepted Rick Greenspan's offer to coach Indiana basketball and assume the ultimate program rebuilding project?

All of those days are significant and in some ways played a role in IU's basketball resurgence. But ask the players, the guys who were in the trenches and experienced IU's basketball rebirth firsthand, and to a man they'll tell you it all started in the summer.

The summer of 2011, with the aid of the Cook Hall practice facility, IU's players began to hold themselves more accountable.

Will Sheehey worked on his perimeter shooting and put up thousands of shots. Classmate Victor Oladipo focused on ball handling, free throw shooting and becoming a better defender. Watford tried to get stronger and at the same time improve his shooting touch. Tom Pritchard dropped 15 pounds but got stronger in the weight room. Jordan Hulls, already known for his unrivaled work ethic, spent hour after hour in the gym shooting the basketball. Zeller tried to put some pounds on his relatively thin frame and get stronger.

Players talked a lot about how encouraging it was to have everyone together working during the summer to get better.

"It's huge," Hulls said in an August 2011 interview. "A lot of the guys have been here all summer doing workouts and taking classes, getting in the gym and playing open gym. It is nice to have that structure and to know that everyone is here. Coach (Je'Ney) Jackson has put us through some great workouts, and everyone is getting bigger and stronger. We have all gained weight, which will help us in Big Ten games."

The phrase you would hear over and over from players during the summer was that, unlike summer workouts in the recent past, the summer of 2011 workouts were "player driven."

"It is no more of the coaches telling us what to do," said Derek Elston in an interview in mid-August prior to the start of the 2011-12 season. "Jordan (Hulls) has us on the line every day at 3:30, when we're supposed to be there, running the pre-workout before we actually work out.

"I've never seen this team like this. Coming in my freshman year, it was always kind of look at the coaches to see what to do, and now the coaches are kind of getting in there and asking what we're doing and we're already ready to go."

Watford used the same phrase when talking about the summer workouts.

"It's more player driven now because we are a veteran team," Watford said. "We hold each other accountable more than anything. We embrace the hard work—we know the workouts are going to be hard going into it—but we try to attack it. As veterans, we talk to the younger guys and push them through it."

Watford said having veteran players in the program made a big difference.

"When I came in, we didn't really have any veterans," Watford said. "We were kind of on a downside, I guess you could say. But we are the leaders now, and the veterans take on that challenge and that role."

Calbert Cheaney was added in late spring as IU's director of basketball operations. One of the things IU's all-time leading scorer said he tried to share with Indiana's players was that there was simply no substitute for hard work in the offseason.

"It really comes down to good, old-fashioned hard work," Cheaney said. "There is no substitute for hard work. There is no secret formula for getting better, except for hard work. You have to go out and work hard and be the best you possibly can and try always to be consistent."

Clearly one of the big differences during the summer leading into the 2011-12 season was that Hulls had taken on more of a leadership role. When the 6-foot guard from nearby Bloomington South High School talked, his Hoosier teammates listened.

"For sure I have been trying to be more vocal this year," Hulls said in an interview in August. "In high school, I was more of a guy that would lead by example, not as vocal or yelling at guys. I'm not necessarily yelling at guys here unless they need to be, but I'm just trying to encourage everybody and get things organized and be a leader the way they want me to be here.

"Verdell (Jones III) and some of the other seniors are helping me out as well, but it's something that I have taken upon myself, and it has been asked of me from time to time. Being the point guard, being a leader is something that I have to be."

Crean went to Hulls after the 2010-11 season ended and told him he wanted his point guard to be more vocal.

"I think the team needed someone to be that guy, and I am more than willing to be that guy," Hulls said. "Whether that is getting on someone or directing workouts or whatever the case may be. That's kind of how it came about. I've always been the leader of most of the teams that I have been on, and its something that I need to take control of."

Hulls said it was all about holding each other accountable.

"We have a couple guys that know how workouts should be run and what needs to be done and those kinds of things," Hulls said. "As long as we are all holding each other accountable, that's all we can ask for and it's a big thing for us. We have to come in and work hard every day and not slack off."

Hulls also said he learned that sometimes being a leader is not a popular position. But in the same breath he said he didn't care. Hulls said it was a role that needed to be filled.

"I want to win, so I am going to do whatever it takes to get more wins in the win column," Hulls said. "Like I said, I don't need to yell at them if they don't need to be yelled at. If I say something and you don't like it, though, too bad.

"But that's how we are going to win. That's how my dad and some of the coaches kind of told me that it's all about winning here and that's what we need to do. Being that kind of leader. We can be friends after workouts, but when we are on the field or the court, it is all business and we need to get things done."

It was a direct and sometimes in-your-face approach, but Hulls' teammates agreed that it was a role that someone needed to adopt. And if anyone didn't think Hulls was the guy, they certainly weren't saying anything.

"He is a lot more vocal," Elston said. "He is one of those guys that starts screaming now. During conditioning days, if you're not making it, Jordy is the first one to tell you, and whether you like the way he is saying it or not, he is going to say it. If that doesn't motivate you, he'll get you off the floor. He has had to kick a couple of guys out of the conditioning. Jordy is one of those guys that has stepped it up really big for us, and we hope that it just continues for us during the season."

Oladipo said in early September that he thought Indiana had made big strides in the summer.

"This has been a real big summer for us," Oladipo said. "Bringing in the tools that we have brought in and how we are coming together.

We have made great strides and you will hear that from everybody. From (strength coach) Coach Jackson to the entire coaching staff.

"We are going to continue working because we have to get this thing back. These fans deserve it. The people and the university deserve it and I am ready. And I know my teammates are ready, as well, to get started this season."

As for his own game, Oladipo said he had been working on many different areas.

"My ballhandling was not as sharp as it needed to be (last season), and my shooting was suspect," Oladipo said. "That is something that I have really worked on. When I went home for those six weeks, my dad and I did an hour of ball-handling every single day with bands on my arms, trying to get bigger, stronger, faster and more under control. I think doing that has made me more comfortable with the ball and more able to make better plays. I can see things happening sooner because I don't have to worry about where the ball is while I'm dribbling."

Watford said what he worked on the most was ball-handling with the hope that he could play more on the perimeter.

"I worked on ball-handling and ball moves, things like that," Watford said. "With Cody coming in, I feel like I'm going to be able to step out a little bit more, so I wanted to work on explosion moves and things like that."

80 03

It was an important summer for Elston. He would be the first to admit he didn't have a stellar sophomore campaign the year before. He was injured early in the nonconference season in warm-ups prior to the November 21 game at Assembly Hall against Evansville. The pain was in his midsection. He played through it all season, and later an MRI revealed a sports hernia. Elston had surgery May 26 and by mid-August was finally feeling good again. When he sat down with members of the IU media in mid-August he said he wasn't quite 100 percent, but he was getting close. After rehabbing the injury and working on his legs most of the summer, he had spent the previous weeks playing in open gym. He said it felt good to feel relatively healthy again.

"For me, it is just an excitement to be on there, to be able to play again the way I want to," Elston said. "My defense has gotten a lot better. Some guys still abuse me a little, they know I'm hurt so I can't really go hard all the way.

Derek Elston gets inside for a shot against Purdue at Mackey Arena in 2012.

"After I get done stretching with Tim (Garl), and then I come back on the court, I feel so loose and I feel like I can play with those guys again, and that is probably the best feeling."

Elston said one of the most difficult parts of the sports hernia injury was that he lost any explosiveness he had. He also lost some of his vertical jump.

"It's coming back," Elston said. "Me and Coach (Je'Ney) Jackson were just talking about how I've lost a half an inch from my vertical from when I measured my best back in October. I'm a half an inch away from that and I'm just three weeks into being where I need to be. He is really excited about that, and he is telling me that when I go home and I'm going to California for a couple of days, to get on the beach and run on the beach to get my thighs and my calves bigger.

"He said when I do come back, I should see a good three or four inches of gain from all of the lifting and things we'll be doing. That is always fun to know."

Elston said his primary focus for the summer was to improve defensively. And he knew to do that, he had to concentrate on devoping quicker feet.

"The whole point of my rehab has been putting the bands around my ankles and doing slides," Elston said. "I have got weights on my ankles and swinging them back and forth just to get the motion back. Agility in the sand, agility in the pool. Coach has me running stadiums on the football field. Stuff to get the movements I'm going to be doing on the court, he has got me doing in those situations so it is not as painful. I'm getting my technique back, and then once I get it all stretched out, it is like there is nothing even there."

But Elston said when he looked back at this game following his sophomore season, he knew the one area that needed to improve more than any other was his defense. He said when he got 100-percent healthy, defense would become his No. 1 priority.

"I'm just trying to do the defense thing," Elston said. "My jump shot is going to be there. That is something I can come in and work on, on my own or with the managers. Right now I just want my defense to be to a point where I can guard a three, a four or a five.

"I've got to be versatile, or the team is playing so well right now you're not going to see the floor. I've got to be able to guard multiple positions, and I've got to be able to bang down low. Really, I'm just trying to be able to guard a guard."

Elston said the trick was going to be adding weight without losing quickness.

"I want to try to get my body to where I can guard a five and still guard a three," Elston said. "I can gain a lot of weight and I've always been able to have this big upper body, but Coach Jackson was telling me I could gain 15 pounds and just put it in my legs. So that is really what I want to do.

"I'm jumping rope every day because I've got to have the quick feet to guard the three but still have the strength to guard a big four or a big five, to where if Cody or Tom (Pritchard) got in foul trouble, I could still guard them. But if they wanted to go big but have me guard a three or four, I can go out there and do it."

Watford said he noticed how far Elston had come in a short period of time. He said if Elston could remain healthy, he would give the Hoosiers a major boost in the upcoming season.

"He is very important," Watford said. "As long as Derek stays healthy, he is going to be able to help us a lot. He is going to be able to give us another big body on the inside. He's going to be able to rebound and stretch the defense because he can shoot the ball. As long as Derek stays healthy, I think we will be in great shape."

℀   ℀

Several IU players had busy summers. Hulls and Oladipo played on a team that played nine games in China in mid-May. Later, Hulls plus several others, including Christian Watford and Will Sheehey, participated in the Indy Pro-Am League.

Hulls said the Pro-Am experience gave him a chance to play against some diverse competition.

"I was playing against different competition and guys who have played at the next level, whether it's the NBA or overseas," Hulls said. "Being able to play against stronger and more physical guys and having to play defense against them really helped me out because that was my main goal."

Watford said it provided a measuring stick.

"It was fun and great to compete against those guys," Watford said. "I used it as a measuring tool to see how you compare to (guys that play professionally) and play some different competition and get up and down the court. I felt like I measured up pretty good, but I wasn't able to get up there a lot because of classes and things like that. When I did go up there and play, I feel like I did pretty well."

Sheehey said it was a great experience.

"Jordan and I got to play on the same team so that was good," Sheehey said. "Like Christian said, matching up with different players from different levels was a good time."

With some of the older players, in particular, the summer had obviously provided them some time to think about how quickly their college basketball careers were slipping by.

Hulls talked about the sense of urgency he was feeling with two seasons of college basketball left to play.

"Time is going by fast, and with only two years left, I have to try to make the most out of that," Hulls said. "I think not just my sense but our sense of urgency is that everyone wants to win. The past two years, we have learned a lot and gained a lot of experience.

"There are things that we can take into account—like watching film for example—or all of those things that we need to work on to get to the next level. It is very apparent and urgent that we need to get these wins and get competitive and get to the top of the Big Ten or whatever the case may be. It is something we are working toward every day. We have to make it an emphasis that individual workouts or strength training or whatever we are doing is going to help us get more wins."

Watford echoed Hulls' feelings on that sense of urgency.

"I definitely feel that way," Watford said. "I only have two years left, so I'm on the down slope of my career here. It's going downhill now, so you want to win and win fast.

"We realize that the time is now and we don't have time to wait. We have some senior guys that want to get something done while they have been at Indiana. So we don't want to send them out with a losing record or anything like that. The sense of urgency is definitely there, and we have been working hard."

Hulls was asked if he thought would play more at the point or at the shooting guard position his junior year.

"That is up to the coaches to decide," Hulls said. "Last year, I played a lot of different spots, but I feel the most comfortable having the ball in my hands. We will see what happens this year. We have a very competitive lineup and a lot of guys that can play multiple spots, which is a big key for us. If you want to be able to play, you have to be able to do different things. Playing defense is definitely part of that, so we'll have to see."

Hulls knew that the point guard minutes would likely be shared with Jones and Oladipo. He said both of those players were having big offseasons which he believed would make the competition in the fall even that much more fierce.

"Verdell is 6-5 so he can go in the post, and since he is bigger, he can body guys up more," Hulls said. "He is also very crafty and can get to the hole as well as his outstanding mid-range game.

"Victor is getting huge. He will be a really big force for us. He is handling the ball really well and shooting really well, so we are very excited for that."

₨ ₩

A hot topic throughout the summer was how the three freshmen were developing.

In May, Crean had added a third player to the class of 2011 with the addition of 6-4 guard Remy Abell. Abell, a combo guard from Eastern High School in Louisville, Kentucky, joined Etherington and Zeller in the class. Abell would become just the sixth IU basketball player in history to come from Kentucky, and the first since Tom Boone was on the roster in the 1969-70 season.

When Abell was brought on board, many IU fans questioned the move, not understanding why Crean and his staff wanted another 6-4 combo guard on a team that already appeared guard heavy.

As the season would progress, however, fans got it. Abell was a player who could get to the rim, hit shots from the perimeter, and he was also a solid defender.

At the time of Abell's signing, Crean said Abell was a year-round winner who would bring a great deal of versatility to the IU program.

"He is a big guard who will have an immediate impact defensively with his ability to guard three positions," Crean said. "He can get to the rim on offense, knock down open shots, and will really add to our transition game. I think the most impressive thing about him is his ability to make everyone around him better, and he does not have to have the ball in his hands to be effective. In a lot of ways, he reminds me of Jerel McNeal, who we had at Marquette."

As the summer progressed, IU's veteran players were becoming more and more impressed with the play of the three freshmen.

"Everybody knew Cody coming in was going to be the big guy, and to my surprise he hasn't backed down from anything," Elston said. "He has taken every challenge head on, which is always good to see. Remy and Austin are really good shooters. We kind of mess around with Remy and say that he has a 'spray ball.' So he is working a lot on his jump shot so he can come out and prove to us that he can shoot.

"I played against Austin two to three years in high school, and I always knew that the kid can play. He can shoot, he can drive. Once he gets a little bit stronger, he's going to be able to use his body to get to where he needs to go. Right now those freshmen are pretty surprising."

Hulls said he was most impressed with the work ethic of IU's three freshmen.

"Cody and the other two freshmen have been working their tails off at getting bigger and stronger," Hulls said. "But Cody has a lot of skill and room to get bigger. We are excited to have him. He is another big body to throw in there and he can shoot from 15-17 feet, which is always key in the pick-and-roll and pick-and-pop game. He is really athletic and long—I don't think some people realize how long he really is—and he will just go get the ball, which is important when it comes to rebounding."

Oladipo said he thought the freshmen had made the necessary adjustments and were feeling more comfortable in the program as the summer wore on.

"They are getting better at it," Oladipo said. "When we first started, they struggled at it like most freshmen do. The lifting at 6 a.m. and playing every single day is a little different than high school. But they have adjusted real well and are starting to get the hang of things."

Watford said he knew before Zeller arrived that he was going to be an instant impact player. But he said even he was surprised at how polished Zeller's game was coming into college.

"He is going to draw a lot of attention, more than anything," Watford said. "He's a big guy that can pass the ball and can see the floor. That's what we need. He can also finish down there so that's going to help us, too."

Sheehey was asked to pick one player who had made the biggest strides in summer workouts. He said he couldn't do it.

"I can't pick just one guy," Sheehey said. "Christian has been working hard and Victor as well. The three freshmen coming in, too—trying to figure out the program and how things work—they have done a great job. Everyone has done a great job of working hard progressively this summer."

In early September, after school had begun and players had started individual workouts, Sheehey and Watford sat down with media members to talk about how the team was progressing.

"Workouts have been going great," Sheehey said. "With the group practices having started, it really helps us with the team unity because before, we could just go in groups of three or four. But now we all get to go together and can see how everyone is playing together."

Watford said having more players involved had picked up the competition and raised the level of intensity.

"We get the chance to go after each other a little bit," Watford said. "Instead of only having four guys in there, we get a chance to go four-on-four or three-on-three a little bit more. It has been fun, and we have been getting after it."

Sheehey said just one year of being together makes the workouts that much better.

"I think guys are more comfortable, in a sense, because they are veterans and they know what to expect and what is expected from them, so they can give the maximum effort," Sheehey said. "For the freshmen, it is better for them because they get to learn from what the older guys do. So it's an advantage that we have."

Both Sheehey and Watford talked about what it means to have a strong staff of assistant coaches in the program. Both Steve McClain and Tim Buckley had been Division I head coaches in the past, and Bennie Seltzer would be hired as a head coach at Samford in Birmingham, Alabama following the 2011-12 season.

Add to that Calbert Cheaney, and it was a star-studded staff.

"It helps because you get different views on different things," Watford said. "Some guys relate to some guys differently. So if you are doing something wrong, another coach can come and point it out. So it works out great."

Sheehey said the overall knowledge of the staff is what stands out for him.

"They have so much knowledge of the game from being in the same position as a head coach before they came to Indiana," Sheehey said. "They can take a step back now and focus more on things that can help you improve."

Watford said he was also impressed having Cheaney back at Indiana.

"He is a great motivator and an icon to look up to," Watford said. "As director of operations, he really can't tell us too much about basketball, but he can tell us about life and pushing through the tough times. I'm sure when he was here, he went through a lot of tough things, so having him here is a great experience."

Watford said that coming from Alabama, he really didn't know that much about Cheaney's IU accomplishments before he arrived in Bloomington. Sheehey said that once you've been around the program, though, you knew about Calbert Cheaney very quickly.

"You see the pictures around the offices and locker room and you know he is the all-time leading scorer in the Big Ten," Sheehey said. "It's something that you hear a lot and when you talk about the tradition at Indiana, his name is at the top of the list. You kind of have to know."

As for the upcoming season, Watford said he sensed that he and his teammates had prepared themselves well over the summer and were now ready to take the next step.

"I know we are ready," Watford said. "We have a lot of veterans that have played a lot of minutes. I have been on the court since I was a freshman and Jordan has, too, so the sense of urgency is there. I almost feel like a senior, as many minutes as I have played, and Jordan as well and other guys that came in with me. So there's definitely a sense of urgency."

Chapter 18

The 2011-12 Indiana University basketball season will long be remembered as IU's season-long coming-out party.

After three tough years, the Hoosiers would get it all together, find themselves ranked in the top 25 for the last three months of the season, and eventually make it to the Sweet Sixteen of the NCAA Tournament.

But the season didn't exactly get off to a good start.

A week before Hoosier Hysteria, IU's annual kickoff event to the season, the IU Nation received devastating news about a player who was expected to be a major contributor.

Once again, the bad news involved Maurice Creek. Creek, IU's tough luck junior guard, suffered a torn left Achilles tendon that would end his season and require surgery. One report was that Creek suffered the injury running up a flight of stairs at his apartment complex. Another was that he hurt it in a pickup game.

Whatever the case, it was a cruel blow to a player who at one time was expected to be perhaps the best player in an IU recruiting class that also included Christian Watford, Jordan Hulls and Derek Elston.

Since arriving at Indiana in the summer of 2009, Creek had spent more time rehabilitating injuries than he had on the court.

He suffered a fractured left kneecap driving for a layup against Bryant on December 29, 2009. He had started the first 12 games of his freshman season and scored a career-high 31 points against Kentucky. Through the first nine games of that season, he had led the nation in freshman scoring with a 17.3 average.

As a sophomore, Creek suffered a stress fracture in his right knee in a Big Ten game January 20 against Michigan and missed the remainder of the season.

Because those injuries happened well into those seasons, Creek would not be able to get either of those years back.

If there was a silver lining to his Achilles tendon tear it was that it happened before the season began. Creek would have surgery, miss the entire 2011-12 campaign, but would then have two full years of eligibility remaining beginning with the 2012-13 season.

Still, the latest injury was like a punch to the stomach for Creek, his teammates and coaches, and IU fans everywhere. It just hurt to see someone who had worked so hard go down again with a freak injury.

"This is a devastating blow for someone who has worked so hard to get himself in a position to help this program again," IU coach Tom Crean said. "He is going to receive the best medical care possible, and we will take his recovery one day at a time. I think the most important thing that we can do is to make Maurice know that despite his injury, he can serve a very vital role in helping our program, and we will actively keep him involved every day."

The Achilles is fibrous tissue that connects the heel to the calf muscles. It's the thickest and strongest tendon in the body.

Shortly after surgery the Monday before Hoosier Hysteria, Creek began sending Twitter messages, thanking people for their support.

"One thing I ask from everyone IS NOT TO SHED NO TEARS ... I LOVE Y'ALL ... THIS IS JUST ANOTHER BUMP IN THE ROAD ... I WILL BE BACK ... BELIEVE THAT," one of Creek's tweets read.

Crean said IU is devoted to helping Creek recover.

"I know he and his family have always appreciated the thoughts and prayers they receive from Hoosier Nation," Crean said.

In 30 career games for the Hoosiers, Creek had averaged 11.5 points and shot 37.1 percent from 3-point range. He averaged 16.4 points in 12 games as a freshman and 8.3 in 18 games his sophomore year.

While Creek's injury was the biggest preseason blow for the Hoosiers, a day before Creek got hurt IU had to deal with a misstep in recruiting when Crean committed a secondary violation.

The violation occurred on Thursday, October 6, when Crean met with a recruit during a no-contact period. The recruit was Hamilton Southeastern senior Gary Harris, the most sought-after recruit in the state, who would eventually earn the state's *Indianapolis Star* Indiana Mr. Basketball award and sign with Michigan State.

Crean reportedly met with Harris during a prep period in which he was an office aide.

Truthfully, secondary violations are common. IU had 18 of them in 2010, two by the men's basketball team. But when it happened so close to the Kelvin Sampson mess, this one got headlines.

Crean said the violation was a communication mix-up between himself and Assistant Coach Tim Buckley. Within an hour of making the improper visit, Crean had realized the error and had called IU's compliance office to report it.

According to the report filed by IU, Assistant Coach Tim Buckley advised Crean the previous day that he could have an off-campus contact the next day. Buckley thought Thursday was the final day of the contact period. It was the first of the evaluation period.

Within an hour after Crean had made the improper visit, Buckley realized the error and contacted Crean. The IU compliance office reported it to the Big Ten and the NCAA that same day. Buckley received a letter of admonishment from IU.

Because of the incident, IU said it has reduced its number of recruiting person days by two for the 2011-12 academic year to 128 total. In addition, IU will only have one contact opportunity with the prospective student-athlete for the 2011-12 academic year.

The day after the news came out, I wrote this blog about Crean's appearance on the "Dan Dakich Show" in Indianapolis on radio station 1070-The Fan.

Tom Crean was on the "Dan Dakich Show" today at 12 p.m. on 1070-The Fan in Indianapolis to explain what happened last week that resulted in a secondary NCAA recruiting violation.

The one thing we know here for certain is this: People are going to believe what they want to believe.

Fans of competing programs are going to insist that there is no way that Crean didn't know that Oct. 5 was the deadline for the contact period. They will insist it was a willful disregard for the rules. Nothing Crean does or says moving forward will change that opinion.

Indiana fans will likely believe their coach made a mistake. That's what he said today on the radio. That's his story and he's sticking to it.

That said, here's what Crean had to say today about the situation:

(Dakich asked him to take him through the events of what happened on Thursday, Oct. 6, the day that Crean stopped by Hamilton Southeastern High School and had contact with 2012 recruit Gary Harris when he was an office aide during his prep period.)

"We had a miscommunication on Oct. 6 as to what the last day of the contact period was. My thought was that the last day of the contact period was Thursday. I had a school visit, so to speak, which is just part of the contact period which I thought and had a day planned. We had a Media Challenge which you (Dakich) missed, by the way, which you could have dominated in. We had that in the afternoon and had a full day of recruiting planned around it. We just went about business as usual, and then about 15 minutes later, I realized after talking to Tim that we had made a mistake.

"And rather than get mad, we just handled it. We handled it immediately with everybody that was involved, starting with

compliance. And you know Tim Buckley, and I know Tim Buckley, and I know myself and the coaches that we have here, and everybody is extremely serious about the rules. Certainly when you walk into a situation like this you're already serious and it just turns it up that much more in the way you pay attention to things. And it's an ongoing process. We spent 45 minutes this morning talking about some of the things we can and cannot do with Hoosier Hysteria and on official visits, and you're constantly learning new things. But that was just a total miscommunication, and like I said, we handled it immediately. That has been really the only distraction to it. Revamping the day. Being upset with myself for making a mistake and then just trying to move forward right away."

(Dakich then asked if Crean or his staff understands the people's reaction to his news. He said 'How in the hell can this possibly happen, because this is the set day and it has been set for a long time.' So let me ask you, Dakich said, how does it possibly happen?)

"It just happened. There's no excuse or let's try to rationalize it. It just happened. We got screwed up on what the last day of the contact period was and it was a mistake. But it certainly wasn't ... That's not how you break a rule if you're looking to break a rule. You know that. You've been in this business a long time. If you're looking to circumvent something you don't do it that way. But it happened. As direct as I can put it, it was an honest mistake. It was owned up to immediately. We handled it and we moved right on. Everyone here handled it accordingly. I think we have a track record here of trying to do things the right way. And when mistakes happen, because it's not the first and the longer you coach there's going to be more, as long as you aren't doing them knowingly and willingly and as long as you try to handle it immediately there's really not a lot of other things you can do."

(Dakich asked how IU figured out it was a violation.)

"Oh, about 15 minutes into it I was on the phone with Tim (Buckley) and we realized it. Obviously we can sit here and split hairs, but it was just a matter of getting it done right now. We screwed up, let's handle it and not let it sit here."

Dakich then had Crean explain the whole recruiting period situation, how many contacts/evaluations you're permitted to have, etc. ... Crean explained that in detail. Then Dakich tried to come back and re-ask many of the same questions again, but Crean wasn't going to provide different answers. Eventually, Dakich turned the subject to first Maurice Creek, then Victor Oladipo and Will Sheehey and eventually Cody Zeller.

Crean said that with Zeller, in particular, that he has gained two inches on his vertical since arriving at IU over the summer. He has also added 40 pounds to his squat and 18-19 pounds to his frame in terms of weight gained just in the short time since he's been at Indiana.

So that was basically Crean's response in a nutshell. What do you think?

It is always been said that things happen in three's. The third one for Indiana wasn't as big as the other two, but the day before IU was to officially open practice with its Hoosier Hysteria festivities at Assembly Hall, it was learned that Christian Watford was nursing a foot injury and his foot was in a walking boot.

Because of that, Watford would not participate in Hoosier Hysteria. The injury wasn't believed to be serious and Watford was expected to be ready for the November 11 season opener against Stony Brook.

But still, for IU fans who wanted to believe that 2011-12 was going to be a different kind of season for their Hoosiers, things certainly weren't getting off to a great start.

ဆာ ၦ

Hoosier Hysteria, or Midnight Madness as it was once referred to, is always a big night on the calendars of Indiana basketball fans. It signals the start of the college basketball season. And for Indiana it usually means Hoosier fans can stop thinking about football and concentrate on the ball that bounces back to you when you dribble it.

By the time IU had its 2011 Hoosier Hysteria, the football team was 1-6, having lost at Wisconsin earlier in the day, 59-7, in Kevin Wilson's debut season with the Hoosiers. IU would go on to lose its final five games and finish 1-11.

As so often is the case, IU fans were clearly ready for basketball to begin.

For as long as anyone can remember, the Hoosiers had taken advantage of the official beginning of the college basketball season by having a practice that began at exactly midnight on the first allowed date. Crowds of more than 10,000 fans have annually attended the event. Admission has always been a canned food item that is donated to the Hoosier Hills Food Bank.

Over the years, the event had moved from a pretty straightforward introduction of the team, a few drills and a scrimmage when Bob Knight was the IU head coach to a full-blown production by the time Tom Crean was on the sideline.

Some fans can still recall the stir that freshman Andre Owens caused in Mike Davis' first season as the IU coach, when the guard took off his shirt and flexed for the crowd before participating in the slam dunk contest. After that, it became a fully clothed affair.

In the Tom Crean era, IU had an appearance from the national recording act Straight No Chaser, and its members actually participated in the scrimmage with the Hoosiers — and held their own.

The 2011 Hoosier Hysteria was a little different, as Indiana abandoned the usual protocol of starting at midnight of the first official day and moved it to Saturday night after IU had already had its first official practice. With that change and the fact that IU football was on the road at Wisconsin, I missed Hoosier Hysteria for one of the few times in my 14 seasons covering Indiana basketball.

It was a night to see and be seen as a big group of recruits was on hand, including all five members of IU's 2012 recruiting class that would officially sign their letters of intent a month later. Hamilton Southeastern's Gary Harris was also there, and IU fans made sure he knew it, chanting his name and giving him some old-fashioned Hoosier love.

Kyle Neddenriep, our fine staff writer who covers high school sports and the recruiting scene for the *Indianapolis Star*, covered Hoosier Hysteria for us that night, and here's what he wrote the next day.

BLOOMINGTON, Ind. — Turntables at midcourt, a spot-on impression of singer Usher by Victor Oladipo and a full-throated ovation for heralded Indiana University freshman Cody Zeller were among the highlights at a festive Hoosier Hysteria gathering on Saturday night at Assembly Hall.

It was quite a party, interrupted only briefly by roars of "Ga-reee, Har-risss," as Coach Tom Crean addressed the fans. The chants referred to uncommitted Hamilton Southeastern star Gary Harris. The 6-4 senior had a front-row seat while on his official recruiting visit.

Harris has taken an official visit to Purdue and also will visit Kentucky next weekend and Michigan State on Nov. 5.

Crean lauded the 16,100 fans in attendance for their fervor.

"If we play close to as good as you cheer, we'll be cutting down nets very soon," Crean told the crowd.

Progress has been slow for Crean, who is 28-66 in his three seasons at IU. The Hoosiers finished 12-20 last season and last in the Big Ten Conference at 3-15.

Prospects look better for this season, though, as some outlets have pegged Indiana as a fringe NCAA Tournament pick. Despite losing junior guard Maurice Creek to a torn Achilles tendon, Indiana returns six of its top seven scorers.

But perhaps the biggest reason to think the worst is behind the program is the addition of the 6-11, 220-pound Zeller, last year's Indianapolis Star *Indiana Mr. Basketball from Washington, Ind.*

Zeller is clearly a fan favorite already. His ovation came last as the players were introduced in alphabetical order.

It was rivaled in volume only by the cheers for Crean, Eric Gordon, D.J. White and Calbert Cheaney. Gordon and White are former Hoosiers and current NBA players. Cheaney, a former IU and NBA player, is in his first year as the school's director of basketball operations.

"Indiana fans are great," Zeller said. "Whether it's 'Hoosier Hysteria' or a Big Ten game, the fans are going to come out and give it their all. It's definitely a fun crowd to play in front of."

Sophomore Will Sheehey marveled at a nearly full house, despite coming off a 12-win season.

"It's hard to put into words, but it's a good feeling to know that many people back you up," he said.

Though Harris was the marquee name, Indiana had a number of other recruits in attendance. Among them was Derek Willis, a 6-9 junior from Kentucky, who at one time was committed to Purdue.

Willis, considered one of the top players at his position in the country, attended Purdue's practice earlier Saturday.

All of Indiana's 2012 recruiting class was present: Hanner Perea of La Lumiere; Broad Ripple's Ron Patterson; Lawrence Central's Jeremy Hollowell; Peter Jurkin from North Carolina; and Yogi Ferrell of Park Tudor. Jurkin and Ferrell are taking their official recruiting visits this weekend.

Two juniors committed to IU, Warren Central's Devin Davis and Cathedral's Collin Hartman, were also in attendance. Other in-state prospects were Wapahani sophomore Grant Evans and Greensburg sophomores Bryant McIntosh and Sean Sellers.

Sheehey defeated Oladipo in the finals of the dunk contest, though Oladipo may have delivered the performance of the night with his rendition of Usher's "U Got it Bad" prior to the player introductions.

Another highlight was a soccer-style header pass from Daniel Moore to Sheehey during the dunk contest.

TV analyst Bill Raftery emceed the event, at one point telling the crowd, "This is going to be the start of something beautiful."

Pete DiPrimio of the *Fort Wayne News-Sentinel* added a few other notes at the end of his story the next day.

Crean said that school officials reserved 6,800 student tickets and that by Saturday morning student ticket sales had surpassed 7,600. He talked about the team's grade point average of 3.0 (a huge turnaround from the academic mess he inherited from former coach Kelvin Sampson).

He also addressed the optimism that this will be the year the Hoosiers return to their winning ways after three straight 20-loss seasons.

"We will be men of action," he said. "We will do everything at a high level. If our last two practices are any indication of how badly these guys want to win, we're in for a great, great year."

Freshman Austin Etherington won the 3-point shooting contest. In the 20-minute scrimmage, the red team led by Cody Zeller, Jordan Hulls and Verdell Jones III beat the white squad 45-43.

"I had fun," freshman guard Remy Abell said. "It was my first time at Hoosier Hysteria. I never even watched one (as a recruit). I expected it to be packed, but not that packed."

෨   ൽ

A few weeks later was the annual Big Ten Basketball Media Day in Chicago where coaches from all 12 Big Ten teams and a few of the top players from each squad spend a day talking about the upcoming season.

Not surprisingly, my story the next day focused on the one guy who many believed would be the reason that Indiana basketball would be able to take a step forward in the 2011-12 season—Cody Zeller.

Now it was clear from the Big Ten writer's preseason poll, however, that most of the scribes didn't think that Zeller's presence was going to help Indiana that much. The writers had Ohio State as the overwhelming pick to win the Big Ten followed by Wisconsin, Michigan and Michigan State. Purdue was fifth. Indiana was picked ninth, ahead of Iowa, Nebraska and Penn State.

But my story the next day focused on Zeller and what people inside and outside of the program were saying about him.

ROSEMONT, Ill. – *Indiana's basketball teams in recent years haven't had to worry much about feeding the post. The big players they have had, guys such as Tijan Jobe or Bawa Muniru, looked better getting off the bus.*

IU's offense was more guard-oriented, and frontcourt players were dominated by opposing big men. With 6-11 freshman Cody Zeller, all of that is expected to change.

"Indiana getting Zeller was like us getting Mateen Cleaves," Michigan State coach Tom Izzo said. "It just brings in a marquee guy to say, 'Yep, we're going to get this thing going.'"

But IU coach Tom Crean said Thursday at Big Ten basketball media day that it hasn't changed quickly enough. He said he had to stop practice one day last week to remind his team it needed to get the ball to Zeller.

Crean said the team Zeller was on during scrimmages was losing consistently, and the big freshman wasn't getting enough scoring opportunities. Crean instituted a rule that a basket wouldn't count unless Zeller had at least one touch in a scoring position on that possession.

The players got the message. The ball started going in to Zeller, he became active going to the basket, and his team couldn't be beat.

"The point was, no matter what you think you have been as a player here at Indiana, you're not somebody that has made it easier for everybody else," Crean said. "Cody makes it easier for everybody else.

"You can go at him and give him the ball and something can happen. Or you can play through him. That's what our team has got to learn to do right now."

Will Sheehey said that he was one of Zeller's teammates in that practice scrimmage and that it was too bad Crean had to stop practice to remind them.

"With a guy like Cody you look a lot smarter if you get him the ball," Sheehey said.

Verdell Jones III went one step further. He said getting the ball to Zeller is a must if Indiana wants to be successful this season.

"We just haven't been used to getting the ball inside, but it's something we need to learn quickly," Jones said. "Cody brings a dimension that we haven't quite had: a 7-footer who can score in the post. A 7-footer who can make plays and dish it. He's going to be a big, big part of our offense this year."

Zeller wasn't one of the three Indiana players on hand for interviews at media day. But he was the only player anyone wanted to talk about ... and it wasn't just the sentiment from the Hoosiers.

"Any time you bring in a 7-footer that was a McDonald's All-American, good things are going to happen," Izzo said. "Cody is just such a talented kid and it's going to be great for Indiana."

Some think it is unfair to put unrealistic expectations on Zeller, but Crean doesn't think his big freshman will put any undue pressure on himself.

Purdue coach Matt Painter said he wouldn't worry about Zeller feeling any kind of pressure.

"I don't think there's pressure on great players," Painter said. "I think there's pressure on limited players. I was a limited player. I was running around saying, 'How am I going to stop Jalen Rose?'

"A guy like (Zeller) doesn't have pressure. He's good. JaJuan Johnson gave a lot of people trouble because he had size and skill and athleticism.

"I think Zeller will do some of the same things."

Next up after Big Ten Media Day for the Hoosiers was a closed scrimmage with Indiana State at Bankers Life Fieldhouse in Indianapolis, and then IU's lone exhibition game against the University of Indianapolis at Assembly Hall on November 5.

As exhibition games against Division II opponents go, playing the University of Indianapolis was probably a good move for Crean and his staff.

It was only an exhibition game, but Crean didn't want Indiana to fall less than a week before opening the regular season against Stony Brook.

Fall to U of I, you might say? Are you kidding me? Well, tell that to the University of Tennessee. The year before, the University of Indianapolis went to Knoxville and beat Tennessee in an exhibition game, 79-64. The Greyhounds went on to post a 19-9 record.

So for an Indiana program that had suffered three consecutive 20-loss seasons, nothing was a given. And so Crean had his team ready to play in the final exhibition tune-up.

As people who watched IU through the 2011-12 season would come to realize very quickly, though, the Hoosiers with Zeller were a completely different animal than they were without him.

In the exhibition game, Zeller scored 16 points and pulled down eight rebounds in 30 minutes of action in a 90-72 victory before a crowd of 16,516 at Assembly Hall.

Indianapolis coach Stan Gouard was impressed.

"Zeller is unbelievable," Gouard said. "He's large. We tried to (double-team him) and he never panicked. He did a great job of kicking the ball out to shooters, and those guys knocked shots down. If they keep doing that, they're going to be tough to beat because he's going to draw a double-team every night."

Indiana shot 64 percent from the field in the first half and 54 percent for the game. But Crean wasn't particularly happy with the opening effort.

"We're not a team that understands yet how to put that throttle down and keep it down," Crean said. "We're working through that. We're not going to be a seven-man team or an eight-man team. If we're going to play the way we want to play defensively and pressure the ball and have the activity we want to have, we're going to have to play a lot of people."

Oladipo was singing Zeller's praises after the game. While admitting it wasn't a real game, Oladipo said Zeller was impressive.

"It just shows his presence and how much he's going to help us win," Oladipo said. "They were doubling every time he got the ball, sometimes when he didn't. That opened up the flow for everybody and helped us share the ball. Like I said before, we did recruit him for a reason."

With the exhibition game under its belt, Indiana was ready to start playing them for real in six days against Stony Brook.

Chapter 19

A few weeks before the regular season begins each year, I always do a little prognosticating. First I do a blog where I pick what I think will be the ultimate order of finish in the Big Ten, and then later I come back with a game-by-game prediction of what I think Indiana's regular-season record will be.

I always caution it by saying that it's nearly impossible to really know how teams are going to fare before they've even played a single game. But it's water-cooler talk, and the blogs generally get lots of people responding.

Whenever I have people at the end of a season saying that they told me so when it came to my predictions being off or theirs being on, I always ask them if they put up a prediction in my blog. Those are the people I have the most respect for. The ones that go out on the limb and make a prediction at the same time that I do, given the information at hand.

When the Big Ten writers made their annual preseason predictions, Purdue was picked fifth and Indiana was selected ninth. When I did my own picks, that appeared in my blog on October 25, I picked IU sixth and Purdue seventh.

Did I know this might ruffle the feathers of a few Boilermaker fans? Sure. But if I did anything else, they would be disappointed. As it turned out, Purdue fans came out of the woodwork telling me what an idiot I was for making such an outlandish claim. It was clear to them that I was just a homer and trying to give Indiana unnecessary props.

I tried to explain my way of thinking, but it did no good. They weren't on me as much as they were when I suggested years ago that Robbie Hummel would be nothing more than a role player at Purdue (an opinion I clearly got wrong), but they let me have it nonetheless.

As an aside there, I tried to say years later that what I meant was that Hummel's role would be to be the Big Ten player of the year but they weren't buying that one, either. Oh well, sometimes we say things we regret and that was one of them.

My IU prediction to finish ahead of Purdue, however, was one that I really didn't think was that farfetched.

My feeling, and I explained it in the blog, was that if Cody Zeller could make an impact right away, and if Victor Oladipo and Will

Sheehey, in particular, could take their games up a notch, that there was no reason Indiana couldn't be a middle-of-the-pack Big Ten team.

Now, as it would turn out, Indiana would actually finish fifth in the Big Ten at 11-7, one game ahead of sixth place Purdue at 10-8, so perhaps I evened the score with Boiler fans.

But then again, probably not. I'll always be the hated writer of their rivals, writing for what they like to call the "IU Star."

As for my preseason prediction for the Hoosiers overall record, I went with 19-12, which I thought would be a major step in the right direction.

I explained that record this way in my blog that ran a few days before IU opened the regular season with Stony Brook.

It's that time of year. IU opens the season Friday night at home against Stony Brook. With Cody Zeller in uniform, there's a new buzz surrounding the Indiana basketball program this season.

I go back and forth between IU winning 18 or 19 games heading into the Big Ten Tournament. Either way would be a strong improvement over 12 wins a year ago. Obviously, my prediction is based on nobody getting hurt. Once you start losing key players for long periods of time I think it's much more difficult to get a handle on a team. Maurice Creek's injury last year was a good example. With him the last two months, IU would have had a better shot at winning some of those games, especially the three- and four-point losses it sustained late in the year.

So I'll go with 19-12 which, considering this is a team that has won a total of eight Big Ten games the last three years, is likely quite ambitious. Still, looking around the Big Ten, I think the Hoosiers will match up better with a lot of teams now that they have Zeller in the middle.

My prediction is based on IU going 10-3 in the nonconference portion of the schedule and 9-9 in Big Ten play. Obviously this means the Hoosiers are going to have to get a few of those elusive road victories, especially two or three in conference play.

But that's what I'll stick with. If the Hoosiers can go 9-9 in Big Ten play, they would likely play in a Thursday game in the Big Ten Tournament and be favored to win that 20th game. If IU can win 20 games, I believe the Hoosiers will be participating in postseason play for the first time in four years.

ᔓ   ᔕ

Indiana's schedule for the 2011-12 season was once again set up to give the Hoosiers a good chance to get off to a good start.

Five of the first six games, all in November, would be played in Assembly Hall. The exception was a true road game at Evansville, where the Hoosiers would be the second team to play in the Purple Aces' new arena, the Ford Center.

IU would also have a good true road test in the Big Ten/ACC Challenge against a much-improved North Carolina State team. There was the Kentucky game looming in early December as well as a neutral site matchup against Notre Dame in the first Crossroads Classic at Bankers Life Fieldhouse in Indianapolis. IU would then play two more cupcake home games at Assembly Hall before opening the Big Ten season in late December on the road at Michigan State.

The season opener against Stony Brook wasn't expected to be much of a test—and it wasn't. Crean had talked the day before the game about how Stony Brook was a potential NCAA Tournament team and that they were picked second in the America East Conference. But you weren't sure if he was saying that so his kids wouldn't get overconfident or if the Sea Wolves were really that good.

When Indiana put a 96-66 beat down on Stony Brook, most thought it was likely the former. But to Crean's credit, when Stony Brook finished the 2011-12 season 22-10 overall and 14-2 in its conference and won the regular season title, people looked at that game a little differently.

Zeller recorded a double-double in his Indiana debut with 16 points and 10 rebounds. He had three steals, including one from three-quarters court where he dribbled the ball the length of the floor and dunked it.

In what would be a regular occurrence at home games in Assembly Hall, the crowd spent a lot of time chanting his name.

As good as Zeller played, Oladipo gave an early glimpse of what people could expect from him for the 2011-12 season. It wasn't so much his offense, though Oladipo did equal his career high with 16 points, but rather his lockdown defense that was most impressive. Oladipo drew the assignment of guarding Stony Brook's best player, Bryan Dougher, who was considered a lights-out 3-point shooter.

Oladipo got up into him right from the start. Dougher hit a contested 3 on Stony Brook's first possession. After that he didn't make another shot the rest of the way. He missed his last seven attempts.

"I just tried to make him play fast, make him work and try to get him tired," Oladipo said. "I thought I did a pretty good job of that tonight."

Indiana shot 65.4 percent from the field for the game and 70.4 percent in the second half.

The 96 points scored by Indiana left Stony Brook coach Steve Pikiell scratching his head. And for good reason. In Stony Brook's final 31 games of the 2011-12 season, no team would score more than 74 points against the Sea Wolves. They would eventually play in the NIT, where they lost to Seton Hall 63-61 in the first round.

"Believe it or not, our defense is usually pretty good," Pikiell said. "Obviously that's the most we've ever given up in points and that's the highest percentage ever given up, and that's because of Indiana."

Two days later, IU was back in action against Chattanooga in the first of what would be four games at Assembly Hall in the first Hoosier Invitational. The way the tournament was set up was that both Indiana and Butler would play three home games against Chattanooga, Savannah State and Gardner-Webb in a 10-day span. At the end of those games, IU and Butler would then meet in the final game at Assembly Hall.

As good as IU's offense was in the season opener against Stony Brook, Indiana's defense came up equally big against Chattanooga.

The Hoosiers held the Mocs to 27-percent shooting and came up with 15 steals in a 78-53 victory to improve to 2-0.

Sophomore guard Victor Oladipo had a career-high 21 points, hitting six of nine shots from the field and eight of 11 free throws.

Jordan Hulls had 18 points on six 3-pointers, and Verdell Jones III had 16 points. IU's starting guard trio combined to hit 17 of 25 shots (68 percent) and scored 55 points.

All were good numbers, but Tom Crean was happiest with IU's defense. The 27-percent shooting was the second-best defensive effort in four seasons under Crean at Indiana.

Crean said he wanted IU to hold Chattanooga senior guard Keegan Bell in check. With Oladipo drawing the first assignment, and later Jones, Bell was held scoreless, missing all five of his shots in 30 minutes.

"The key for us was the Bell kid, and to hold him scoreless was a really big deal," Crean said. "When you have four guys (on Chattanooga's team) that scored 25 points or more in a game last year, then you know they've got some high-level scorers.

"I think a win like this could really come back and help us down the road, because that's a team that is picked to win their division, and I didn't see anything on film to make me believe they wouldn't be capable of that."

The Mocs may have been picked to win the North Division of the Southern Conference, but in reality they would finish last. They went 11-21 overall and 5-13 in conference play.

Still, Indiana had done what it had set out to do. It posted two easy wins over opponents that it was expected to beat, and now the Hoosiers were ready to take their show on the road for the first time. Up next was a mid-week game in the new Ford Center in downtown Evansville against the Purple Aces.

Evansville was looked upon as being IU's first true test. Not so much because the Aces were considered a powerhouse or anything, though they did knock off Butler 80-77 in their opener, but more because IU simply had not won many true road games in the Tom Crean era.

And saying "not many" was actually putting it lightly. The answer was one. And that was one out of the first 31, or in other words, a 1-30 record in true road games. The lone win had come at Penn State on January 21, 2010.

So when the Hoosiers went to Evansville and dominated play from start to finish in a 94-73 victory, IU fans began to take notice.

Sure, the 3-0 start was hardly against the toughest competition but all three wins had been by 20 points or more. In Crean's first season, IU did not have a single victory of 20 or more. In year two, the Hoosiers had three. So in three games, IU had equaled the number of 20-point-or-more victories from the first two seasons.

Which was a start. And that's all it was. IU only had to look back one season to a team that had opened 6-0 and 9-2 before finishing 12-20. No one was ready to put the cart before the horse, but at the same time, a 3-0 start was still noteworthy.

Jones paced five IU players in double figures with 17. Watford, who had scored a total of nine points on three-of-14 shooting in the first two games, had 15 points against Evansville. And the Hoosiers shot the ball well again. IU made 55.9 percent of its shots from the field and 52.4 percent from 3-point range on 11-of-21 shooting.

While it was a capacity crowd at Evansville's new downtown arena, there were also plenty of Indiana fans on hand. Zeller, who had 14 points and nine rebounds, guessed that a good number of IU fans made the 50-minute drive from his hometown of Washington, Indiana.

"There were a lot of Indiana fans here," Zeller said. "I think half of the town of Washington was here."

After the Evansville game, Indiana would play back-to-back games in the Hoosier Invitational on Saturday and Monday of that same week. First up was Savannah State and then Gardner Webb.

When that stretch was complete, Indiana had played five games in 10 days.

Much like the first three games, Indiana barely broke a sweat against Savannah State. The Hoosiers raced to a 94-65 victory.

Zeller posted a career-high with 23 points and added five rebounds and three steals. He hit six of seven shots from the field and 11 of 13 from the foul line.

"I'm feeling really comfortable," Zeller said. "I'm just trying to get used to these guys. I scored a lot of easy buckets tonight off dump-offs where we were able to penetrate."

Good shooting was another common theme. Indiana had shot better than 50 percent in each of the first four games, including 57.1 percent against the Tigers. And the streak of beating teams by 20 points or more was now up to four games. IU had an average victory margin of 26.3 points per game.

Crean was particularly happy with Zeller's play.

"You can go at him and you can go through him," Crean said. "When you have a player like that, he makes everyone better. He's a really good basketball player. That's one guy that took some really big strides from Wednesday night (at Evansville) to tonight, and I think he showed that."

Two days later, IU would wrap up the five-games-in-10-days stretch with a convincing 73-49 victory over Gardner Webb. It was IU's third victory in the Hoosier Invitational, and the Hoosiers would play host to Butler in their next game, six days later.

The standout in this game was Derek Elston, who a year ago to the day had suffered a sports hernia against Evansville that had hampered him throughout his sophomore season. In this one, he scored 10 points and pulled down nine rebounds in 15 minutes off the bench to help lead the Hoosiers to the win.

Another 20-point victory marked the first time in Indiana basketball history that IU had opened the season with five consecutive 20-point wins. Besides the 1974-75 season, it's the only time it had happened at any point in an IU season.

Sheehey had 13 of his game-high 15 points in the second half, and Zeller and Oladipo each had 13 points to lead IU.

But the talk of this game was Elston. Five games in, the junior forward simply was looking like a different player than he had at any point in his IU career. He was averaging 8.4 points and had made 17 of 25 shots from the field, 68 percent. From beyond the 3-point line, Elston had hit four of his first five, including one against Gardner Webb. The year before, Elston made three 3-pointers all season on 17 attempts.

Crean had been saying for some time that he really thought Indiana had seven starters on this team. Along with the starting five of Hulls, Jones III, Oladipo, Watford and Zeller, Crean believed that Sheehey and Elston belonged in that company, too.

"I've said this before, and that's that I think we have seven starters and (Elston) is one of them," Crean said. "He has really improved. We can feel him and see him getting better constantly inside of our practices. He's a product of his work and his health."

The 5-0 start advanced Indiana to the final game of the inaugural Hoosier Invitational against Butler. Unfortunately, this wasn't the same Butler team that had advanced to back-to-back national championship games. Had Shelvin Mack stuck around, it would have been a much more interesting matchup. Still, a rivalry between the two schools had been brewing for a while. And a lot of people were interested to see what would happen when the two tangled at Assembly Hall.

The day of the Butler game I wrote a story about how different the Hoosiers and Bulldogs would be if Zeller had opted to attend Butler instead of IU. Zeller's final three were IU, Butler and North Carolina.

IU basketball color commentator Royce Waltman said sometimes all it takes is one decision to change the course.

"I think a lot of times fans will quickly forget the players you weren't able to get and quickly move on with the team you have," Waltman said. "But those recruiting decisions, often times a coach's fate hangs upon those decisions of one or two kids. It's a big thing."

It clearly had been a big thing for Indiana through the first five games. With Zeller as the team's centerpiece, IU was 5-0. Butler was 3-2 and had had a much more difficult time, even with many of the same opponents. Five games in, the teams had four common opponents. IU defeated the other three teams in the Hoosier Invitational by an average of 26 points. Butler picked up three wins, too, but by an average of 9.3 points.

Zeller was leading Indiana in scoring (14.6), rebounding (7.6) and steals (13), and he was shooting a staggering 80.6 percent from the field.

Waltman said Zeller meant more than just what he was doing statistically.

"I think he has made a tremendous difference with the team, not only in what he brings with his scoring and rebounding, but I just think it brings a confidence to the team," Waltman said. "I just think the rest of the guys are much more aggressive mentally just feeling they have that little bit of an eraser there with Cody Zeller. I don't think there's any question that the day he made his mind up was a pivotal one for Indiana."

One of the most consistent players for Indiana throughout the Hoosier Invitational wasn't even in the starting lineup. Sheehey had turned in one consistent performance after another, and the Butler game was certainly no exception. He came off the bench to score a career-high 21 points Sunday night to lift Indiana to a 75-59 victory over Butler.

Zeller had 16 points and eight rebounds, and Hulls added 14 as Indiana (6-0) matched its longest winning streak in Crean's four seasons at IU.

But as had been the case in recent games, Sheehey was once again a difference-maker for the Hoosiers. He had yet to start a game, but his contributions had been significant. He was averaging 13.3 points per game and had averaged 17 points the past three games. That kind of production earned him Most Valuable Player honors for the four-game Hoosier Invitational.

Sheehey, the 6-6 sophomore from Stuart, Florida, had clearly bought into his nonstarting role.

"Coach really wants me to come in and provide that energy off the bench, and that's something I try to bring every game, not just rivalry games like this one," Sheehey said.

Louisville Courier-Journal columnist Rick Bozich had this to say following IU's victory over the Bulldogs.

BLOOMINGTON, Ind. – You knew where to find Butler basketball coach Brad Stevens at the climax of the last two seasons. He was hanging out with Mike Krzyzewski and then with Jim Calhoun in the NCAA championship game.

It was an irresistible story, a reminder that everybody can win in college basketball, proof that top 50-recruits are not essential for success.

There has been one location where the story was not considered so enchanting — Indiana University, a program sagging with NCAA probation and zero scholarship players when Tom Crean arrived in 2008.

While Stevens was explaining the Butler Way, Crean was being asked to explain why his Hoosiers backtracked from four Big Ten wins to three during his third season. Patience is a principle dropped into introductory press conferences — and then forgotten.

You didn't need a Google search to hear what people were saying before Crean's unbeaten IU team played host to Stevens and Butler in Assembly Hall Sunday night.

"It's a game Indiana has to win," ESPN basketball analyst Dick Vitale said. One national columnist took that concept up a notch. He wrote that Stevens was the guy Indiana would call if the outlook remained overcast in Bloomington this season.

Time to rip up that silly script. The final was IU 75, Butler 59 — the same 16-point gap that separated the Bulldogs and Louisville eight days earlier.

Crean's team was tougher than Stevens' team, knocking away 74 deflections. Crean's team defended better than Stevens' team, limiting Butler to 38-percent shooting. Crean's team was more balanced, getting at least 10 points from four players.

And Crean's team will carry a 6-0 record to North Carolina State on Wednesday.

"We matched their toughness with even more toughness of our own," Indiana athletic director Fred Glass said.

The easy story around the Hoosiers has been that freshman center Cody Zeller, a McDonald's All-American, was the reason that Indiana was ready to move into the middle of the Big Ten standings.

But against Butler, the Hoosiers showed they are more than just Zeller, even though he had 16 points, eight rebounds, two blocks and three steals.

The guy Butler couldn't slow was Will Sheehey, a sophomore guard. Check the recruiting rankings. Sheehey didn't show up on any top 100 lists when Crean fetched him out of Florida in 2010.

In Sheehey, Crean saw a player with the toughness and resolve, a guy he could develop into a relentless defender. Sheehey lived in the gym last summer, commuting to Indianapolis to compete in a summer league against NBA players.

It shows. Ask Butler.

Sheehey shot with confidence, making three of four three-point shots and scoring 21 points, the best of his career.

When Butler guard Chrishawn Hopkins hurt Indiana with 13 quick points in the first half, Sheehey asked Crean for that defensive assignment. Hopkins finished with only 19.

Indiana won a game the Hoosiers would not have won last season, and not simply because the Bulldogs lack Shelvin Mack and Matt Howard from the national runner-up team.

Butler played good defense. Indiana played better defense. Butler threw the ball away 21 times. The Bulldogs' starters made only 11 of 34 shots.

"We knew that rebounding and defense would get us a win, and that's exactly what happened," IU guard Jordan Hulls said.

ᔅᔢ ᔤᔥ

The win over Butler gave IU a perfect 6-0 record heading into what many believed would be Indiana's biggest test to date: North Carolina State in the Big Ten/ACC Challenge.

It didn't help that the Big Ten/ACC Challenge hadn't been good to Indiana in recent years. Part of the reason was that even if Indiana was slightly down in a year, the networks always wanted the Hoosiers to be part of a marquee matchup. So IU's opponents had been Duke and North Carolina a lot more than any of the bottom feeders in the ACC.

And over the previous eight seasons, IU was 1-7 in the event.

North Carolina State came into the game 5-1 and had recently beat Texas. The Wolfpack's only loss was to Vanderbilt, a team that later would be the only other team besides Indiana to knock off Kentucky.

But for Indiana, this was a perception game. Beat North Carolina State on its home floor, and not only would the Hoosiers be 7-0 but they would be 2-0 in true road games on the season. Considering they were 1-30 the previous three seasons, that would be a monumental win.

Moreover, the reality was that even though IU was 6-0, it didn't really have a signature win. A win over a North Carolina State team that was expected to be an upper division ACC team could go a long way toward giving IU a little respectability. It also wouldn't hurt a future NCAA résumé to have a road win like this in the non-conference season.

And what the Hoosiers didn't know at the time was that by the time the season was wrapping up, North Carolina State would be part of the same Sweet Sixteen lineup that the Hoosiers would find themselves in.

With just under eight minutes to play, the Hoosiers trailed by seven points, 63-56. In past seasons, that lead, especially on an opponent's floor with the crowd on its feet going crazy, would have been too much to overcome. But Indiana was showing once again that the 2011-12 Hoosiers were a much different team than IU fans had seen in a long time.

From that point on, IU outscored North Carolina State 30-12 and won the game going away, 86-75 at the RBC Center in Raleigh, North Carolina.

In many ways, the victory was a return to relevance for the Hoosiers. It wasn't Kentucky-esqe, but it was big, nonetheless.

Hulls had 20 points, including a huge 3-pointer with 1:37 to play that gave IU a 79-75 edge. Zeller added 19 points and seven rebounds, and Watford had 16 points and nine boards.

Crean called the victory "monumental."

"This win was monumental for our program because we had never won in this game," he said. "And we hadn't been to an atmosphere like this. Our guys felt like they could compete, but to compete is one thing and to come away with a victory is another.

"It's a landmark win for us as a program and certainly one of the bigger wins for us in our time at Indiana."

After N.C. State took a 63-56 lead with 7:48 to play, Watford and Zeller each made two free throws, and Oladipo's dunk with 5:45 to play pulled IU within 65-64. Watford put IU on top for good at 71-68 with a 3-pointer from the right wing with 3:58 remaining. The lead grew it to 76-70, but the Wolfpack closed to 76-75 with 2:03 left on a drive by C.J. Williams. Indiana then scored the final 10 points, with Hulls' 3-pointer from the left wing being the backbreaker.

"The shot clock was running down, I got a pick-and-roll, and they went under the screen and I backed off and pulled the trigger," Hulls said. "Fortunately it went in, because we needed that spark right there."

IU's next opponent was a home game against Stetson, where the big thing the Hoosiers needed to guard against was not looking ahead to the following weekend's matchup with No. 1 Kentucky.

It was an emotional day for the Hoosiers anyway, because the 1987 national championship team was honored at halftime on the 25th anniversary of IU's fifth and last national title.

Crean wasn't happy with IU's energy level in the game as the Hoosiers were clinging to a 33-29 halftime advantage over the overmatched Hatters. Looking for a spark, Crean turned to Daniel Moore, and the senior guard started the second half and helped lead IU to an 84-50 victory. The victory improved IU's record to 8-0.

Oladipo said people who didn't think Moore was an important part of the IU team didn't know what they were talking about.

"I've said this before, but without (Moore) we can't win," Oladipo said. "He brings us a spark in practice, and when he's there (in the game) he brings a spark, too. A lot of the stuff he does, people don't even see, but when he gets in there he gives it all he's got."

Moore didn't score but had three assists, three steals and 10 deflections in nine minutes. His energy at both ends of the court kick-started the Hoosiers in the second half. By the time Moore came out of the game with 16:44 to play, Indiana had increased its lead to 44-33 and would not trail by less than 10 points again.

"I just try to do what I do well, and that's defend and provide a lot of energy," Moore said. "I'm not going to score a lot or do anything much more than that. I know my role and I try to do that well. Most importantly, I've got to help guys in practice. I won't play a lot, but if I can keep getting the other guys better in practice, that's the best thing I can do."

The game also included the 25th anniversary celebration of IU's 1987 national championship team. Twelve members of the team, including all five starters, were in attendance and honored at halftime.

Despite the rain, IU fans stood in a line that extended outside the arena for a one-hour autograph session with the players. One member of that team, Steve Eyl, who now lives in San Diego, said he was completely taken aback by the response from the IU faithful.

"When I heard we were going to have an autograph session, I thought a few people might come by," Eyl said. "The next thing I know, it's a solid one-hour event and the people were unbelievable. It was crazy. I had no idea it would be anything like this.

"It's been a long time. A lot of these fans weren't born when we won the title. But everyone who came up to us was thanking us, and I just wanted to thank them."

Chapter 20

At 8-0 it was time for the Hoosiers to climb up on the national stage with their December 10 victory against the No. 1 Kentucky Wildcats.

The first three chapters of this book dealt in detail with Christian Watford's shot that sent Hoosier Nation into a frenzy and announced to the college basketball world that Indiana basketball was indeed back.

Some Kentucky fans, and even coach John Calipari himself, said later that IU had won on a fluke shot. First of all, it wasn't like it was a half-court heave or a shot with a particularly high degree of difficulty. It was a 3-point shot from just beyond the line at the left wing. And it wasn't like it was Tom Pritchard, Cody Zeller or even Victor Oladipo, a 20-percent 3-point shooter, who had hoisted up the shot.

Watford would finish the season shooting at a 43.7-percent clip from 3-point range. When Watford, Hulls or Matt Roth were launching 3-pointers during the 2011-12 season, it was far more a case of money in the bank than a case of a missed opportunity.

It also wasn't like Indiana had trailed the whole game and then came up with a lucky shot at the end. It could be argued that IU was the one that was in control of this game for most of the second half and it was Kentucky that had done enough right things in the final few minutes to come from behind and take the lead.

Indiana led by eight late in the first half after Hulls hit a 3-pointer to put the Hoosiers up 30-22 with 2:33 to play. Another Hulls 3-pointer with 14:36 to play in the game gave IU a 10-point lead at 48-38. It was still a nine-point advantage at 9:51 after a Victor Oladipo dunk put IU up 60-51. When Will Sheehey hit a 3 at the 9:05 mark, IU led 63-53. And finally, a 3-pointer by Jordan Hulls at the 7:52 mark in the game gave Indiana a 66-57 advantage.

When Kentucky put on a run of its own and took a 69-68 lead with 2:01 to play, it marked only the Wildcats' second lead of the second half. The other one, at 35-34, lasted a total of 43 seconds.

So the 'Cats could call Indiana's victory a fluke if they wanted to, but to IU fans it all sounded more like sour grapes.

Let's don't forget some of the missteps that Kentucky took in the final few minutes of that game.

With Kentucky leading 69-68 with 1:16 to play, Michael Kidd-Gilchrist had a costly turnover that gave IU the ball back. Thirteen seconds later, Watford scored on an inside move to put the Hoosiers back on top 70-69.

Let's not forget the missed one-and-one free throw opportunity by Anthony Davis with 20 seconds to play with Kentucky leading 71-70. Let's also not forget that Doron Lamb could have made it a three-point game when he had two free throws with six seconds to play. Make them both and even if Watford hits his 3-pointer, the game goes to overtime. Instead, Lamb missed the first and made the second to put Kentucky up 72-70.

And then let's not forget the biggest faux pas of them all, when Kentucky opted not to foul on IU's final possession. The Wildcats had two fouls to give and their coach had just reminded them of that in the huddle, yet Kentucky allowed Verdell Jones III to dribble down the middle of the court, pick up a screen at half court from Cody Zeller and then flip the ball back to Watford for *The Shot* that rocked the college basketball world.

When it was all said and done, Kentucky coach John Calipari stood back and said he was proud of his team's effort. It was the first true road game for a team dominated by freshmen, and the Wildcats had almost pulled out a win in what was a lion's den of emotions at Assembly Hall.

"I'm proud of my team," Calipari said. "How they gutted it out in the second half (and) how they played to win. We're pretty good. I've got a good team. We can win in different ways of playing."

Calipari also gave Indiana and its crowd some props as well.

"Indiana and the crowd made us play the way we played," Calipari said. "It's not like we were awful."

As for Crean, as much as he was basking in the limelight of IU's back-on-the-map victory over the top-ranked team in the nation, he wasn't ready to say that beating Kentucky was the end all for his Hoosiers either.

"This is not an exclamation point to our season," Crean said. "We have a lot of the season left. There's a lot of room for growth. That's what I'm most excited about."

೮ಾ   ೮ಽ

The Monday after Indiana had knocked off the No. 1 team in the land to improve to 9-0 on the season, Hoosier fans everywhere couldn't wait for the national polls to be released. The one thing everyone knew was that the longest run in school history of not being ranked in the *Associated Press* top 25 had come to an end for the Hoosiers.

Indiana debuted in the *Associated Press* poll at No. 18. In the ESPN/ USA Today Coaches Poll, Indiana entered in the No. 20 position.

A Twitter post by IU junior guard Maurice Creek, who was out for the season with a torn Achilles, seemed to sum it up.

"The Hoosiers are ranked 18th in the country," Creek wrote, moments after the poll was released. "It feels good."

Indiana had had little to feel good about in the three-plus years since it was ranked No. 18 in the AP poll on March 10, 2008. In the past three seasons, Indiana had a combined record of 28-66, including an 8-46 mark in Big Ten play.

IU coach Tom Crean said being ranked was a significant step. He said he was happy two weeks before when his team simply picked up a pair of votes in the polls. He was happiest for his five seniors — Verdell Jones III, Tom Pritchard, Matt Roth, Daniel Moore and Kory Barnett — because of all they have endured at Indiana.

"I just found out today that since 1950, every four-year player at Indiana had been ranked in the top 25 at some point in their career," Crean said. "That lets them be a part of the IU tradition in a special way, and there are no players who are more deserving of it than they are."

Just over a month into the season, Indiana (9-0) was basking in success as one of just nine teams in the country that were still unbeaten, joining top-ranked Syracuse, Louisville, Baylor, Missouri, Illinois, Marquette, Xavier and Murray State.

A closer look at the results of the AP poll found a large disparity in where voters believed Indiana should be ranked. Eight of the 65 did not rank IU at all. Three others had Indiana in the top 10. One of those, Ray Fittipaldo of the *Pittsburgh Post-Gazette*, ranked Indiana No. 5 in the nation.

My own thought was that No. 5 was too high, but then unranked wasn't right either.

Indiana was one of just nine unbeaten teams in the nation. For me, that didn't mean that IU should necessarily be in the top nine. I'm one of the 65 voters in the AP poll. I've voted in the poll for more than a decade. I usually look at the teams I rank ahead of a school and try to decide if I think the higher-ranked team would beat the lower one. This isn't always the most important criteria, but it's part of the equation.

That week I ranked IU No. 16. I felt like the No. 18 ranking in the AP poll was fair. I thought the Hoosiers probably deserved a better ranking in the other poll, but those things take time.

Indiana had a big game coming up next against Notre Dame, and I strongly believed that if the Hoosiers could get past the Irish that they would have a chance to move up in those rankings by the time the conference opener against Michigan State rolled around on December 28.

There were a few other notes that I found interesting about IU's 9-0 start. It was the first time an Indiana team had opened 9-0 since the 1989-90 team started 10-0. That team struggled in Big Ten play, however, finishing 8-10 and 18-11 overall.

The last time an IU team won 11 or more games to open the season was in 1975-76, when the eventual national champions won all 32 games.

When Indiana beat Kentucky, it marked the first IU win over a No. 1-ranked team since the Hoosiers defeated top-ranked Duke 74-73 on March 21, 2002, in the NCAA Tournament's Sweet Sixteen. That team went on to lose in the national championship game to Maryland.

The win over Kentucky was also IU's first over a top-10 team since an 80-61 victory over Michigan State on February 16, 2008.

Late in the afternoon on that Monday, Watford appeared on 1070-The Fan in Indianapolis in the afternoon slot with JMV. He said he thought IU had plenty of motivation moving forward.

"We don't want to be looked at as a one-hit wonder," Watford said. "It's pretty easy to focus when you know there's more out there for your team."

8 3

Up next after finals week was Notre Dame in the first Crossroads Classic at Conseco Fieldhouse (which would later change its name to Bankers Life Fieldhouse) in Indianapolis. The doubleheader that day would feature Butler against Purdue, and Notre Dame against Indiana. In the 2012-13 season IU would face Butler and Purdue would get Notre Dame. A few months after the 2011-12 season came to an end, athletic directors from the four schools announced that the event would be extended through the 2014 season.

Funny how that works when you get a capacity crowd of more than 19,000 to attend the inaugural event.

During the Big Ten weekly teleconference in the week leading up to the Notre Dame game, Crean talked about the importance of his team maintaining their focus after the win over Kentucky. He said there were a lot of students patting his guys on the back this week and putting them on a pedestal. He wanted them to enjoy it, but he also wanted them to come back down to earth very quickly.

"The most important thing is that if we get concerned with other people's expectations then we get away from what's most important, which is ours," Crean said during the Big Ten teleconference. "It's the same when you're not winning. You can't get caught up in what you're not doing and what you're not supposed to do. You've got to get caught up in what you can do and what's out there. That's an important ingredient for success in any endeavor."

Crean said it was a matter of keeping perspective.

"There's no way getting around the fact that this game did take place, there's no way around the fact that it was an incredible moment, and there's no way around the fact that people are going to be talking about it. The bottom line is, do we want to build on the opportunity and have the chance to do things again down the road? Or do we want to stay standing? And I don't think any of us want to stay standing. We want to keep moving."

The next step was against the Irish, a team that would catch fire in January and February and make a big run in the Big East. When this game was played in December, however, Notre Dame was still trying to find itself after losing top scorer Tim Abromaitis to a season-ending injury.

Notre Dame was 7-0 at home and 0-4 on the road. The Irish had gotten blasted by Missouri, 87-58, and also had a 20-point loss to Gonzaga. The other two losses were also respectable as the Irish had lost to Georgia and Maryland.

On game day, it was clear that Indiana had a simple goal against the Irish. It was a ploy that would make ESPN's Dick Vitale proud. The week before, when Vitale called the Kentucky game, he spent most of the broadcast pounding home the point that the Hoosiers needed to get Zeller more touches.

Apparently, Crean had the same point of emphasis in practice the week before the Notre Dame game. With Zeller demanding the ball and scoring a game-high 21 points, No. 18 Indiana was able to overcome a sluggish performance and defeat Notre Dame 69-58 in the second game of the Close the Gap Crossroads Classic before a capacity crowd of 19,064 at Conseco Fieldhouse.

The victory gave IU a perfect 10-0 record, and with UNLV's 64-48 win over Illinois earlier in the day, it left the Hoosiers as the only remaining unbeaten team in the Big Ten.

As for the game, Hulls repeated what he and his teammates had talked about before the season even began in terms of getting their big freshman center more involved in the offense.

"We have to play through Cody all the time because he can do so many different things," Hulls said. "You throw it in and he can either score or pass. We just have to cut off of him and find the open spots. It's very crucial that we do that every game, and it showed. He'll do whatever he needs to do to win."

The previous three times that Zeller had stepped on the floor at Conseco Fieldhouse, his Washington High School teams won state championships. He pointed that out to Hulls and Victor Oladipo before they appeared in the postgame interview room.

"I was just telling them, I think it's the worst game I've ever played here," Zeller said. "But it's a fun place to play."

When Zeller's Washington team won the state title at Conseco earlier in the 2011 calendar year, Zeller had 20 points and 18 rebounds. As a junior, he had 20 points and 26 rebounds. His freshman season at Washington, he got into the game for only the final minute and didn't score. Brother Tyler Zeller, however, scored 43 for Washington.

Against the Irish, Zeller had eight rebounds to accompany the 21 points. He hit eight of 14 shots from the field. Zeller scored 12 of IU's first 22 points and kept the Hoosiers in it early. Notre Dame tried to be physical in the post early, until center Jack Cooley picked up his second foul. He fouled out with 2 minutes, 57 seconds to play.

"Early in the season, I played against a few guys who tried to be physical and I just tried to take whatever they would give me," Zeller said. "Whether they're backing off me or playing physical, I just try to stay active, and these guys do a good job of getting me the ball."

The big question for Indiana going into the game was how the Hoosiers would bounce back after their emotional 73-72 victory over then-No. 1 Kentucky. Early on, the results weren't good. Notre Dame (7-5) led 15-6 with 13:10 to play in the first half.

"Our guys never wavered when we got down," Crean said. "We made a lot of mistakes early in the game, and a lot of them were communication mistakes. We were waiting for other people to help us out of a situation rather than being a participant in our own rescue. Our guys did a great job of picking that up and gaining confidence. And then a few baskets for us started to go in."

Oladipo, who battled foul trouble throughout the game, scored 16 points in 24 minutes. He hit six of seven shots from the field. Hulls had 12 points, and Watford had 10.

Rick Bozich, the columnist for the *Louisville Courier-Journal*, wrote the next day about how IU's payback machine continued to roll on.

INDIANAPOLIS – The Indiana University basketball Payback Tour rolled relentlessly forward at Conseco Fieldhouse on Saturday. Add Notre Dame to the teams that had embarrassed the Hoosiers during the last three seasons and have now discovered that Tom Crean's team is no longer inclined to retreat or flinch.

Even on a day when Christian Watford didn't take a single 3-point shot, much less a buzzer-beater. And when the Hoosiers barely made 42 percent of their field-goal attempts. And Cody Zeller and Verdell Jones found themselves benched with foul trouble. And Crean received only six points from his subs.

All that happened, and the Hoosiers still dispatched Notre Dame 69-58 to move to 10-0. This is the same Notre Dame program that beat Indiana by 38 in Crean's third game three seasons ago, when the Zeller on the court played for Notre Dame (Luke) instead of Indiana (Cody).

"They've been kicked around," Notre Dame coach Mike Brey said. "Now it's time to deliver, and they're ready to do it."

It wasn't the Hoosiers' most spectacular game of the season. But that made it more impressive, because it was a legitimate 40-minute statement about why Crean's team is the last remaining unbeaten in the Big Ten.

Think of it this way: The Hoosiers should begin Big Ten play at Michigan State on Dec. 28 with as many victories (12) as any of Crean's first three teams won in an entire season.

On Saturday, they did it with defense, holding the Irish without a field goal for a 14-minute stretch. They did it by insisting that Zeller, their precocious freshman center, got about a quarter of IU's field-goal attempts. That enabled him to score 21 – and joke that he was the only member of the family that didn't travel to Maui for Notre Dame's 88-50 victory over IU in 2008 because he had a game at Washington (Ind.) High School.

"I had Thanksgiving alone," he said, shaking his head.

This was a perfect opportunity for Indiana to play like a team still intoxicated by the adulation that has surrounded them in the week since upsetting Kentucky 73-72, a game ESPN analyst Dick Vitale said he ranks as one of the five most exciting games he has ever called.

Kirkwood Avenue was closed into last Sunday morning as it raged with celebration. The Hoosiers moved into the Top 25. Fans purchased the last 3,000 or so tickets for the Crossroads Classic, which opened with Butler's 67-65 victory over Purdue.

As students kept telling the players they were wonderful, Crean showed them a video of all but the final 5.6 seconds of the UK game. Look at this. And this. He found a dozen spots when they could have lost.

"An immature team wouldn't have wanted to hear that," Crean said. "But they did. I could see it throughout the whole week of practice."

There were still early signs of a hangover. The surprise wasn't that Notre Dame surged ahead 15-6. The surprise was Notre Dame wasn't ahead by more. An Indiana team that made 9-of-15 3-pointers against UK didn't make any in the first half against Notre Dame. Brey aligned the Irish defense to squeeze hard on the perimeter.

Last season Indiana could not adjust. Now, with Zeller and a cast of veterans, the Hoosiers can.

"They've been toughened by it and they've stayed together," Brey said. "It's really what college athletics is all about."

ဆ   ൚

At 10-0 the Hoosiers had two more preconference home games at Assembly Hall to use as final warm-ups for the Big Ten season which was only 11 days away.

IU had moved up one spot in the AP poll to No. 17. The first of the final two pre-conference games was against Howard, two days after the victory over Notre Dame.

Four of Indiana's previous five opponents had all been games where Indiana had an emotional stake. The first was Butler, which was an instate rival. The second was North Carolina State, and a chance to capture a rare true road victory. Then came Kentucky, one of IU's biggest rivals, and finally Notre Dame, another quality opponent from within the state of Indiana.

The Hoosiers were due for a laugher, and that's exactly what they got with Howard. Hulls scored 16 points, leading six players in double figures as Indiana raced to a 107-50 victory over the Bison at Assembly

Hall. It was IU's second-most lopsided victory in school history. It fell eight points short of the record, a 65-point 94-29 victory over Notre Dame the night Assembly Hall was dedicated in 1971.

Indiana (11-0) was off to its best start in a season since the 1975-76 national champions won all 32 games. While a lot of other milestones didn't seem nearly as significant to this Indiana team, having something in common with the '76 team was different.

"That means a lot," Sheehey said. "Even though we're taking this one game at a time, it is nice when you look back on the games you've already won. It does feel good, and coach talks about making history, and that's what we're trying to do."

The 107 points were the most scored by a team coached by Crean in his four seasons at Indiana, and the most by any Indiana team since the 1999 NCAA Tournament, when the Hoosiers scored 108 against George Washington.

On a night where Indiana shot 67.3 percent from the field, had 27 assists on 35 baskets, and led by 37 points at halftime, a superlative individual effort stole the show.

It wasn't enough that Hulls beat Howard with his right hand, but he did it with his left hand, too. With the shot clock running out in the final minute of the first half, Hulls dribbled to his left, ducked under a defender, and tossed up a running 3-pointer from the left wing with his left hand.

As Hulls ran back on defense, he wore an ear-to-ear grin. His teammates shared high fives on the bench.

To those who know Hulls, it's not that big of a deal. He often practices shooting left-handed as well as right. But it was rare to see him shoot lefty in a game. Describing the replay on the Big Ten Network, play-by-play announcer Gus Johnson said, "That was a HORSE shot there."

Jones said the first time he saw Hulls shooting with his left hand, he looked at him and said, "What are you doing?"

"But I guess what you guys don't know is that he's practicing for games like this where he can do his trick shots," Jones said with a laugh.

Crean said the play simply showed off Hulls' athleticism.

"That was pretty impressive," Crean said. "The guys that aren't shocked are the coaches and the teammates. They see him do that a lot. He's very gifted with both hands and I don't think he would have taken it if he didn't think he could make it."

Joining Hulls in double figures were Jones, Sheehey and Zeller each with 12, while Watford had 10.

The final tune-up before the start of Big Ten play came three days later when the Hoosiers faced the University of Maryland, Baltimore County (1-10). As good as Indiana was playing, it was almost unfair to face another opponent of this caliber. Indiana used a 42-7 run over an 11-minute stretch in the second half to post an easy 89-47 victory over UMBC.

In two games in a three-day stretch, IU had won by a total of 99 points.

But IU fans could have cared less about how much the Hoosiers won this one by. In a few short days, Indiana basketball had gone from the "Hurryin' Hoosiers" to the walking wounded. First it was Elston, who sustained a broken nose in practice. Next it was sophomore Will Sheehey, who rolled an ankle when he stepped on a ball in practice. Against UMBC, it was Jones, who suffered a hip flexor late in the first half.

Many of the crowd of 12,665 spent the second half with one eye on the locker room entrance to see if Jones would emerge. He never did. Jones went down in a heap late in the first half and limped to the locker room.

No timetable was given for his return. Jones emerged from the locker room after the game to sign autographs — without crutches.

"I haven't really had a chance to talk to the doctors, but Verdell did seem to be moving around a little bit better when I left to come (to the news conference)," Crean said after the game. "Our injuries are all day-to-day things."

The biggest injury occurred during the week to Sheehey. Crean said Sheehey suffered a "freak injury" when he stepped on a ball the day before the UMBC game. He said the IU staff was waiting for the swelling to go down. Crean said he did not expect the injury to be long term.

IU found others to step up against UMBC. Watford had 22 points and 10 rebounds, Hulls had 16 points, and Matt Roth came off the bench to score a season-high 14.

Crean praised Roth, a senior guard who had scored only 22 points on the season before Thursday.

"His play was big because he's a veteran and it was great to see him do that," Crean said. "It's great to see him go into this break and into the next wave of the season with confidence, because we're going to need him."

One funny aside that came out of the UMBC game was a story involving Elston, who had broken his nose earlier in the week in practice. It had been determined that Elston would wear a protective mask, much like ones worn by several Hoosier players in recent seasons. Crean, though, insisted it would be a clear mask. He said Elston had wanted it painted.

"He had some ideas, but we shut that down real fast," Crean said with a smile. "Derek is a real treat. No, that will just be a regular plastic face mask. He's not painting it like a hockey goalie, I know that."

Crean was asked what paint scheme Elston had suggested.

"This is a G-rated place," Crean said. "He's at a different level. I wouldn't have understood it. It's some character, some movie, or something from *Tour of Duty*, I don't know. But we're not doing it."

One other interesting note from the UMBC game was that Hulls' free throw streak, that had lasted for more than a year ,came to an end.

Hulls, who hadn't missed a free throw since the Kentucky game in 2010, missed the first of two technical free throws with 4:50 to play in the first half. That ended his Big Ten record streak of 58 consecutive free throws.

Hulls wasn't happy about it, either.

"That was terrible," Hulls said. "They're free for a reason."

Chapter 21

One of the nice things about my preseason predictions is that I usually allow myself a mulligan right before the conference season begins to re-evaluate. I've always thought it was almost unrealistic to make picks when you had not even seen a team play a single game.

But the preconference picks are something. Now, you're armed with data, and you feel like you can make a more educated guess.

I wrote a blog on that very topic a day or so before IU opened the Big Ten portion of the schedule with its December 28 road game at Michigan State.

Before the season began, I thought Indiana had a good chance to go 9-3 in the preconference schedule. I figured the losses would be to Kentucky and North Carolina State, and then the Hoosiers would lose to either Notre Dame or Butler. The fact that Indiana was now 12-0 and had cracked the top 15 with its No. 13 ranking heading into Big Ten play was beyond my wildest dreams. But as I said in that blog, Indiana was clearly making a believer out of me. I wrote:

> Do I think IU will go on the road Wednesday and knock off Michigan State, a team it hasn't defeated at the Breslin Center since 1991? Probably not. What about Ohio State on New Year's Eve? Not really sure. I think IU will put up a fight, especially with a sold-out crowd. But it's going to be a tough one. Likely an Ohio State win. What about Michigan on January 5? Now, that's one I think Indiana can win.

After that, I broke down the schedule in a little more detail. I said that I thought Indiana could go 8-1 in conference home games with the loss being to Ohio State. On the road, I thought IU had a good chance to go 4-5 with wins over Penn State, Nebraska, Iowa and Minnesota.

If that prediction came true, Indiana would end up with 12 wins in Big Ten play. Which, when you think about it, even with the Hoosiers off to a 12-0 start, was mind-boggling. This is a program that over the past three years had a combined record of 8-46 in Big Ten play. The road record was 1-26.

But as I pointed out in that blog, 12 wins seemed like a possibility. That meant IU could lose to Michigan State, Ohio State, Wisconsin,

Purdue and Michigan on the road, and Ohio State at home, and still finish 12-6 and be solidly in the NCAA Tournament field. That would put IU at 24-6 plus a nonconference win over North Carolina Central in the middle of Big Ten play that would make the Hoosiers 25-6 going into the Big Ten Tournament. Think about what an accomplishment that would be. Three years ago, IU was 6-25 for the season in Tom Crean's first year.

So that was my pick: 12-6. In that scenario, IU would open the season 0-2 and be 3-3 as of January 15. Indiana would improve to 5-3 before losing at Wisconsin. The Hoosiers would be 6-6 through February 4 before rallying to win their final six Big Ten games.

I had a lot of people weigh in with their own comments and predictions at the end of that blog. I've included a few of those here.

George McLaren, a big IU fan who lives in Indianapolis, wasn't ready to take the 12-6 leap of faith, but he thought the Hoosiers were more than capable of finishing above .500 in Big Ten play.

"12-6 would be amazing—an unbelievable turnaround," McLaren wrote. "But I think 10-8 is more likely. And should get the Hoosiers back into the tournament."

Rob Kimmell weighed in from Atascadero, California. He was going with a 14-4 conference record.

"I'm going out on a limb, but I'm going to say 14-4, with one home loss vs. OSU, road losses vs. MSU, OSU, and... argh... Purdue," Kimmell wrote. "But the 12-6 prediction is probably more realistic. And 25-6 overall, like Terry predicted, would be just peachy heading into the B1G tourney."

Michael Baber said the current Indiana team reminded him of the 2002 squad that made it to the Final Four.

"(They have) a blue chip underclassman, an athletic energy guy, and a group of hard-nosed upperclassmen emerging from years of adversity," Baber wrote. "That team, too, found ways to win when nobody expected it—and also went 11-5 in conference play. I don't feel qualified to make predictions. But I feel like this year will bring more surprising wins than surprising losses."

Mike Fields, of Bedford, Indiana, said he thought Indiana could go 16-2 in the Big Ten.

"Undefeated at home, losing on the road to Wisconsin and Ohio State. Can't believe I'm saying that. Just really like the team and how they are playing."

Sharon Hickman, from Jacksonville, Illinois, said she would take 12-6.

"You never know, but 13-5 is a possibility," Hickman wrote in her blog comment. "All I know is I really enjoy this team, and no matter what, I will be rooting for them the rest of the season. I do believe we will get in the big dance, if we have no major injuries. What is the status of our injured players? Go Hoosiers! Oh, I do think IU will beat OSU at home!"

Michael Coriell, who lives in Clarksville, Indiana, was thinking one more win than my prediction.

"I have to go with 13-5 for Indiana and I will smile all year long," Coriell said.

Rob Schuman, from Churubusco, Indiana, was afraid Indiana fans were getting too far ahead of themselves.

"Before we start the spirit of '76," Schuman wrote, "let's temper expectations and remember we still have little depth and a team that is still learning how to win, both in tough close games and on the road. This has been an amazing nonconference season, but let's get into February before we go too nuts. My hope is that when the season is over, there is a single digit number in the 'L' column. If that happens, there should be some major hardware heading to B-town in the form of year-end awards."

The injury bug was on a lot of people's minds, especially the uncertainty of Will Sheehey after he rolled his ankle by stepping on a rolling basketball in practice the day before the UMBC game, as they formulated their predictions.

"If the injury demon continues to haunt IU, I say 8-10," said Bill Madden. "If we can get a break there, I think 13-5 with a sweep of Purdue."

Alan Winterrowd, of Bluffton, Indiana, was taking a bit of a wait-and-see approach.

"12-6 sounds like a reasonable number, but I am still a bit worried about Zeller's stamina through a long season, so I will go with 11-7," Winterrowd wrote. "A lot of this will depend on the team's mental toughness. I think many of us expect the team to be tough, but how they react to these first tough games and any losses that come from them, will show us a lot."

ଚଠ ଓଷ

The day before Indiana opened Big Ten play at Michigan State, Spartans coach Tom Izzo said he couldn't remember many December games holding the importance of IU-Michigan State right out of the gate.

"Right now Indiana is playing as well as anybody, and it's gonna be a helluva test for us," Izzo said in a story in the *Detroit Free Press*.

"You have two teams that have an 11- and 12-game winning streak (going). They are 12-0. We are 11-2. This starts the Big Ten season. I don't think it gets any better than that."

One thing that was certain for Indiana right from the start in conference play is that all eyes were going to be on 6-11 freshman center Cody Zeller. Zeller had passed every test to this point but now came the rigors of the Big Ten schedule. Like his older brothers Luke and Tyler before him, Zeller had come to college with huge expectations. Luke played at Notre Dame and Tyler at North Carolina. All three were 6-11 or taller and all three were Indiana's Mr. Basketball going into college. But 12 games in, Cody had been the most impressive to date.

"I think Luke was more of a perimeter big man who spent more of his time facing the basket, and Tyler is very skilled with a great jump hook and runs the floor as well as any big man in college basketball," said ESPN college basketball analyst Jay Bilas.

"But I think Cody is the strongest at that age and has a more developed body. Of the three, at this point in his career, he's the best rebounder and the most complete player. He's a good passer and he's the type of guy that even at his age you can play through him."

Zeller was leading Indiana in scoring (15.1), rebounding (7.3) and shooting from the field (66.3 percent). He was averaging 27.7 minutes per game. He had a double-double in his college debut against Stony Brook and had a high game of 23 against Savannah State. And he had already been named the Big Ten's freshman of the week four times.

Putting up the numbers that Cody had against IU's nonconference foes was one thing, but now came an 18-game grind in the Big Ten. Everyone wanted to know just how Zeller would hold up against more rigorous competition.

"I think Cody will do very well in the Big Ten," Bilas said. "To those who question IU's schedule, I would just say there are a lot of guys who are playing that schedule that aren't doing anything against it. Cody is going to get better and better. We haven't seen his best, but what we've seen is pretty darn good."

Steve Zeller, Cody's dad, said he was looking forward to seeing how the entire IU team dealt with whatever adversity might be part of league play.

"This team has yet to experience its first loss, and the older players haven't had much experience with success, so it will be interesting how they handle things," he said. "It's going to be fun because the one person they have who has experienced that success is coach (Tom)

Crean. He's the one who will lead them, and I feel very comfortable with his leadership."

As it would turn out, Indiana would experience a little bit of everything in its Big Ten debut at Michigan State.

Fifteen minutes into the game, Michigan State had built an 18-point lead, and it looked like the game would turn into a rout. The Hoosiers, however, closed the half on a 13-2 run to get within seven at 36-29 at the break. The first nine minutes of the second half was all Indiana. In fact, when Watford hit a 3-pointer with 11:14 to play in the game, Indiana led 54-45, and they were beginning to get nervous in the Breslin Center.

But that's when the Spartans had a run for the ages.

In a span of just over six minutes, Michigan State went on a 20-0 run to take control at 65-54. Keith Appling scored on a drive to the basket and hit a free throw to start the run. Two free throws by Adreian Payne at the 5:13 mark ended it. Indiana would not get closer than eight points the rest of the way. Michigan State went on to win 80-65, handing the Hoosiers their first loss of the season.

And how did Zeller fare in his Big Ten opener? Not so good. Zeller was limited to a season-low four points and three rebounds.

"Cody saw what this game is like in the sense of this league when you go against some of the physical five-men that are in the league," Crean said. "But he'll make some adjustments. He made some in the second half. It didn't turn out to be a great game for him, but he is a quick learner."

Some of Zeller's problems were because of foul trouble. He picked up his second with 7:27 to play in the first half and didn't return until the second half. His third came on a reach foul in the lane at the 15:16 mark. He didn't get his fourth until 1:14 to play, but the fouls limited his ability to get in the flow of the game. "They were very physical, and (Cody) is not used to dealing with teams that have that kind of size," Crean said. "They did a very good job of three-quartering him inside of the post, and we didn't do as good of a job creating angles."

Two-thirds of Indiana's injured players made contributions. Jones, who suffered a hip flexor against UMBC, started and played 28 minutes. He scored 11 points on five-of-10 shooting from the field. Elston, sporting a plastic face mask to shield his surgically repaired broken nose, played eight minutes off the bench.

The third injured player, Sheehey, did not make the trip. Sheehey was expected to still be out another game or two.

Watford led Indiana with a season-high 26 points and 10 rebounds. He hit nine of 16 shots from the field including four of six 3-pointers.

He also eclipsed the 1,000-point barrier for his career at Indiana late in the second half.

But Indiana clearly didn't have any time to feel sorry for itself after suffering its first defeat. In three days, the No. 2-ranked team in the nation, Ohio State, was coming to Bloomington on New Year's Eve, and the Hoosiers had to figure out how they would be able to avoid an 0-2 start to conference play.

ಬಿ ೞ

In the days leading up to the visit from Ohio State, the Hoosiers were saying all the right things. They felt like they had something to prove after falling in the Big Ten opener to Michigan State.

"It was a rude awakening for us at Michigan State, and I think we've definitely gotten our edge back and we're hungry more than ever," Verdell Jones III said. "We want to prove to people that we're for real and that the nonconference wasn't just a fluke. We really want to get back after it. We really got after each other these past two days in the film room and on the court with the mistakes we made and the defensive errors we had."

While Jones was preaching all the right things, the reality was that it was going to be tough for Indiana to avoid that 0-2 start to Big Ten play. No. 2 Ohio State (13-1, 1-0 Big Ten) was coming off a dominating 87-54 conference-opening win against Northwestern and was considered one of the most talented teams in the nation.

The Buckeyes were led by sophomore Jared Sullinger, who was averaging nearly a double-double with 16.3 points and 9.6 rebounds per game. The defensive assignment on Sullinger would likely fall on Zeller, and after his less-than-stellar conference debut all eyes would once again be on Indiana's 6-11 freshman to see how he would handle his next big test.

The truth is that Zeller was limited to four minutes in the second half by foul trouble as he attempted to guard Sullinger. Zeller fouled out with 2:24 to play, having scored 14 points. Sullinger, who sat the final 11 minutes of the first half with two fouls, finished with 15 points and nine rebounds.

That was one of the games within the game.

But as Crean would point out later, this one wasn't about any one player making a big play on offense or defense. Instead, for the Hoosiers, it was a game of multiple contributions. Five IU players scored in double figures, led by Hulls with 17 and Oladipo with 15.

Oladipo made big plays on both ends of the floor in the final 36 seconds, and Watford sealed it with two free throws with 2.9 seconds to play, as the No. 13 Hoosiers knocked off No. 2 Ohio State 74-70 before a capacity crowd of 17,472 at Assembly Hall.

The victory allowed IU to complete the double beating of the No. 1 and No. 2 teams in the nation in the same season. In IU's storied basketball history, it had never been done before. IU became the ninth team in college basketball since the 1996-97 season to accomplish the feat.

"We never flinched when we were down throughout the game, especially the last five or six minutes," Crean said. "We made plays. We made the defensive plays especially. We had 58 deflections tonight. That is coming off (the Michigan State game), where we had 34 deflections, which was a season low. I was proud of the way our guys came home and made adjustments."

Christian Watford dunks against Ohio State on New Year's Eve when the Hoosiers beat the No. 2 Buckeyes at Assembly Hall.

In a game that included 10 lead changes in the second half, IU used its defense to create its offense on the play that put the Hoosiers ahead for good. Hulls stripped the ball from Ohio State's Aaron Craft 30 feet from the basket, Elston tipped it, and Jones came up with the steal. Jones threw the ball to Oladipo, who drove and put up a contested reverse layup with 36 seconds remaining to give IU a 71-70 lead.

"Our defense needs to be our key," Hulls said. "Our defense is what really got us the lead in the first place, and that's what kept us in the game. We were just staying active. Our defense is something we've been harping on all week, and pretty much all year."

Craft, who led the Buckeyes with 16 points but also in turnovers with six, committed another turnover on the next possession when he attempted to make a pass to Sam Thompson inside. After IU inbounded, Hulls was fouled and hit one of two free throws with 13.4 seconds to play.

Then came Oladipo's defensive gem. Ohio State got the ball in the frontcourt quickly, and senior guard William Buford launched a 3-pointer for the win from the right wing. But Oladipo went up high to contest the shot, which caromed off the back of the rim and into the hands of Watford.

"I knew (Buford) was going to get the ball, and I just wanted to contest it without fouling him," Oladipo said. "I just got there. We're lucky he missed."

Indiana was now 1-1 in Big Ten play, but there was still no time to take a deep breath. Next up was Michigan.

I caught up with former IU basketball player Pat Graham and had a conversation with him after the Ohio State game. We talked about how IU was getting the winning feeling back at Assembly Hall. Indiana was 13-1 going into the Michigan game, including a 10-0 record at Assembly Hall. The wins over Kentucky and Ohio State were obviously the highlights of that run. During the five seasons when Graham played at IU, the Hoosiers only lost six games at home. That was a stark contrast to Crean's first three seasons at Indiana when the Hoosiers went 25-25 at home.

Cody Zeller dunks against Michigan at Assembly Hall early in 2012.

Graham told me a story about being in Assembly Hall on New Year's Eve for the win over Ohio State, when his 10-year-old son turned to him in an electric atmosphere with about three minutes to play.

"Is this what you said Indiana basketball used to be like?" Cade Graham asked.

Graham just had to smile.

"You don't realize how much you take for granted all of that winning at Assembly Hall until it's not that easy anymore," said Graham, who helped the Hoosiers go 42-0 at home his final three seasons. "But when my son said that, I told him, 'Yep, this is exactly what it was like.' And you know what, I couldn't be happier for all of the current players who are experiencing that again."

Indiana's good fortunes at home would continue against Michigan, which came into the game ranked No. 16 in the nation.

But it wasn't without a little drama.

Watford hit one of two free throws with 2.9 seconds remaining, and Indiana survived a half-court heave by Zack Novak at the buzzer to win 73-71.

Watford scored a game-high 25 points on eight-of-11 shooting, including three of four on 3-pointers. Zeller had 18 for the Hoosiers, hitting eight of ten shots.

That's 16-of-21 shooting from IU's two big men.

IU looked like it was headed for an easy win. The Hoosiers led by as many 15 in the first half and were ahead 65-55 with 7 minutes, 20 seconds to play after Oladipo scored on a slam dunk from the left base line. On the previous possession, Watford had hit a 3-pointer from the left wing.

But Michigan used a 13-3 run to tie the game at 68-all with 3:06 to play.

Indiana had another good shooting game. The Hoosiers hit 55.2 percent of their shots in the first half, 55.0 in the second half, and 55.1 percent for the game. It was the fifth time in 15 games that Indiana had shot 55 percent or better from the field, but the first in Big Ten play.

At 2-1 in conference, the Hoosiers were now off to play Penn State where they would try to get that elusive true road victory in Big Ten play. Remember, the Hoosiers under Crean were now 1-28 in true road games in Big Ten play over four seasons. The lone win, however, had come at Penn State in 2010.

One of Indiana's biggest weapons in the 2011-12 season was the 3-point shot. And IU had plenty of guys who could make them: Hulls, Roth, Watford, Sheehey, Jones, and even Elston.

Penn State played a game of pick-your-poison against the Hoosiers. One game after Watford and Zeller had been a dominant force inside against Michigan, the Nittany Lions decided they were going to play some zone against IU and make the Hoosiers beat them from the outside.

And that's exactly what happened. Hulls knocked down seven 3's en route to a career-high 28 points. Hulls was seven of nine from 3-point range. But he got some help from Roth. Roth hit five of six 3-pointers and scored a season-high 22 points. All together, Indiana hit 16 from beyond the arc in its 88-82 victory over Penn State.

"It's huge to get Matt involved in the game, because he can open the floor up so much once he hits a couple of 3's, and he was able to hit a lot tonight," Hulls said. "I was just trying to penetrate and drive and find him for a 3 because he's always ready to shoot. He was huge for us tonight both offensively and defensively."

Earlier in the week, Watford and Zeller combined to score 43 points on 16-of-21 shooting against Michigan. Against Penn State, Hulls and Roth combined for 50 points on 12-of-17 from the field.

The 16 3-pointers were one away from Indiana's school and Big Ten record of 17 against both Illinois and the Nittany Lions. In this one, the Hoosiers made 16 in 24 attempts, 66.7 percent.

"I thought it was just a testament to how well we moved the ball," Roth said. "We had a lot of inside/outside stuff to get us started, and that's always the best shot to get when you're shooting 3's. You want to get it from the inside or from the middle.

"They ran a little zone on us, and I thought we attacked it well. In transition, we did a great job running the floor and getting lost in the game."

It was a big win for Indiana (15-1, 3-1 Big Ten) on many fronts. Getting the elusive road victory was big. But this was also a Penn State team that was coming off a 20-point home victory against Purdue a few days earlier. It was also big in a week during which five teams that were ranked ahead of the Hoosiers lost. Indiana was expected to move into the top 10 when the rankings came out that week. And finally, the victory was important because the Hoosiers continued to win without sixth man Will Sheehey, who had now missed five games in a row with a left ankle injury. Sheehey dressed for the Penn State game and participated in warm-ups but did not play. IU was 4-1 in his absence.

Indiana was now on a roll, and it looked to continue that run with an upcoming four-game stretch that included a home game with Minnesota, road games at Ohio State and Nebraska and a home game with Penn State. While the road test at Ohio State would be no easy task, the Hoosiers had to feel as if they had positioned themselves to do some damage.

The reality, however, was that the next three games, in particular would be one of Indiana's most difficult stretches of the season.

છ   ભ

When Indiana prepared to play Minnesota at Assembly Hall on January 12, everything appeared to be weighing in the Hoosiers favor. IU had cracked the top 10 with a No. 7 ranking a few days before. The Hoosiers were 3-1 in Big Ten play and had posted home victories over

Ohio State and Michigan, two of the better teams in the conference. Minnesota, on the other hand, had dropped its first four conference games, and the Golden Gophers were reeling. Add to that the fact that Indiana was 11-0 at Assembly Hall, and it seemed as if the stars were aligned in IU's favor.

None of it mattered. Indiana played without emotion, and Minnesota looked like the team that should have been ranked. The Golden Gophers had 16 offensive rebounds, including 12 in the second half. They never trailed in the second half and stunned IU, 77-74.

There were two major keys in this one: IU's inability to knock down shots and Minnesota's offensive rebounding.

One game after lighting it up from 3-point range against Penn State, IU, the nation's best 3-point shooting team, made four of 18 shots against Minnesota. That's 22 percent. That's not going to get it done.

"We just didn't have our edge tonight," Hulls said. "We didn't get stops when we needed to, and we gave up too many good looks. And you've got to come up with the big rebounds at the end of the game, and we just didn't do that."

Indiana somehow managed a 35-33 rebounding edge, but the Golden Gophers picked up one big rebound after another on the offensive glass.

"It was deflating to give up that many offensive rebounds," said Zeller, who had 23 points and eight rebounds. "We just have to do the little things better. That one was on us."

As bad as Indiana played, the Hoosiers trimmed a nine-point deficit with 1:11 to play to just one point with 17.3 seconds remaining. And trailing by three at the end, Christian Watford had a 3-point opportunity from the right wing but missed with seven seconds to play.

The only positive in the game was that Will Sheehey played in his first game since December 19. He scored 12 points in 15 minutes off the bench.

Crean wasn't happy in his postgame press conference.

"This game starts with our lack of awareness defensively," Crean said. "Communication, weak side, ball side, challenging shots, block outs, the awareness never got where it needed to be until the end of the game. What I said to this team before the game, what I said to them all week, it's a step that they have to take.

"They're shooting the ball well and getting a lot of attention for winning and things like that, but teams that take the next step totally get that defense is what comes first in every situation. Defense creates the offense, defense creates more opportunities, defense creates the fast break, you name it. The best teams gain confidence from their defense, not the other way around."

Crean said winning is easy when you're making shots. But it's the teams that figure out how to win when the shots aren't falling that are the most successful.

"The easiest thing in the world to do is be sky high when you're making shots," Crean said. "The hardest thing to do is to understand how committed you have to be to the game of defense and rebounding when you're not. Tonight was one of those nights where we didn't make as many shots, and we're going to watch the film and see that the ball didn't move as well and that our movement, our screening, some of those things weren't nearly as good.

"Again, that's how I see it. We played hard, but we didn't play as smart as we needed to. We were prepared, our guys had really good practices, but as I look at the game, now we weren't playing on edge the way that we have. Those might sound like buzz words, but those were real."

Three days later, Ohio State punched the Hoosiers in the mouth. The Buckeyes came out hot, played suffocating defense, and held Indiana to 14 first-half points.

The result was an 80-63 victory.

Ohio State led by 21 at the half and never looked back.

"They got up into us," Crean said. "It sounds simple, but it's not. We weren't as strong as we need to be with the ball. Feeding the post is all about angles. We didn't get to (the right) spots, and when it became hard to make cuts, we let them be the aggressor instead of just plowing through."

In the first half, Indiana had twice as many turnovers (12) as it did made shots (6). Indiana was six of 22 from the field.

Suddenly, IU was on its first two-game losing streak of the season and at 3-3 was now tied for sixth in the Big Ten standings.

"Like when we were winning, we've just got to take it one game at a time," Hulls said. "It's been a rough week for us, but we had a good eight weeks. We have to take that into account from the standpoint of getting back to the basics and what got us the victories."

The good news for Indiana was that the next game was at Big Ten newcomer Nebraska. When you looked at the schedule before the season began, the two road games that looked most likely for Indiana to be able to win were Penn State and Nebraska.

Penn State was already in the books, and now IU would travel to Lincoln with a definite sense of urgency. The Hoosiers hoped that a win over the Cornhuskers might help them start to turn things back around.

80 CB

Instead, the nightmare continued at Nebraska.

When IU had played Minnesota and Nebraska this season, those teams were a combined 1-9 coming into the games. The Cornhuskers were 1-5 in Big Ten play coming in and had been manhandled by just about everybody. And Indiana did much of the same in this one and had an 11-point lead with seven minutes to play.

But then the bottom dropped out.

It was a particularly tough final few minutes for Hulls.

Two free throws by Brian Jorge Diaz with 11 seconds to play gave the Cornhuskers their first lead since the 14-minute mark of the first half at 70-69.

Hulls hurried the ball into the frontcourt, turned the corner, and had a drive to the basket. When the defense shifted over, Hulls was forced to put up an off-balance shot in the lane, and he missed. The rebound went to the floor and rolled toward the IU bench; Hulls picked it up and hoisted a desperation shot at the buzzer that missed the mark.

The last possession was tough for Hulls.

The one before it, however, was even worse.

Hulls, who came in shooting 89 percent from the free-throw line for the season and 88 percent for his career, had a one-and-one free throw opportunity with 23.8 seconds to play and his team clinging to a 69-68 lead. Hulls had hit his first four free throws.

This one bounced hard off the right side of the rim and was rebounded by Nebraska.

"He's a human being, and nobody is more disappointed than he is," Crean said. "But we wouldn't trade having him at the line again. You all know that he has been phenomenal at the line. He just missed a free throw. I hope he gets that same opportunity here again in the near future."

Crean said the fact that Nebraska was able to score 16 points off of IU's 15 turnovers was a pivotal statistic. Ten of those turnovers came in the second half.

"We've got to take care of the ball better," Crean said.

"I think we're going to go back and look at the film, and we're going to look at the turnovers in the second half and just see how excruciatingly painful those were for us. They turned into easy baskets for Nebraska." All of a sudden Indiana was 15-4 overall and 3-4 in conference, with a couple of ugly losses on itsNCAA résumé.

IU could only hope a home game with Penn State could turn its fortunes back in the right direction.

Chapter 22

Indiana's midseason skid had reached three games and the Hoosiers had dropped to 3-4 in Big Ten play before they played host to Penn State on January 22. As it would turn out, IU's woeful play would extend for another half before it got better.

In the first half against the Nittany Lions, Indiana couldn't find its offensive rhythm. It trailed by as many as five points, shot 41 percent from the field, and was out-rebounded by six. Penn State, however, was barely able to capitalize and led by only two points at the break, 29-27.

In the second half, Indiana looked a lot more like the team that had opened the season 15-1 with wins over No. 1 Kentucky and No. 2 Ohio State. The Hoosiers resembled much more the team that just a few weeks before had cracked the top 10 in the nation.

Indiana took charge of the game quickly in the second half. The first two offensive possessions would set the tone. On the first, Verdell Jones III made a hard drive to the basket and didn't hit the shot, but Cody Zeller followed it in. On the ensuing defensive trip, Hulls made a steal from Jon Graham and drove as though he was going to take a contested layup. At the last moment, while in the air, Hulls passed to Jones, who scored to make it 31-29.

"We knew coming out of the locker room that we needed to have a good start in the second half," Hulls said. "We knew we had to play hard and physical, and there were just things we had to get corrected. I thought we did that with our defense and turning up our intensity."

A 16-4 run in the first 10 minutes of the half put the Hoosiers in control. And with Victor Oladipo playing lockdown defense on high-scoring guard Tim Frazier and Hulls scoring all 14 of his points in the second half, Indiana ran away for a 73-54 victory over Penn State.

It was the first win in two weeks for Indiana, which had dropped games to Minnesota, Ohio State and Nebraska. The Hoosiers' previous victory had also been against the Nittany Lions. The season sweep over Penn State was the first in Coach Crean's four years at IU.

It was a tough day for Penn State in more ways than one. A few hours before tipoff, the Nittany Lions learned that legendary Penn State football coach Joe Paterno had died of lung cancer in a State

College, Pennsylvania hospital. Penn State coaches wore black ribbons to honor Paterno, and there was a moment of silence before tipoff.

As for the game, IU shot 65.2 percent in the second half, the fourth time this season that the Hoosiers had shot better than 60 percent in a half. IU shot 53.3 percent for the game.

"I thought we played with a toughness and energy and for the most part played with the intelligence that you have to have," Crean said. "I think to hold a team to the shooting percentage that we did, especially in the second half, says a lot about our guys' resolve in the defensive end. And we were probably a little more anal than ever about closing a game out—I know I was—and making sure we didn't take a lot of chances at the end."

Jordan Hulls and Matt Roth pose for a photo with Tom Crean moments after the pair combined to hit 12 3-pointers in a road victory at Penn State in 2012.

After evening their Big Ten record at 4-4, the Hoosiers went back on the road to a hostile environment at the Kohl Center against Wisconsin. It would be the only meeting between the two teams in the 2012 conference season.

IU hadn't won at the Kohl Center since 1998, and this trip wouldn't be any different. Wisconsin, ranked No. 25, scored the final six points of the game and hung on for a 57-50 victory over an Indiana team that had dropped to No. 16 with its recent play.

But Indiana had some encouraging signs on the road in this one. IU led by two at halftime and by five points in the second half. The Hoosiers led 46-45 at the 5:38 mark after Watford knocked down a 3-pointer from the left wing in transition.

Wisconsin quickly regained the lead and didn't give it back.

IU cut its deficit to 51-50 with 2:08 remaining, following Watford's steal and pull-up jump shot. But then the Hoosiers stopped rebounding.

Ben Brust misfired on a 3-pointer with 1:40 to play but got his own rebound. Brust again missed a 3, but Ryan Evans rebounded for the

Badgers. Evans was fouled and made both free throws to make it 53-50 with 1:04 to play.

Indiana had one more chance, but when Jordan Taylor missed a long 3-pointer from the top, the Badgers came up with another offensive rebound. Mike Bruesewitz then made two free throws to make it 55-50.

The final rebounding totals were even at 24 and Wisconsin had only a 7-6 edge on offensive boards, but the timing of those boards was key.

Zeller was limited to seven points and three rebounds in 19 foul-plagued minutes. He was an uncharacteristic 2-of-7 from the field.

So as the Hoosiers left Madison that night, having lost in the Kohl Center for the 11th time in a row, IU was once again struggling to find a way to stay in the Big Ten's upper division.

For a team that had lost four of its last five games, and in the past six games only had two wins over Penn State to show for its troubles, it was time to put a string of victories together to get in a better position for postseason play.

Most felt that with the victories it had posted to this point in the season, Indiana would be an NCAA Tournament team just as long as it could find a way to either be at .500 or slightly above for the season.

To do so, the Hoosiers needed to find their winning ways again.

ᴆᴐ   ᴄᴈ

The next five games would turn out to be a stretch where Indiana was able to regain its momentum.

It started on Sunday, January 29 when the Hoosiers played host to Iowa at Assembly Hall.

If these were the only numbers you knew about this Indiana-Iowa game, what would you have thought the outcome would have been? The Hawkeyes hit 63 percent of their shots for the game including an incredible 79.2 percent in the second half. In those final 20 minutes, Iowa made 19 of 24 shots. Hearing those numbers, you would have at least thought it was a close game and likely believed that Iowa had run away with a victory.

The truth was anything but that.

First of all, Indiana scored 54 points in the first half. Against Wisconsin three days earlier, the Hoosiers had scored 50 for the game.

Next, Indiana was unstoppable inside. The Hoosiers scored 58 points in the paint. That was 20 more than their previous season high of 38 against Ohio State on New Year's Eve.

Zeller had the big numbers with a career-high 26 points on 11-of-12 shooting from the field. Eight of those baskets were dunks. He also had four assists and three steals, including one where he stole the ball at half court and dunked it at the other end.

"I had a pretty easy job of just catching it and dunking it," Zeller said. "Our guards did a really good job of finding me in the alley a couple of times. Verdell (Jones III) did a really nice job of passing tonight. I thought it was a good team effort."

The result was actually an Indiana rout. The No. 16 Hoosiers never let off the gas and rolled to a 103-89 victory over Iowa at Assembly hall.

But back to the bottom line. IU had eight more points in the paint Sunday than it did for the game Thursday against Wisconsin.

"The bottom line is that you have to take what the defensive is giving you," Crean said, "and they were giving us the opportunity to get the ball inside, get the ball dropped off, get it kicked out, and our guys did a really good job of recognition."

Iowa coach Fran McCaffery was more than a little impressed with Zeller.

"He is a terrific freshman," McCaffery said. "He is the best freshman center I have seen. He can score. He can rebound. He can pass. You don't see many 7-footers who have as good of a feel for the game as Cody has. He doesn't go looking for stats. He knows that he is going to get his stats every night. He just does whatever the team needs him to do."

The next game was a nightmare at Michigan, but luckily for the Hoosiers they would rebound from that effort and go on to put together a little streak over the following three games.

But the first day of February at Crisler against the Wolverines was bad news from the start. Michigan scored the first 13 points of the game, led by as many as 20 in the first half, and held on for a 68-56 victory at Crisler Center. As poorly as Indiana played early, the Hoosiers did get the lead down to two at 52-50 with 3:20 remaining, but Michigan was able to pull away at that point.

Crean was livid after the game. He went as far as to say his starting lineup of Hulls, Jones, Sheehey, Watford and Zeller was a joke.

"At the start of the game, we allowed a very good team to play like a great team," Crean said. "And our players came out playing like they had seen a ghost."

It was the second game in a row where Crean had used that lineup. The only difference between this lineup and the one that started the first 21 games was Sheehey in place of Oladipo.

"Our starting lineup was a joke," Crean said. "That's why we didn't play that lineup much longer after the initial start of the game. We've just got to continue to get better. I'm looking for guys in February that are playing with a warrior spirit. You just have to have it. It's the same guys that started out great the other day against Iowa. They're human beings. Young ones. I'm not going to make an excuse for them. It just wasn't good enough."

Crean said you simply cannot come out and play the way Indiana did and expect to be successful.

"You can't come out and not have a physical presence right off the bat. You can't come out and give that much space to a team that is as good as Michigan," Crean said.

Crean didn't single out anyone but said it was obvious why that group did not see much time on the floor together the rest of the game. Sheehey, who didn't score and had three turnovers in 10 minutes, played only two minutes in the second half.

Now 5-6 and one game under .500 again in Big Ten play, Indiana's next game may very well have been its turning point for the season.

If Indiana fell on the road against rival Purdue at Mackey Arena, the Hoosiers would slip to two games under .500 in conference play and the chances of finishing .500 or better in the conference might have been slipping away.

A win at Purdue, however, would have been Indiana's first true conference road win under Tom Crean in any building other than the Bryce Jordan Center in State College, Pennsylvania. To call this game big would have been a complete understatement. It wasn't a must win because it was on the road against your rival, but it was pretty close. As it turned out, there would be big road victories for Indiana during the season, but none was bigger than winning at Mackey Arena.

Crean talked late that Saturday night about the watershed moments that led to the No. 20 Hoosiers' impressive 78-61 victory.

There was a huge block by Sheehey in the closing minutes, as the Boilermakers tried to cut IU's lead to two. There was also a clutch 3-pointer from the left corner in front of the Indiana bench by freshman guard Remy Abell that extended the lead to nine.

Then there was Oladipo.

Forced to handle the ball more than at any time in his IU career because of a shoulder injury to Jones the game before at Michigan, Oladipo took on the challenge and excelled. The sophomore guard scored a Big Ten season-high 23 points and pulled down eight rebounds.

There were a couple of areas of Oladipo's performance that were particularly remarkable. Coming into the game, he had made 11 of 19 free throws in conference play, 57.9 percent. Against Purdue, he hit 10 of 12 from the line. He also made his only 3-pointer. Coming in, he was three of 22 in Big Ten play from beyond the arc.

"I just felt like I needed to come and attack tonight," Oladipo said. "I felt like I could drive it against their big men, and I felt I needed to do that for us to be successful."

Indiana, which improved to 18-6 overall and 6-6 in the Big Ten, had a season-high 53 rebounds, though no player had more than eight. The Hoosiers had a 53-35 edge on the boards.

The first half proved that IU had clearly caught Purdue on an off shooting night. The Boilers were eight of 40 from the field in the first 20 minutes, including missing all 11 of their 3-point attempts.

But IU wasn't much better. The Hoosiers were 11 of 34 (32.4 percent). At one point midway through the half, IU was two of 17 and Purdue three of 17 from the field.

Purdue coach Matt Painter actually said that the way the Boilermakers played most of the game, it would have been a shame in many ways if his team had found a way to come back and beat IU.

"I thought (Indiana), in general, was quicker to the basketball and, to me, it looked like it meant more to them," Painter said. "Right from the start, looking at guys' facial expressions and reading body language, I thought they were more engaged.

"If we could have made that play there at the end when we were down four and they had wound up losing, it would have been a shame. Because they deserved to win the game. They were tougher than us, they were quicker than us, and, like I said, they definitely deserved to win."

Indiana was clinging to a 65-61 lead with less than three minutes to play when Purdue senior guard Lewis Jackson came up with a steal at midcourt and drove to the other end with a chance to cut the lead to two. But Sheehey caught up on the play and made a big block over Jackson's right shoulder, and Watford retrieved it in the corner.

Watford was fouled and hit both free throws to make it 67-61. In fact, that keyed a 13-0 game-closing run for IU to end the game and make it look much more lopsided than it actually was.

The back-breaker was supplied by Abell, who hit a 3-pointer from the left corner with 1:27 to play to put IU on top 70-61. Abell had a career-high 13 points in 19 minutes off the bench.

Zeller had 16 points and eight rebounds for IU.

But the point in this game that could not be emphasized enough was the difference between IU leaving Mackey Arena with a 6-6 Big Ten record or what would have been a 5-7 mark had the Hoosiers lost. A 6-6 record, with a win over your rival on the road, was as good as it could get at that point for the Hoosiers.

The next two games against Illinois and Northwestern would mark the only time IU would play those teams in the Big Ten in 2012. Both games were at home and both were must win situations.

Indiana didn't disappoint on either count.

Against Illinois, and facing 7-1 center Meyers Leonard, Zeller simply took over in the second half. The 6-11 freshman scored 14 of his game-high 22 points in the second half and consistently took the game to Leonard as No. 23 Indiana ran away from the Illini to post an 84-71 victory before 17,389 at Assembly Hall.

Watford, who had made three of his past 14 shots and didn't make a field goal the game before at Purdue, snapped out of his mini-slump. Watford had 18 points on six-of-11 shooting and hit a big 3-pointer from the right wing with 5:48 to play that put the Hoosiers on top 73-61.

IU would not trail by less than 10 points the rest of the game.

Oladipo, who had a career-high 23 points at Purdue, bounced back with 18 against the Illini. For the second game in a row, Oladipo hit 10 of 12 from the line. In the previous 11 games, Oladipo had attempted a total of 19 free throws but appears to enjoy handling the ball more and driving.

As good as Watford and Oladipo played for IU on Thursday, Zeller stole the show, especially in the second half.

He hit five of eight shots from the field, 12 of 14 from the foul line and was consistently on the attack inside. He also made it difficult for Leonard to get the ball. Leonard, after scoring 15 points in the first half, was limited to two points and just two shots in the second half.

"I thought Cody did a great job, especially in the second half," said Hulls, who had 15 points and seven assists. "He didn't let (Leonard) post deep. When we fed the ball to Cody in the post, he was really patient like he always is and he was trying to find people. If not, he attacked the basket and got them in foul trouble. He was definitely huge for us."

Indianapolis Star columnist Bob Kravitz wrote in his column the next day that, after watching IU beat Illinois, there was no question in his mind that the Hoosiers would eventually be NCAA Tournament bound for the first time since 2008.

Here's what he wrote the next day:

Not that an NCAA Tournament berth was ever a question for Indiana University's restored basketball program, but ... now, there's NO question.

The only issue is where the Hoosiers will be seeded.

On a night IU faced a desperate Illinois team, a talented group that has gone into its annual swoon of underachievement, the Hoosiers punched the Illini in the teeth, winning 84-71.

Currently, ESPN bracketologist Joe Lunardi has the Hoosiers as a No. 4 seed. But if they keep playing the way they've played in victories at Purdue and Thursday night against Illinois, that number could improve.

There's never a soft spot in the Big Ten schedule; just ask Illinois, which lost at home recently to Northwestern. But now the calendar gets favorable as the Hoosiers head toward March.

The Hoosiers have games against Northwestern, at Iowa, home against North Carolina Central, at Minnesota, then finish at home against Michigan State and Purdue. They should be favored in most of those games, if not all of them.

Keep in mind, with the new 12-team Big Ten, the top four teams get first-round byes in the Big Ten Tournament. IU is currently fifth, 1½ games behind Wisconsin (plus Wisconsin holds the head-to-head tiebreaker). But the Badgers still must travel to Michigan State and Ohio State.

This is where Coach Tom Crean wanted his team to be, toughened up by a 2-5 midseason slump, a better team, he said, than the one that started the year 12-0.

"I'm seeing a lot of individual improvement, and the biggest improvement as a team is we've gotten mentally tougher," Crean said. "We went through that little drought where we kind of forgot that edge you've got to have after we beat Ohio State. Any time you have success like that, it's easy to fall off, but I think we got it back.

"Guys are adding things to their games. We're better in the post, especially post defense. Our awareness is improving. Our rebounding is much better. We're continuing to move the ball.

"... Our guys have come through this a little bit more hardened."

This was a good, solid, smart, tough physical victory. The Hoosiers got the Illini in deep foul trouble early in the second half, chased Illini big man Meyers Leonard early, and simply kept attacking.

The difference-maker?

It was Jordan Hulls, who had a special night both as a scorer and as a facilitator, finishing with 15 points, seven assists and four rebounds (and just two turnovers).

They also had balance: Cody Zeller with 22 points, Christian Watford and Victor Oladipo each with 18.

This was still a game, tied at 46, a dangerous-looking game, when Hulls knocked down a 3. The next possession, he pushed the ball upcourt to Zeller, who finished off a 3-point play. From that point on, the Hoosiers never looked back, outscoring Illinois 38-25. In the process, they got Illinois in foul trouble and began to fluster Leonard.

"We know Leonard has been getting in foul trouble during the Big Ten (season), so we just kept attacking," Zeller said.

"We got in the bonus early, so we knew if we kept attacking, we'd get the one-and-one or two shots."

It's scary to think where Zeller will be a year from now, two years from now. We all knew he could play at this level, but his toughness has been on display virtually every night in the most physically taxing league in the nation.

"I think he relishes (the physicality), I really do," Crean said. "I think it gets him going. He's a tough young man — mentally, physically, and he's getting stronger all the time. I think the more you come at him, the better it is. If you want to be physical, he's going to respond.

"I'm sure a lot of it has to do with the way he was raised, playing against his older brothers. The only thing about Cody that's soft is he's too soft spoken on the court sometimes."

Free throws?

They had a bunch.

And they made a bunch.

The Hoosiers made 16 of 16 in the first half, earning a two-point lead at the half despite Illinois' 54-percent shooting. They finished 35 of 42, missing some late free throws after the outcome was decided.

They are one year ahead of schedule now. After winning six, 10 and 12 games, and inspiring some dim-witted questions about Crean's coaching ability, the Hoosiers are now just one victory short of the magical 20.

It's been fun to watch them grow. Hulls, from a skittish freshman who wouldn't shoot the ball if you bribed him with a hundred-dollar bill. Watford, who has developed an NBA game to go with those NBA physical skills. Victor Oladipo, who was a bundle of misguided athleticism before blooming this year.

The knock on Crean had been that his players hadn't developed within the program, certainly not the way Purdue's Matt Painter got major improvement from the likes of E'Twaun Moore, JaJuan Johnson and Rob Hummel.

That can't be uttered any longer.

This is a good college basketball team. And after a couple of slip-ups, one that appears to be getting better.

Next, IU won its third game in a row with a 71-66 win at home against Northwestern.

Here's how *Louisville Courier-Journal* columnist Rick Bozich summed it up in his column on the game the next day as the Hoosiers had reached the 20-win plateau.

BLOOMINGTON, Ind. - Don't say this is the 20-victory season that you expected from Tom Crean's Indiana University basketball team, because it isn't.

Not if you're the editor of a preseason magazine that picked the Hoosiers to finish 10th (Lindy's) or 11th (Basketball Times) in the Big Ten.

You can only imagine what opposing recruiters said. It wasn't that they expected the Hoosiers to follow their wins over Kentucky, Notre Dame, Ohio State, Michigan and Purdue by defeating Northwestern, 71-66, in Assembly Hall Wednesday to make it 20 wins in 26 games.

Some coaches might shrug at 20 wins and an 8-6 Big Ten record. Not Crean.

Not after all the lovely things he heard while knocking on the doors of the recruits he's collected since arriving to lift the Hoosiers off the NCAA probation discard pile in April 2008.

"The fact that we've had to live through the 20-plus losses the last couple of years, and we owned them, there's no doubt about that,"

Crean said. "It was brought up many, many times. We've read about it. We've heard about it.

"We've heard about it from recruits that heard about it from other recruiters. That's just the way that it was.

"To get that 20th win, for this team ... it's a good benchmark for us."

Actually, it's more than that. It's a sign that IU is bound for the NCAA Tournament for the first time in four seasons – and doing it in a season when the wise guys were convinced the NIT was IU's ceiling.

Skeptics howled that they couldn't remember a big man Crean had ever coached. Now they have to howl about something else, because his big man, Cody Zeller, is one of the nation's best centers, regardless of class.

Odds are that Zeller took 23 giant steps toward being named the Big Ten Freshman of the Week for the seventh time by pinning 23 points, seven rebounds, three assists and a steal on Northwestern.

What they'll probably say about Crean now is that anybody could win with Zeller, just as they tried to say anybody could win with Dwyane Wade after Crean found, developed, and won with him at Marquette.

Except this isn't just a Cody Zeller IU team. It's a team with numerous functioning parts, a team that showed Northwestern that it can win when Jordan Hulls doesn't score and the Hoosiers make two of 13 3-point shots.

Check the recruiting files. Verdell Jones was a marginal prospect still unsigned when Crean took the IU job. Two years later, Victor Oladipo was ranked in the fringe of the Top 100, even though he performed at DeMatha High School in Hyattsville, Maryland, one of the nation's most prominent programs.

Crean has molded Oladipo into the Big Ten's most fearless defender, a guy who can defend point guards, wings or centers. When Crean switched Oladipo to John Shurna with about 12 minutes to play, the Northwestern forward had 26 points.

Shurna finished with 29 – and a sense of what brand of mouthwash Oladipo used.

Don't forget Jones. IU fans have made a career banging on the senior, even though he has scored more than 1,300 points. After

Jones left the Michigan game with a shoulder injury Feb.1, the chatter began that Indiana was better with its new lineup.

Crean doesn't listen to the chatter. Never has. Never will.

Guess who scored his only six points in the final 4:04 and broke the tie at 63?

Verdell Jones III.

"This game fit the bill of 20 different wins and 20 different ways for us," Crean said.

Just as nobody predicted it would.

Chapter 23

Indiana was hitting the stretch run of the regular season schedule with four Big Ten games remaining and one nonconference game against North Carolina Central.

The Hoosiers had won three games in a row and were about to face an Iowa team on the road that the Hoosiers had scored more than 100 points against just three weeks earlier.

With 20 wins and victories over Kentucky, Ohio State and Michigan on its résumé, IU looked like a team that was clearly headed to the NCAA Tournament, but again, I think it continued to be one of those things where people really didn't want to express that out loud. Get through the last five games, put the finishing touches on the résumé, and we'll talk about the NCAA Tournament when the time comes. But with that ultimate goal within reach, IU fans seemed just happy to remain cautiously optimistic coming down the stretch.

Things didn't start out well, though, thanks to a performance by Iowa senior guard Matt Gatens when the Hoosiers played the Hawkeyes at Carver-Hawkeye Arena on February 19.

Gatens poured in a career-high 30 points against Indiana, including 22 in the second half, as Iowa took control early and upset the No. 18 Hoosiers 78-66.

It was a big win for Iowa, as it got the Hawkeyes to one game over .500 overall at 14-13 and 6-8 in the Big Ten. But the loss snapped IU's three-game win streak and moved IU's conference record to 8-7.

The magic number for IU fans to feel safe about the NCAA Tournament was nine Big Ten wins. That would mean the worst IU could finish would be 9-9 in Big Ten play. After the loss to Iowa, the Hoosiers were still one game away from the nine-win mark with three to play.

Only one of those would be on the road, and that would be the following Sunday at Minnesota. IU was now 2-6 in Big Ten road games. The other two games were against Purdue and Michigan State, but at least those were at Assembly Hall.

At Iowa, IU coach Tom Crean wasn't happy with the way his team attacked, and even less pleased with the way IU let Gatens take control of the game. Crean said the Hoosiers had their best two defenders—Victor Oladipo and Will Sheehey—on the Iowa senior, but Gatens still created enough space to get the shots he made.

"We want to be there on the catch, there was no doubt about that," Crean said in the postgame press conference. "The 3's late in the second half, it wasn't that we didn't know he was going to catch it. He was just in a great flow, a great rhythm. He's not only one of the better shooters and guards in this league; he's one of the better ones in the country. That's a four-year guy that has been doing it at a high level."

Cody Zeller had 15 points and a career-high 13 rebounds for his third double-double. But he also struggled around the basket, hitting just five of 12 shots. It was only the fourth time in 27 games that Zeller had shot less than 50 percent from the field. The first time the teams met, Zeller had a career-high 26 points and made 11 of 12 shots from the field, including eight dunks.

After the Iowa game, IU came home to play a midweek non-conference game against North Carolina Central. Even though it wasn't much of a game, it would be one that IU's players would reference after they got to the NCAA Tournament because they had to prepare quickly for an unknown opponent.

Some people like playing nonconference games in the conference season, others think it takes away from the flow of the year.

Crean didn't feel as if he had a choice.

When the Big Ten released its schedule in the summer, IU would have had a stretch late in the conference season where it would play just four games in a 22-day stretch. In the previous 28 days, IU would have played nine games. And so Crean asked North Carolina Central if it would give up a previously scheduled December 7 date with IU and move the game to late February. Both sides reached an agreement and the game was set for February 22. Had IU not done it, it would have waited a full week from a bad game at Iowa before it played at Minnesota the following Sunday.

"We didn't want to be in a situation where we would be playing just three games in three weeks," Crean said on his weekly radio show. "You're not practicing that long this time of year, anyway. But there's a physical part to it, there's an execution part and a fundamental part. But there's also a mental part, and the mental one is the one you're most concerned about this time of year."

North Carolina Central came into the game on a two-game win streak and winners of five of the last six, but the game itself wasn't much. Indiana won by 19, 75-56, and picked up its 21st victory of the season.

But what turned out to be entertaining for the Indiana fans who watched IU improve to 16-1 at Assembly Hall was an appearance from a guest manager.

San Francisco 49ers head coach Jim Harbaugh, Crean's brother-in-law, was in town for the NFL Scouting Combine. Not only did he make the short drive from Indy to Bloomington for the game, but he became a participant.

He sat at the end of the bench and at timeouts would bring the chairs on and off the floor for the players to sit.

"I've never sat on the bench before, so I felt like I should be contributing in some way," Harbaugh said.

At halftime, I cornered Harbaugh and asked him about his chair duty.

"I've been practicing," he said with a grin. "And I'm getting better. It's taking me some time, but I'm getting better."

Crean said Harbaugh and 49ers general manager Trent Baalke spoke to the IU team before and after the game. As for Harbaugh's managerial duties, that was all on his own.

"I think it goes to show why he's a very successful leader as a player and certainly now as a coach," Crean said, "because there's no job above him and there's no job beneath him, and it's all about winning."

As for the game, it was good for Indiana to get its performance against Iowa out of its system.

Crean pointed out the play of his two sophomores — Victor Oladipo and Will Sheehey — as being dominant on both ends. Oladipo consistently drove to the basket and got good looks, and Sheehey played one of his best games since suffering the ankle injury in late December.

Oladipo had 16 points and Sheehey, who was in the starting lineup, had 12. The duo combined to hit 11 of 17 shots from the field and played ball-hawking defense. Oladipo had a straight-down block against Jeremy Ingram that led to a layup by Sheehey at the other end.

It was the third year in a row that IU and North Carolina Central had played. IU won the other two games by 23 and 16 points, but Eagles coach LeVelle Moton said this Indiana team was clearly much better than the previous two.

"That's a great basketball team," Moton said. "The key is that everyone got better, and then there's the addition of Zeller. That kid is big. I didn't know he was that tall. Normally in basketball they give you two or three inches (in the program), but he's big.

"The big difference (with Indiana) is they don't have to work as hard anymore to get a shot."

Zeller had 17 points and seven rebounds.

Watford's latest mini-slump continued. After scoring one point and missing all five of his shots at Iowa, Watford missed all eight of his attempts against North Carolina Central and had two points from the line.

But Crean still found a silver lining with his junior forward. He was pleased with Watford's effort on defense.

"I thought Christian really impacted the game in the second half with the way he defended," Crean said.

    ♊   ♋

Next up was a trip to The Barn (Williams Arena) in Minneapolis to play Minnesota.

Indiana had struggled at Minnesota for years. Going into this one, IU hadn't won there since 2008 and was 4-11 against the Golden Gophers in the last 15 road meetings. Add the fact that Minnesota had already beaten IU once this season, handing the Hoosiers their only loss at home, and everyone knew it was going to be a particularly tough place to get a win.

Still, it was an opportunity on a variety of fronts.

Again, conventional wisdom was that IU was going to make the NCAA Tournament. Even with a total collapse at this point, which would mean losing to Minnesota, Purdue and Michigan State to end the regular season and then losing in the first game of the Big Ten Tournament, IU would be 21-11. The Hoosiers had a ratings percentage index of No. 18 in the nation, and all the bracketologists still had IU comfortably in the tournament field.

But still, lose the last three games of the Big Ten and any NCAA Tournament momentum would have a completely different feel.

IU entered the Minnesota game tied for fifth in the conference with Purdue at 8-7. And because Iowa had upset Wisconsin a few days earlier, a chance at earning one of four first-round byes in the Big Ten Tournament was still a possibility. The Badgers were just one game ahead of IU and Purdue at 9-6 in Big Ten play, but Wisconsin did hold any tie-breaker against IU because the Badgers had won the only meeting of the season between the schools.

The Minnesota game was big not only because of what it would mean to win but how much it would hurt to lose. Iowa was now 7-8 in the Big Ten and trying to increase its Big Ten Tournament seeding.

And with IU wrapping up the conference season with first-place Michigan State followed by Purdue, a lot of things could still happen in terms of movement in the Big Ten standings.

That was the backdrop as Indiana headed for a date with the Gophers in The Barn.

It seems like every season I've covered Indiana, which is 15 and counting as I write this book, there are always a couple of games that turn out completely different than you would have expected.

And not always, but they seem to balance each other out during the season. Indiana had clearly had a couple of those games to this point in the 2011-12 season.

The first Ohio State game, for example, could probably fall in that category. Even though it was a home game for the Hoosiers, Ohio State still came in as the odds-on favorite to win the conference, not to mention the Buckeyes were ranked No. 2 in the nation at that point.

But IU had definitely had a couple of games on the other side of the ledger, too. The loss at home to Minnesota was clearly unexpected, as the Gophers were winless in the conference before they stunned IU 77-74. And the debacle in Lincoln, Nebraska where Indiana squandered a late lead and lost to the lowly Cornhuskers, was the biggest of games like that on the list.

IU would quickly add another one—though this time it was for the opposite reasons.

Indiana dominated Minnesota throughout the game, particularly on defense, and left The Barn with a convincing 69-50 victory. The No. 23 Hoosiers limited Minnesota to 31-percent shooting from the field.

Conference road wins hadn't come easy for Indiana in a long time. And it had been eight years since Indiana had beaten a team on the road by 19 points or more. The last time IU had held a Big Ten opponent to 50 points or less on the road was in 2002 against Northwestern.

Zeller never got untracked and managed just seven points, but IU got one of its most balanced scoring efforts of the season. Watford, Oladipo and Hulls all had 12 points, and Jones chipped in 11 off the bench. When these teams played in January, Jones was held scoreless.

The victory also gave Indiana the magical ninth conference win with two games to play. In the previous three seasons under Crean, IU was 8-46 in Big Ten play. This team had now eclipsed that win total in one year.

Crean was happiest with the defense that day. Minnesota's previous worst shooting day of the season had been 37.7 percent at Illinois. So holding the Gophers to a 31-percent day was significant.

Crean put Watford, at 6-9, on 6-4 Minnesota point guard Andre Hollins. It was a practice that IU would employ more and more as the regular season wrapped up and the postseason began. And with Watford being able to guard a point, Crean said the Hoosiers had three players (Sheehey and Oladipo were the other two) who could guard all five positions on the floor.

"When you have three guys that are like that, you really have a chance to make your team better," Crean said. "Our switching was real good. As I said to them before the game, we're going to find out real quick where our communication is in the game. And I thought our communication was very good."

IU led by 11 at the half and by as many as 24 with 5:39 to play.

Indiana now only had two days before conference-leading and No. 5-ranked Michigan State would come to town and Crean would get another shot at a first victory at Indiana against his former mentor, Spartan coach Tom Izzo.

                                                         ஐ ௸

As Michigan State entered the final week of the season, the No. 5 Spartans had a great opportunity ahead.

Sixteen games into the conference season, Michigan State was 13-3 in Big Ten play. The Spartans had already clinched a share of the Big Ten title and had a two-game lead on both Ohio State and Michigan.

All Michigan State had to do was win one game and the Spartans would win the conference outright. That would be no easy task, however, because they would have to first travel to Indiana and then face Ohio State.

Indiana's motivation was significant, too. IU was still hoping Wisconsin might trip up and the Hoosiers could slide into the fourth and final spot in the Big Ten standings. That was big in the new 12-team Big Ten because it meant that IU could secure one of the four first-round byes in the tourney and not have to play on Thursday.

To do that, IU would have to win out and hope the Badgers would lose their final two games.

In the meantime, Indiana just wanted to post another résumé-building victory. The Hoosiers had already knocked off No. 1 Kentucky and No. 2 Ohio State in the season. Now they wanted the trifecta with No. 5 Michigan State. Who cares if all three games were at Assembly Hall? They were still high-quality programs that people would take notice of come NCAA Tournament selection time.

The first time the two teams had played in the Big Ten opener, Michigan State had won a wild one by 15 points, 80-65. But that was in December. IU had played 16 games since that first meeting. In many ways, these were two different teams.

The rematch wasn't so wild. Indiana jumped out to a quick 10-point lead, built it up to 14 at the half, and went on to post a 15-point victory of its own when the No. 18 Hoosiers defeated the No. 5 Spartans, 70-55.

I wrote the next day that Victor Oladipo said he drew a little inspiration earlier on game day when he watched film from the first IU-Michigan State game.

It wasn't something the Spartans said or did or anything like that. No, these were problems Oladipo detected with his own team. He said he thought they stood around too much in the first game and were passive at both ends of the floor. He felt they settled too many times for jump shots. This time, he consistently drove the ball to the basket and was the difference maker.

"I was just trying to be aggressive and take it to the basket," Oladipo said. "I just felt as if I could go past a lot of the guards that were checking me. Jordan (Hulls) did a good job of setting me up early coming off the handoffs. He gave me the room to blast off the handoffs and get to the rim."

Oladipo had 13 points. His three baskets were all drives, and he also made seven of eight free throws. In the past seven games, Oladipo was 47-of-55 from the free-throw line.

The win was Indiana's sixth in the last seven games, and the Hoosiers were now 17-1 at Assembly Hall. It marked the first time any IU team had ever beaten three top five teams during the regular season. The only other time Indiana came close was when the unbeaten 1976 national champion Hoosiers beat three top five teams, but two of those wins came in the NCAA Tournament.

The first time the teams met, Zeller had been given a rude awakening to Big Ten basketball. He was held to four points. The second time, he led Indiana with 18 points on seven-of-12 shooting. Watford had 10 points and a career-high 14 rebounds. His previous career best was 11. Jones came off the bench to score 12. Hulls had 10 points and three steals. But it was Oladipo, especially in the first 10 minutes, that set the tone for Indiana. Three times in the first five minutes, he drove to the lane, got fouled and shot two free throws. He made five of six.

"That's what we need out of Vic all the time, and he's been good at that," Hulls said. "He has been aggressive off the pick-and-rolls. When he explodes to the rim, it just opens up a lot of things for us."

Michigan State coach Tom Izzo said earlier in the week that the play of Oladipo was a big reason IU had been having recent success. He felt the same Tuesday night.

"Give Indiana credit. They did a great job," Izzo said. "I thought Oladipo did a great job in there, and they worked on some things with their big guys. We just didn't respond the way I would have liked to have responded."

That set the Hoosiers up for the Big Ten finale against Purdue on Senior Night.

As I wrote in my advance the day of the game, you could have made the argument going into the IU-Purdue game that the Hoosiers and Boilermakers were playing the Big Ten's best basketball.

In the previous three weeks, Purdue was 5-1 and had posted road victories at Illinois and Michigan. For the Wolverines, that was their only home loss in 16 games. Indiana had also won five of its last six Big Ten games and six of seven games overall when you included North Carolina Central.

Since February 8, four Big Ten teams had only had one loss. IU, Purdue and the two Michigan schools. Michigan State's loss was to Indiana and Michigan's to Purdue.

"I don't look at things so much in terms of the whole body of work as much as who is playing the best basketball at this point in the season," said Dan Dakich, a former IU player, assistant coach and interim head coach, and now a college basketball analyst for ESPN.

"But I think Indiana and Purdue are playing better than anybody right now. Purdue went up to Michigan and played a great game and got a big win. And Indiana just played what I believe is the toughest team in the Big Ten in Michigan State, and went out and out-toughed them. I think that says a lot."

On the line in this one was the fifth seed in the Big Ten Tournament. The winner would be the No. 5 seed and the loser would get No. 6. It would also mark the difference between playing Penn State or Nebraska, the teams that would be the No. 11 and No. 12 seeds in the conference tournament.

It would also be Senior Day at Assembly Hall, where IU would honor Verdell Jones III, Tom Pritchard, Matt Roth, Daniel Moore and Kory Barnett.

Like they did against Michigan State earlier in the week and Minnesota exactly a week before, Indiana sent a message to Purdue that this was a team you didn't want to be playing in either the conference tournament or the NCAA Tournament.

Watford scored 19, and Sheehey added 16 as No. 18 Indiana built a big second-half lead and held on for an 85-74 victory over rival Purdue.

Indiana's five seniors were on the floor for the final 22.4 seconds. Two of them, Jones and Roth, combined to score 16 points and hit four 3-pointers. Jones had two assists, two blocks and two steals as well.

"I think collectively we're playing some of our best basketball," Jones said.

The victory gave IU a final home record of 18-1 at Assembly Hall. It also gave the Hoosiers their first sweep against Purdue since the 2006 season.

IU appeared to have the game in hand throughout, but Purdue made a valiant rally at the end. IU led 75-62 with 2:44 to play following two free throws by Zeller. But a 9-2 run cut the lead to 77-71 with 1:19 to play. Five free throws allowed IU to build the lead back up again and hold on for the win.

Verdell Jones III thanks his teammates while at the microphone during Senior Night festivities following regular season finale victory over Purdue at Assembly Hall, March 4, 2012.

Indiana now advanced to the Big Ten Tournament where it would face No. 12-seed Penn State. The Hoosiers had swept the Nittany Lions in the season series.

Bob Kravitz's column in the *Indianapolis Star* the following day talked about the five IU seniors and the role they had played in the turnaround.

Before Cody Zeller, before The Movement, there were The Survivors. Those are the five young men — Verdell Jones III, Tom Pritchard, Daniel Moore, Kory Barnett and Matt Roth — who came to Indiana University when its basketball program was at a low ebb and heading toward even greater depths.

None of the five will be recalled as legendary players; none will have jersey numbers lifted to the rafters. But all five were representative of the kind of toughness and perseverance that has taken this Hoosiers program from the very bottom of the Big Ten to a solid fifth in the conference, with a real chance now to make noise in March.

All of them lived through three 20-plus-loss seasons.

All of them heard boos, especially Jones and Pritchard, who were thrown into the deep end without water wings.

All of them have been central to a team that is now 24-7, a team that knocked off Purdue 85-74 Sunday on Senior Day at Assembly Hall.

From Barnett, the self-styled Human Victory Cigar, to Jones, the one-time string bean who has grown into a man. From Moore, the Carmel kid who turned down a scholarship at Boston University so he could walk on and wear the candy stripes; to Roth, one of the sickest 3-point shooters in college history; to Pritchard, who remained committed even as his playing time dwindled, who drew the biggest cheer of the night when his jump hook found the bottom of the net. (And when he introduced his attractive girlfriend, which drew another round of sing-song "Tom Pritchard" chants.)

"I always tell our (young) guys, 'You have it made,' " Jones said last week. "Way back in the day, man, we were doing football drills, getting hurt every day. I tell Cody (Zeller), 'You're all finesse now. You don't have the hard life like we did.'

"To see now where we have 7-footers and athletic wings and to think to back in the day when you had two walk-ons who were starting and Kyle Taber with two bad knees was our starting center."

Hard to think back and imagine it now:

Three seasons ago, Pritchard led IU in playing time, averaging 29 minutes a game as a freshman.

"I remember our third game against Notre Dame (in Hawaii), they were double-teaming Pritchard," IU coach Tom Crean remembered with a smile. "We lost by 38."

Two seasons ago, Jones was IU's leading scorer.

For the better part of three years, they stood steadfast as their team often got rolled by opponents with superior talent. None of them flinched, though. None of them transferred or ran from hard times. They honored their commitments, despite the fact that the program was about to be torn apart after the Kelvin Sampson departure. They fought, they competed as better recruits came along, and now, they are part of an IU team that is playing the best basketball of anybody heading into the much-anticipated Big Ten tournament at Bankers Life Fieldhouse.

How can you fail to share their joy?

"They're all a big part of what we've become," said Jordan Hulls, who suffered through some of the hard times himself the first two seasons. "Now it's great to see them reap the rewards."

Their freshman year, they couldn't beat anybody. Now they're part of a team that has swept the state of Indiana, has beaten Kentucky and Ohio State and Michigan State, and is heading into the Big Ten Tournament on a big-time roll.

Every four-year player at IU since 1973 has competed in the NCAA Tournament, and now this group, survivors of seasons with six, 10 and 12 victories, will get a chance to play deep into March.

"It's about never staying down," Crean said of his seniors during postgame festivities. "It's about never letting it be over. It's about fighting back day by day so that you can have moments like these."

For the first time in the seniors' IU careers, there will be a March that matters, a March when they have a real chance to win.

This week's Big Ten Tournament looks like it will be the best we've ever known. With Ohio State's semi-stunning victory at Michigan State, there's a three-way tie (with Michigan) for the regular-season championship. And you can't dismiss Wisconsin, which always finds a way to make noise during the tournament.

IU, winner of seven of eight, is playing better than anybody in the conference right now.

Purdue, despite a defensively leaky performance at IU, has a chance if it gets the requisite shot-making from the perimeter.

Shoot, Northwestern still has faint NCAA Tournament hopes and can barge its way in with a couple of victories.

Who knows what you're going to get with Illinois, a massively talented group that has epically underachieved most of this season?

Late in Sunday's game, there was the memorable picture of all five IU seniors, all standing on the floor and playing together. Jones broke out a Cheshire smile: "Yeah, that was nice."

Yeah, it was.

ഇ ന

Indiana would go on to split its two games in the Big Ten Tournament.

The Hoosiers beat Penn State 75-58 on Thursday at Bankers Life Fieldhouse in Indianapolis and then on Friday lost to Wisconsin 79-71.

But Indiana basketball had a major setback in the first game against Penn State, one that would impact the remainder of the season. Put it this way, IU wasn't celebrating a lot after posting its first Big Ten Tournament victory in six years.

That's because late in the first half, Verdell Jones III would suffer a torn ACL in his right knee. On a very innocent-looking play, Jones' dream of playing in the NCAA Tournament came to an abrupt end.

"We have a really close team, and when somebody goes down like that, you just feel helpless," Zeller said. "You can bet there's a lot of prayers going out his way tonight."

Jones pulled up after a jump stop with 5:45 to play in the half and then quickly crumpled to the floor, screaming in pain. The university said at the time it was a right knee sprain and that Jones would be re-evaluated the next day. Early the next day, IU announced that Jones was done for the year. He had averaged 7.5 points per game.

This was how Bob Kravitz described things in the beginning of his column the next day in *The Star*.

As Indiana basketball coach Tom Crean motioned for a wheelchair to take Verdell Jones III off the floor, the Hoosiers senior shook his head. There was no way he was going off in a wheelchair, no matter how badly his right knee was injured after a noncontact first-half jump stop.

"No chance," said teammate Kory Barnett, one of two Hoosiers to help Jones off the floor Friday afternoon at Bankers Life Fieldhouse. "He's a tough guy. He's gone through too much in his time here to go off in somebody's wheelchair."

The initial diagnosis was a sprained right knee. But sitting just yards from where Jones went down, it was hard not to imagine the worst. The minute his right foot hit the floor, he crumpled and screamed, then began to cry. He was evaluated further Thursday night.

Listening to an emotionally distraught Crean on the radio broadcast after the Hoosiers' 75-58 win over Penn State in the Big Ten Tournament's first round, things didn't sound hopeful.

"It was a great win because of the way we dealt with adversity, and once Verdell went down, we had to deal with that again," he said tearfully. "They're more composed than I am."

Composure did not come easily.

"It's just hard," Crean said. "Verdell means so much to this place, so ..."

Radio play-by-play man Don Fischer saw Crean struggling and intervened, saying how hard it must be to see a noble senior's career possibly end on such a sad note.

"I don't know if it's definitive (that Jones' season is over)," Crean said. "But he's meant a lot to the program. I just want our fans to think of him, pray for him. You don't want to see anybody go down, especially somebody who's persevered for so long to get to this point.

"We wouldn't be in this position because of all the things he's meant."

His voice cracking, Crean walked away.

Later, talking to the media, Crean said, "There's no worse feeling than when your own children are sick or hurt, and it's really a lot like that when you're a coach."

Indiana basketball fans had very likely never heard of Wisconsin's Rob Wilson before the Hoosiers faced the Badgers in the Big Ten Tournament quarterfinals.

And why would they have? Wilson, a senior reserve guard, was only averaging 3.1 points per game. His high game of the season had been 11. His high game for his career was his sophomore year when he scored 13.

Against Indiana, he scored 30. No typo. Yes, 30 points. Wisconsin won the game 79-71. Indiana finished the regular season 25-8.

Wilson made 11 of 16 shots from the field, including seven of 10 from 3-point range. Whenever Wisconsin needed a big shot, he was there to step up and hit it.

Wisconsin coach Bo Ryan said he never envisioned Wilson's offensive eruption but was quick to point out that he didn't think it was luck, either.

"You look at those shots, he was open," Ryan said. "His teammates got him the ball. He was squared up. I think he might have forced one shot. And if you want to write down that I should have been playing him sooner, feel free. But where were you earlier to say, 'Hey, how come?' "

Whether it was luck, a fluke, or whatever the case, it was done. IU was done in the Big Ten Tournament basically because of a guy named Rob Wilson and his day in the sun. Indiana had about 48 hours before it would sit in IU's Henke Hall of Champions in the north end zone of Memorial Stadium on Sunday afternoon and watch the Selection Sunday show to see where it would be headed for the NCAA Tournament.

Chapter 24

It had been a while at Indiana since Selection Sunday was a mere formality.

That's the way it had been for countless years, up until about the 2004 season. Indiana had a small hiccup there in the 2004 and 2005 seasons where it was on the outside looking in with the NCAA Tournament. One year was an NIT berth, and the other, Indiana missed out on postseason play all together.

In the two years that Kelvin Sampson was at IU, Indiana played in the tournament twice. And as has been well documented in previous pages here, the first three years of the Tom Crean era was a fish-out-of-water experience for the IU faithful. In a strange reversal of fortune, Selection Sunday became a Sunday like any other. There was no reason for Indiana fans to watch and in fact, watching was often painful. IU fans would find a different Sunday afternoon activity to occupy their time. They would still fill out their brackets for office pools the next day, but watching the NCAA show was like being made to take that teaspoon of medicine when you were young and the aftertaste in your mouth was not appealing. The Selection Sunday show simply provided a dose of reality for Indiana fans that their beloved Hoosiers were no longer on the college basketball map.

Obviously all of that had changed in 2011-12, and as the Hoosiers waited to hear their seed and destination, there was clearly a buzz in the air in the Henke Hall of Champions, in the north end zone of Memorial Stadium.

The players, coaching staff and support personnel were all on the main floor, and chairs were set up so they could watch the action together on a movie screen. CBS had a camera inside the room to capture IU's reaction when its name was revealed in the bracket. On the floor above, there were probably 20 or more media members looking down on the scene like vultures waiting for their prey.

When the time came and the clock hit six, Indiana's players were eager and ready for the moment. Most figured they would be a No. 4 or No. 5 seed, and there was plenty of speculation as to where the tournament committee would send them for the first round. Would they get to be close to home as in Columbus, Louisville or Nashville, or would they get shuttled off to a more far off location? When Indiana had been a fixture in the tournament in the late 1990s and early 2000s, it seemed like IU would often get sent west. San Diego, Sacramento, Salt Lake City were all places IU had been in recent tournaments. So the thought that IU could be sent to a place like Portland, Oregon, was in the back of a lot of minds, too.

I've always felt for the last few teams that get picked on Selection Sunday. Because it's simply a game of hurry up and wait. The announcement of the teams gets strung out in the made-for-TV event, and if your name isn't called in the first region or two, you simply sit there and begin to fidget.

This wasn't a time of tension, because IU knew that its name was going to be called at some point. It wasn't like the Hoosiers were a bubble team or anything like that. IU had the résumé to be seeded in the upper quarter of the bracket.

As it turned out, the Hoosiers only had to wait a matter of minutes before the announcements of pairings and sites finally came.

The South Region came across first, as Kentucky was the No. 1 seed overall in the tournament and in the South. A few moments later, the No. 4 seed in that bracket was revealed, and sure enough it was the Indiana Hoosiers.

Finally, a 28-66 nightmare was in the rearview mirror for good. The Hoosiers were back in the NCAA Tournament, perhaps a year earlier than many expected from a program picked to finish ninth in the Big Ten.

"It's just really hard to put into words the pride and the feeling we have," said Watford, a few moments after the bracket was announced. "It's the first step, and now we need to go and show people what we can do."

Indiana's first round opponent was No. 13-seed New Mexico State, which had finished second in the Western Athletic Conference behind Nevada in the regular season. The Aggies then beat Louisiana Tech in the conference tournament final to earn the automatic bid.

IU would be heading west to the Rose Garden in Portland for a Thursday-Saturday scenario in the opening rounds of play. The other two teams in IU's first pod were Virginia Commonwealth and Wichita State.

Crean did his best to enjoy the moment and the selection show. He and his six-year-old daughter, Ainsley, appeared on CBS about five minutes before the show began.

Later he said he was surprised at how quickly Indiana's name was revealed in the bracket.

"I was stunned at first and then I just wanted to see my family's faces because I've missed seeing that (the previous three seasons)," Crean said. "I think when you're there every year like we were at Marquette the last three years, you almost take it for granted. ... I want this to be in their memories."

CBS Sports analyst Seth Davis predicted that fifth-seeded Wichita State would knock off the Hoosiers in the second round.

"I love it, but that's just Seth. Seth has been giving us ammunition all year," Crean said. "Seth is the gift that keeps on giving right now with his predictions. But I never have a problem when anybody picks against us."

Crean was asked about conspiracy theories that put IU in the region where Kentucky is No. 1. If both teams would win their first two games, they would meet in the Sweet Sixteen in a rematch of IU's 73-72 win December 10 at Assembly Hall.

"(Kentucky coach) John (Calipari) has been saying that," Crean said. "So to see that up there like that, that wasn't a shock. That's fine."

In the next few hours after Indiana's opponent was revealed, the local media started a fact-gathering mission to learn all about the Aggies. We learned that New Mexico State was a solid rebounding team, in fact one of the best in the nation, ranking sixth in the country with an average of over 40 boards per game. The Aggies liked to take the ball inside and get to the free-throw line. They averaged an incredible 33 attempts per game. They didn't shoot a great percentage at the line at 66.7 percent, but they still got a lot of production because of the amount of time they were there. New Mexico State wasn't a particularly good 3-point shooting team. It shot 32.7 percent for the season. The starting backcourt shot 27.3 percent from 3-point range.

The Aggies had a big-time scorer, considered a future pro, in Wendell McKines (pronounced "McKinness"), who had 20 double-doubles on the year and averaged a double-double. In the conference championship game against Louisiana Tech, he had 27 points and 14 rebounds.

While New Mexico State had been to the NCAA Tournament more recently than Indiana, it had been a long time since the Aggies had won a tournament game. Try 1993. Since then they had made four appearances, the most recent in 2010, when they dropped a close game to Big Ten foe Michigan State, 70-67.

As for New Mexico State's NCAA résumé coming in, the Aggies were 24-9 and 10-4 in the WAC. Like I said above, they finished second in the conference behind regular-season champ Nevada. Nevada beat them twice. The Aggies split with Steve Alford and New Mexico. Two of their other losses were to Southern Mississippi, an NCAA No. 9 seed. They also lost to Idaho, Arizona, Hawaii and University of Texas-El Paso. New Mexico State's RPI was 63. Its strength of schedule was 116. It had a road record of 7-5, and it was 5-1 on neutral sites.

But here were some of the more telling statistics: The Aggies were 0-2 against the top 25, 1-1 against teams ranked 26-50 and 0-3 against teams rated 51-100 in the RPI. Basically that told you that New Mexico State didn't play anybody. The Aggies' record against the top 100 was 1-6. That means they were 23-3 outside of the top 100.

Indiana, on the other hand, was 5-6 on the road and 2-1 on neutral sites. But IU was 4-5 against the top 25, 4-0 against 36-50 and 3-1 against 51-100. That's 17 games against the top 100 and a record of 11-6 in those games. It was obvious the discrepancy was because IU played in the Big Ten and New Mexico State was in the WAC. No surprises there. But IU's players and Indiana's fans, despite what the prognosticators were saying, just felt like their team was much more battle-tested going into the first round than their opponent.

New Mexico State's best win was against New Mexico. IU's best wins were against Kentucky, Ohio State, Michigan State, Michigan, and Notre Dame. IU also beat NCAA Tournament teams Purdue (twice) and North Carolina State. The Hoosiers had an 8-5 record against teams in the NCAA Tournament. New Mexico State was 1-3.

ಹ೦   ೮ನಿ

The Indiana basketball team got to Portland on Monday and quickly went to work preparing for New Mexico State. They went out a day early simply to get acclimated to their surroundings. It was spring break at Indiana, so it wasn't like they were missing classes.

Crean and the coaching staff believed that getting to Portland and having the team begin to focus on that first tournament game would be the best scenario. They practiced daily at the University of Portland and had meetings and film sessions at their downtown hotel.

One thing that was obvious in their demeanor in Portland was that IU's players were treating it like a business trip. They were locked in and ready to show people the level of basketball they believed they were capable of playing.

"Coach Crean has been saying the last couple of days that we got in the door and we deserve to be there," said junior forward Derek Elston. "Now it's what you do when you're in there.

"We want to make our presence felt. We don't want to be one and done, and wait until next year like everybody has been saying. We want to do something right now with the team that we've got. This group of seniors deserves the best out of everybody. We have to play to the best of our abilities and see what happens. If we play the way we can, it could be a long run for us."

Don Fischer, the longtime radio play-by-play man and a guy who is known as "The Voice of the Hoosiers," traveled with the team to Portland as he does for all IU road trips.

He said the players were excited about the possibilities that were ahead but there wasn't any 'We're happy to be here' look in their demeanor.

"No one seemed to have the mentality that if they won the first game or if they lost the first game it really didn't matter. It wasn't that way at all," Fischer said. "But Coach Crean and the coaching staff made sure they approached it as a business trip. Now they had fun while they were out there, and they were able to do some different things away from basketball, but they kept the same mentality they had throughout the season."

The mentality Fischer spoke of was a belief within the team that they were a lot better than some people were giving them credit for. In some ways, even though they were the No. 4 in the South and the top seed of the four teams in their pod for the first two rounds, they were looking at the situation as if they were being disrespected and were more of the underdog.

"I think our guys like the underdog mentality and the feeling that nobody expects us to win," said Verdell Jones III, who was doing his best not to hide his disappointment that he would not be able to play in the tournament because of a torn ACL. "Our guys just don't believe that a lot of people think we deserve to be here."

Fischer said he thought the older players, in particular, felt like IU still had a lot to prove. Over the previous three seasons they had heard a lot of negativity about the Indiana program, and it wasn't an easy time for them.

Now that things were looking up again, Indiana was ready to play and show it belonged on the stage it was about to play on.

"To say that they had a chip on their shoulder may be as easy a way of any as saying it," Fischer said. "It wasn't cocky or anything, but it was just a confidence level about these guys and a belief they had in themselves as a team. I saw it through the entire year.

"There was obviously a few games throughout the course of the year that gave them that confidence. Kentucky is the obvious one and

Ohio State was big, too, but I think the North Carolina State game had as much to do with their confidence as any game that they played all season."

Hulls said the Hoosiers were approaching the New Mexico State game the same way they had every game all season.

"We have the same mindset and are approaching this like we have all year, whether it has been practice or film sessions," Hulls said. "We're definitely honored to be here, but once we get on the court we know it's game time and we've got to keep our heads level and focus on the details of the game."

೮೦ ಅ

When game time arrived, the Hoosiers were clearly ready.

Here was my description of the game that ran in the *Indianapolis Star* the next day.

PORTLAND, Ore. — Indiana fans have watched in awe for three seasons the abilities of Jordan Hulls from beyond the 3-point line.

Fans in the Pacific Northwest got to experience it firsthand Thursday night.

Hulls made three 3-pointers in a span of just over two minutes midway through the second half and hit four overall as No. 4-seed Indiana defeated No. 13 New Mexico State 79-66 before 17,519 at the Rose Garden.

Hulls had 22 points, while Christian Watford, Will Sheehey and Cody Zeller all had 14 as Indiana got its first NCAA Tournament win since 2007. It was IU's first NCAA appearance since 2008.

"I just got some open looks, and my teammates did a nice job of getting me open," Hulls said. "I hit my first shot and then after that, the ball just started feeling good as it came off my hand. But the key for me was that my teammates were finding me and getting me open with ball screens."

Zeller also had six steals, setting a school record in NCAA Tournament play.

Indiana will play No. 12-seed Virginia Commonwealth at 7:10 p.m. Saturday, with the winner moving on to Atlanta for the Sweet Sixteen. VCU upset No. 5 Wichita State 62-59.

IU shot 59.3 percent from the field overall, including 64.3 percent in the second half. Indiana hit 18 of 28 second-half shots.

Jordan Hulls hits a runner against New Mexico State in first round NCAA Tournament game in Portland, Oregon, in 2012.

"Give Tom (Crean) credit and that's a really good basketball team," said New Mexico State coach Marvin Menzies. "They just shot the lights out. We just lost to the better team tonight."

Hulls hit 8 of 12 shots from the field, Sheehey made 7 of 11 and Watford knocked down 6 of 11 shots. That's 21 of 34 from that group.

IU coach Crean said he thought Indiana's success Thursday started with his team's approach.

"We're a team that hasn't been in this kind of environment in the NCAA Tournament, and I thought we handled it very well," Crean said.

Indiana (26-8) had a 13-point second-half lead when Hulls started to heat up. He hit a 3-pointer from the top to start the run with 13:56 to play. The next time down, he hit a runner in the lane, and then hit 3-pointers on back-to-back possessions. The second of those put the Hoosiers up 62-41 with 11:40 remaining.

Wendell McKines, the Aggies' fifth-year senior who was averaging a double-double with 18.8 points and 10.8 rebounds per game, led New Mexico State (26-10) with 15 points and seven rebounds.

Sheehey said the IU team took exception to comments made by McKines in Wednesday's news conference. He said then that "no mammal can guard me."

"We thought he had some questionable comments," Sheehey said. "He said no mammal can guard him, so I guess Victor (Oladipo) isn't human."

McKines didn't have the supporting cast to keep up with an IU team that has spent the past 12 weeks ranked in the top 25 nationally.

Indiana had plenty of support. In the first half, for example, when the Hoosiers had a 35-28 advantage at the break, IU had picked up *seven points combined from Tom Pritchard, Derek Elston and Remy Abell. That trio finished with nine points.*

In the postgame press conferences, New Mexico State coach Marvin Menzies talked about Jordan Hulls being the difference maker. He was asked why Hulls was able to get one open 3-point look after another.

"I thought he got a few of them in transition," Menzies said. "It was us trying to get back and worry about Cody. This was really kind of the focus, the way he runs the floor so well. And then getting back out to Hulls was difficult at times.

"So they had some transition 3's. You've got to give the kid credit, we tried to go zone for a couple of possessions. We played two or three possessions and I think he hit two 3's in that stretch or at least one, I know for sure. You've got to give up something to get something sometimes. And when they have that two-headed monster working like that, it's tough to battle back."

Crean was asked about what it felt like, not only to be back in the NCAA Tournament, but to get that first tournament win for the program since 2007.

"I think when I look up at the crowd and catch a glimpse of my family, our families … ," Crean said. "I've got some good friends here, Tony La Russa and Dick Strong. I catch a glimpse of them and I think then it hits you just for a brief moment that this is really, really special. It really is.

"We've been through so much to get to this point that it's hard to spend a lot of time reflecting on it. I guess I have the last couple of weeks with some interviews. We've all learned a great deal. Everybody is better. It didn't seem like it at the time, but everybody is better for what we had to endure. I have no question I'm a better coach. The most important thing to me is that I'm a better Christian."

Crean talked about the role Jones played against New Mexico State, even though he didn't suit up and was lost for the season.

"I look at Verdell Jones and I look at the selflessness of him, looking at all he's done as a player and all the points he scored to be like a coach for me tonight, for us tonight," Crean said. "He was talking to Remy (Abell) and Jordan (Hulls), and he was emphatic with things that he sees. I can reflect on that. Those are the kind of things that really lead you to believe that this program has been through a lot. We're better for it and we're just getting started."

In the NCAA Tournament, there's no rest for the weary. In less than 48 hours, IU would be back in action again against a talented VCU team that had upset Wichita State.

And what IU lacked in experience, this VCU team had. This same program had played in the Final Four the season before along with another Cinderella, Butler.

Don Fischer, who sees the team up close and personal every day, said it was important for the Hoosiers to get that first win, but their focus and their preparation didn't change from one game to the next.

"I don't think the first game validated anything particularly for this team because I think they were all pretty sure they were going to beat New Mexico State," Fischer said. "And that's not a cocky thing, it's more of the fact that they felt totally prepared. And I think that's a big factor in how these kids approached every ball game. I think they trusted their coaches to get them ready, they felt like they had found the right formula throughout the season, and I just think that fed their confidence level where they felt whoever they played, they were capable of beating."

Fischer said that something Crean had talked about throughout the season, whether it was on his radio show, in press conferences or privately was that this Indiana basketball team went into every game thinking they could win.

"And that's a huge difference, at least in my opinion, over the previous three years in terms of what they were thinking," Fischer said. "I never saw that same confidence level in the previous three seasons at any point in time.

"As Coach Crean said, the mentality this team had, though, was one where he believed they could win every game that they played and they believed it, too."

And perhaps it was something that was created internally to fire the Hoosiers up, but there was no doubt that even after beating New Mexico State, Indiana felt it was being disrespected. VCU was waiting for another Cinderella run, and the only team standing in the way for a return trip to the Sweet Sixteen was Indiana.

Not to mention that the national analysts were giving Crean and his staff nonstop bulletin board material.

When I got back to my hotel room that night after IU's victory over New Mexico State, I turned on ESPN to get a recap of all the day's games.

Within minutes, ESPN's Hubert Davis was asked in studio for his upset special in the next round.

There was no hesitation.

"How about VCU over Indiana?" Davis said. "They're a much better defensive team this year as opposed to last year. They have depth, athleticism, they pick up full court, create turnovers, they do a great job. And they're going up against an Indiana team that lacks experience."

Like it or not, Indiana basketball was the program that everybody wanted to pick against.

The Hoosiers were the Rodney Dangerfield of college basketball. Whether it was facing No. 13 New Mexico State on Thursday or No. 12 Virginia Commonwealth two days later, very few national analysts liked the fourth-seeded Hoosiers.

Indiana had felt like the unwanted stepchild all season long.

Victor Oladipo and Tom Pritchard on defense against New Mexico State in the first-round NCAA Tournament game in Portland, Oregon, in 2012.

In the preconference poll of Big Ten media, the Hoosiers were picked to finish ninth. When IU knocked off then-No. 1-ranked Kentucky and Ohio State this season, people said it was because the games were in Assembly Hall.

Just moments after IU's name appeared on the screen on Selection Sunday as a No. 4 seed, CBS and SI.com's Seth Davis said Indiana would never get to the Sweet Sixteen.

"We have to get a little chuckle out of what people say," said junior forward Derek Elston. "Right when we were picked to come into the tournament, not 20 seconds had gone by, someone was picking against us.

"Knowing that we went out and won on Thursday meant just a little bit more because we felt like we proved some people wrong. We've been playing the underdog role all year long. We'll just play basketball and let other people think whatever they want to think."

So what is it about Indiana that made the Hoosiers less than the sexy pick?

Some said that VCU had an edge because they were tournament-tested. VCU beat Purdue in 2011 before losing to Butler in the Final Four.

Another reason some thought Indiana wouldn't advance was simply that recent tradition said the Hoosiers wouldn't make it to the second weekend. Since 1995, IU had only made it out of the first two games once, and that was the 2002 run to the national championship game.

"It's fine with me," Hulls said. "We've been doubted all year even before we started playing. ... All I know is that this team is pretty focused. We can only control what we can control, and that's what we focus on."

It appeared VCU was taking the same approach. VCU coach Shaka Smart made a reference to the movie that is endeared by all Indiana fans — *Hoosiers*.

A story in the *Daily Press* in Newport News, Virginia, talked about just that.

"I know we're playing the Hoosiers, but I'll reference the movie Hoosiers, " VCU coach Shaka Smart said. "The baskets are still 10 feet high. The court is the same length."

At this point, big-school teams don't seem to cause the Rams to fret.

"Those schools that we looked at growing up," forward Bradford Burgess said, "when we get the opportunity to play one of those guys, we just see another opportunity to beat the team."

Asked what makes VCU so difficult, Crean said it was the pressure defense — something that reminded him of Rick Pitino's teams most recently at Louisville.

"It's their length," Crean said. "Everyone knows what Rick has done with those presses at Louisville." The Rams, Crean said, have "the intensity of it. They do an excellent job of putting you in a spot."

That organized chaos led the Rams to victories over Southern California, Georgetown, Purdue, Florida State and Kansas on the way to the Final Four last season. Still, the "Cinderella" moniker follows them.

"We can be the 'Cinderella,' we don't have to be 'Cinderella,' " VCU guard Troy Daniels said. "We just want to go out and play hard every game in the tournament, because everybody wants to win."

Still, Daniels said, the little-brother act has a use.

"It helps us win late in games," he said.

The Rams did so Thursday against Wichita State, scoring the last five points in a 62-59 victory. It had the college basketball world remembering last season's run, though there is a difference, according to those on the team.

"Last year, we had so many offensive weapons, we didn't focus as much as we needed to on the defensive end," said Burgess, the only returning starter from last season. "This year, we've done a great job getting teams out of what they do, and enforcing our 'Havoc' style."

Wichita State got a dose of that. The Rams had Garrett Stutz, the Shockers' 7-foot center, so confused that he couldn't decide whether to dunk or shoot with VCU leading 60-59, in the last minute.

Wide open, he did neither, missing a soft layup. Stutz, Wichita State's leading scorer, finished with four points, making only two of 11 shots.

Indiana presents a similar problem, only more so.

Cody Zeller, a 6-11 center, averaged 15.5 points and was a strong inside presence.

"He's as good as any big kid we have played in the three years I've been here," Smart said. "The scary thing is he is only a freshman."

As Indiana prepared to play VCU, the focus was on the Rams' pressure style of defense.

Bob Kravitz had this column the day that IU and VCU tangled, with the winner going to the Sweet Sixteen.

Here's the best way to describe what it's like to play against Virginia Commonwealth's pressing, trapping, eternally annoying defense:

It's like trying to play basketball in a phone booth ... with three people already in there, trying to make a call.

"Their press is the real deal," Indiana coach Tom Crean said of the Hoosiers' opponent today in the NCAA Tournament's third round.

These VCU Rams generally have different players than those who reached the national semifinal. They don't shoot the ball at such a wicked rate as they did when they went 3-crazy last March. But they still play defense, play it all over the floor, and do it better than they ever did last spring.

It won't matter that Seth Davis picked VCU, or that VCU boosters placed a "Busting Brackets" ad in the Washington Post or any of that sophomoric stuff that passes for inspirational material.

What will matter, at least for IU, is how well it handles the VCU press.

What will matter is how prepared the Hoosiers are with this short turnaround, how prepared they are to play a style that is largely foreign to the halfcourt-stifling, hyper-physical Big Ten.

What will matter is how well Jordan Hulls handles the double-teams and the pressure.

What will matter is whether Victor Oladipo, now pressed into more ballhandling duty with Verdell Jones III's absence, can avoid his occasional penchant for turnovers.

"There are some definitive places that VCU wants you to catch the ball, which is like most pressing teams, which is deep in the corner, and then try to get you to throw it back underneath the basket," Crean said. "And this is not a game where I think we're going to be able to bring fatigue to the game. I thought we were able to bring fatigue to the game (against New Mexico State). I think this team is deep. I think they're used to the way they play ... So it's really a lot more about how strong we are with the ball, what our vision is like and what our mindset is like in seeing that press."

VCU is a brutal matchup at any time of the year, but especially now with such a short turnaround.

Wichita State's Greg Marshall tried to prepare his team for VCU's "havoc" by using six players to press his team during practice. In past years, when Crean was in the Big East and preparing for Rick Pitino's pressing Louisville team, he often went eight-on-five, then seven-on-five, six-on-five and five-on-five. The simple idea being, take away time and space, and suddenly five-on-five doesn't seem like such an onerous task.

"There's a lot of reasons that we play the way we do, and one of them is because it's different than what teams are used to practicing against in their own practices and playing against throughout the course of their schedule," VCU coach Shaka Smart said. "... So in theory, our style is something that will be new for them to see.

Sometimes that works out; sometimes it doesn't work out. And in theory, it should be an advantage for us."

There is no way an opponent can hope to replicate VCU's pressure in a practice setting. None.

"You can do certain things in practice (to replicate the press), but I don't think completely," Smart said. "Just like if we play against a team that runs the Princeton offense, it's next to impossible for us to replicate that. We're just not a Princeton offense."

But, then, "We can't replicate Cody Zeller," Smart said with a smile.

When the fourth-seeded Hoosiers played the 12th-seed Rams, they will see something they haven't seen all season.

"Can you compare VCU to any other team you've seen this year or in the Big Ten?" a reporter asked.

Christian Watford shook his head.

"Not really," he said. "Big Ten teams don't pressure, although (VCU's) length reminds me a little bit of Kentucky."

This will be the ultimate challenge for IU, both for the coaches who have to prepare for VCU's uniquely annoying style in two days' time, but also for the players who have got to figure out how to attack a team that pressures you the minute you get off the bus.

"It's not going to be a game with as many sets," Zeller said. "It's just going to be a matter of playing basketball."

If styles make fights, this ought to be an interesting watch.

The question is, how comfortable will IU be when it's forced to play quicker than it is accustomed. VCU will make you play their pace. Unless you're Butler, of course.

"We just try to speed them up," VCU's Darius Theus said. "Some teams like to walk the ball up the court or they just want to play at a slow pace. If our pressure can speed them up a little bit, it can really take them out of their offense. If we're not forcing turnovers, then we're speeding offenses up, and they're not used to doing that."

The pressure is on. And they'll handle it, all the way to the Sweet Sixteen.

℘   ☙

With 12:28 to play in the VCU-Indiana game, all signs pointed toward the Rams getting back to the Sweet Sixteen.

VCU led 57-48 and appeared in control. Indiana, a team that averaged 12.7 turnovers per game would end up turning it over 22 times against the Rams' pressure defense. Twelve of those were in the second half.

But as it would turn out, VCU would only score four more points in the game. IU closed the game on a 15-4 run and posted a 63-61 victory and a trip to the Sweet Sixteen.

I could go through all the details, but sometimes it's simpler just to share how I wrote the account of the game the next day. And I have to admit, I wrote this one at a furious pace at the end of the game myself. That's because when the outcome looked in doubt, I had already written pretty much the entire story with VCU winning and was just waiting to plug in the final score.

That was before IU went on an unexpected run in the closing minutes and forced me to hit the delete button on that story and start over.

Here's the final product:

PORTLAND, Ore. — Indiana had rallied to tie the score in the final minute of its NCAA Tournament game Saturday when Victor Oladipo rebounded a missed 3-pointer with 23 seconds to play.

Hoosier Nation screamed at television sets across the country for Indiana to back the ball out and go for one shot.

Oladipo had other ideas. He drove the ball at breakneck speed down the court and tried to score at the rim, but the ball was deflected to a wide-open Will Sheehey 10 feet from the basket.

Sheehey knocked down a jumper with 12.7 seconds to play, and Indiana survived a missed 3-pointer at the buzzer to score an improbable 63-61 victory over Virginia Commonwealth in an NCAA third-round game at the Rose Garden.

Indiana (27-8) advances to the Sweet Sixteen for the first time since 2002. The Hoosiers will play No. 1 Kentucky in Atlanta on Friday night.

The official statistics show that Oladipo didn't attempt a shot on the final drive but rather assisted on Sheehey's basket. After the game, Oladipo said he took the shot and it was blocked. He also said he never gave a thought to pulling the ball out and going for the last shot.

"No way," said the sophomore guard. "We got back into the game because we were aggressive, and I wanted to continue to be aggressive. I had just scored on the same play a minute before that, and I felt like I could get to the rim again.

"Give their player credit as he made a great defensive play, but the ball went out to Will and I knew when he put it up, that shot was going in."

Sheehey said he was in the mindset of the majority of people when he saw Oladipo get the rebound. He figured the Hoosiers would pull the ball back out, call a timeout, and try to score on a final shot or force overtime.

"I love that (Oladipo) was being aggressive, and he plays the best when he's aggressive like that and it was really a great play, but

Will Sheehey shares a moment with Tom Crean, moments after his 10-foot jumper gave IU a victory over VCU in the NCAA Tournament and sent the Hoosiers to the Sweet Sixteen.

when he got that rebound, I was thinking we were going to (pull it out)," Sheehey said.

When the ball ended up in his hands, Sheehey said he never thought about pulling it back out, either. The shot was too wide open, it was a distance from which he was comfortable shooting, and he knew he was going for the game-winner.

"I knew I was going to shoot it," Sheehey said. "When Vic was coming down, I had pretty much told myself that if it came out to me, I was going to shoot it. I'm just glad I made it."

After a timeout, VCU got the ball to the middle of the court. Darius Theus kicked it out to Rob Brandenberg, who had an open 3-point look from the left wing. It was close to the spot where Christian Watford hit a 3 at Assembly Hall to beat Kentucky on December 10. But Brandenberg's shot caromed off the back of the rim and Indiana had survived.

The final shot aside, the fact that Sheehey was in position to get a go-ahead attempt in the final 15 seconds was remarkable.

The Hoosiers had fumbled their way into a nine-point deficit midway through the second half and still trailed by five with 2:24 remaining. An IU team that averages 12.7 turnovers per game had a season-high 22 on Saturday, 12 in the second half.

VCU (29-7) led 57-48 with 12:28 to play. The Rams would score just four more points. The Rams stopped playing aggressively and consistently missed jump shots at the end of the shot clock. VCU hit 7-of-28 shots (25 percent) in the second half. IU closed the game on a 15-4 run from that mark.

Cody Zeller became more aggressive and took the ball to the basket. Trailing 61-58 with 46.5 seconds to play, Oladipo drove it to the basket, scored and was fouled. When he hit the free throw, the score was tied.

I thought in the last four or five minutes, Cody Zeller just said, 'I'm going to make plays,' " said VCU coach Shaka Smart. "And he really did a good job, first of all catching the ball where he wanted it, and then making plays and getting to the basket and either getting to the line or finishing."

On VCU's previous possession, senior forward Bradford Burgess, an 80-percent free-throw shooter, had missed two foul shots with 59.3 seconds remaining.

Burgess led VCU with 15 points and made four 3-pointers.

Zeller led IU with 16 points and 13 rebounds, posting his fifth double-double of the year. Watford shared high-point honors with 16, including 4-of-5 shooting from 3-point range. Watford scored the final eight points of the first half to pull Indiana within 42-41 at the break.

Indiana had gone two-for-two in Portland to advance to the Sweet Sixteen which set up the much-anticipated matchup between No. 1 Kentucky and No. 4 Indiana at the Georgia Dome in Atlanta.

It was clearly a case of Indiana going from the frying pan into the fire.

IU players celebrate 63-61 victory over VCU in NCAA Tournament that advanced Hoosiers to Sweet Sixteen.

Jordan Hulls, Christian Watford and Cody Zeller at a NCAA Tournament press conference.

Chapter 25

From the moment Christian Watford's shot hit nothing but net on December 10 in Assembly Hall to give Indiana a 73-72 victory over No. 1 Kentucky, fans everywhere had hoped the Wildcats and Hoosiers would get a chance to play one more time.

Ideally, the teams would have been placed in separate brackets and had a chance to play on the highest stage in the Final Four.

But no one really cared, as long as the two played once again.

While Kentucky players tried to downplay Indiana's "lucky shot" victory, there's no question that they would love to have a shot at the Hoosiers on a neutral court. And Indiana players, buoyed by that performance over three months before, were confident they could repeat that effort anywhere, anytime.

Of course, the TV types were praying once the brackets were released on Selection Sunday that both Indiana and Kentucky would win their first two games of the tournament and then square off in the Sweet Sixteen in Atlanta. Fairy tales don't often come true. This one did. And almost immediately the hype of Indiana-Kentucky II became overwhelming.

Watford had to have been asked a hundred times or more about his shot that beat the Wildcats. Kentucky players were asked about that and about the ESPN commercial that had continued to bring the event back to life over and over in the months since the shot went in.

Not surprisingly, they had seen it a few times too many.

But the big question on the minds of Indiana fans as the Hoosiers prepared to face Kentucky for a second time in the 2011-12 season was: Just what would it take to beat the Wildcats? What was the blueprint for a two-game series sweep of Kentucky?

I came up with a list, and it included four points in particular. The list went something like this:

1. Limit easy baskets: Kentucky is at its best when it's getting out and running. IU would prefer the game be played in the half court. In the first meeting, Kentucky managed just six fast-break points.

"You cannot allow transition points off your mistakes, and you can't allow broken plays," said former IU player, coach and current ESPN college basketball analyst Dan Dakich. "You can't get a defensive stop and then allow someone to come in, get a rebound, and kick it

out for an open 3-pointer. Those are the things that can kill you against a team as talented as Kentucky."

2. Shoot a high percentage: One of the things that makes Indiana a dangerous team in the NCAA Tournament is that it can really shoot the ball with Jordan Hulls, Christian Watford, Will Sheehey and Matt Roth.

Indiana ranks sixth in the nation in field-goal percentage (49.1 percent) and second in 3-point percentage (43.7). The Hoosiers won despite shooting 43.1 percent in the first meeting, but did make nine of 15 3-pointers. It also helped that Watford made the last shot.

"I think you can game plan against Kentucky and stop their best players from scoring from the perimeter," Dakich said. "But Indiana just has a bunch of guys that can make shots. And teams like that are always dangerous in the NCAA Tournament."

3. Favorable fouls: For the most part, IU freshman Cody Zeller has avoided foul trouble this season. But playing against an imposing player such as Kentucky's Anthony Davis, it's even more imperative that Zeller stay on the floor.

In the first meeting, Zeller played a season-high 37 minutes, scored 11 points and grabbed seven rebounds. It didn't hurt that Davis was in foul trouble; he had four fouls and played 24 minutes but has not had more than three fouls since that game.

"The one thing that will be different this time is that both of these teams are playing better than they were in December," said ESPN college basketball analyst Jay Bilas. "You have to remember, that was Kentucky's first real road game, and I think a player like Davis was affected by that.

"But Zeller is a completely different player, too. I think that will be one of the real interesting matchups to keep an eye on, and foul trouble will be a big part of it."

4. No dribble penetration: Marquis Teague put on a clinic in the second half of the first game taking Hulls to the basket. This time it will likely be Victor Oladipo, Sheehey or even Watford guarding Teague, but the point remains the same.

Kentucky is a team that wants to drive the ball to the basket for a score. Force the Wildcats into becoming a jump-shooting team, and you've taken one of their biggest threats away.

"You have to stop all of their guys from penetrating," Bilas said. *"They do run pick-and-roll, they do get into the lane, and when they do, if you help uphill, they're just going to pitch that ball up to the rim for a lob."*

       ᔆ   ᔆ

Indiana returned home from Portland on a Sunday afternoon, had a day or two to rest at home, and then headed for Atlanta on Tuesday night. The game was scheduled for Friday.

Don Fischer, Indiana's play-by-play voice, said the demeanor that IU had during the trip to Portland was repeated with the Sweet Sixteen trip. Once again, it was all business.

"The preparation for the Kentucky game was identical," Fischer said. "The only difference was they were in a different location. Every place that they went to practice they had that same mentality."

But Fischer said that was really nothing new. It was an intangible that was a staple with this IU team.

"I never saw a variance with this team in terms of how they approached games," Fischer said. "Maybe that's as important as anything we saw all year because I think that consistency is very important for a basketball team."

Fischer was a strong believer that everything IU went through the first three seasons under Crean was paying off in the current NCAA Tournament run. He said there was no doubt that the addition of Zeller had been huge, but beyond that, this was the same team from the year before, just better.

"This team did have Cody Zeller and he was a humongous difference," Fischer said. "But the rest of these guys were the same guys that won six, 10 and 12 games in three years. So obviously Cody made a huge difference, but also I think what they learned during that three years of struggle really helped them prepare the right away.

"And again, a tremendous amount of credit has to go to Crean and that coaching staff for getting them to understand just how hard it is to win. They learned that firsthand. Especially those juniors and seniors."

       ᔆ   ᔆ

Both Kentucky and Indiana had won games on Saturday night to advance to the Sweet Sixteen. Indiana had defeated VCU and Kentucky had beaten Iowa State.

In the postgame locker rooms for both teams, players were peppered with questions about Watford's shot that had turned the college basketball world on its ear.

Not surprisingly, Watford was front and center talking about the shot on numerous occasions. People asked him repeatedly to relive *The Shot* and talk about how that one event had changed his life.

When the bright lights were on, and he was surrounded by a sea of reporters, Watford did his best to give the impression he had moved on. He said he didn't think about it nearly as much as he did in the weeks just after it. He said students on campus still brought it up all the time and that everyone had been real nice about it.

He said the times he thought about it the most were when he saw it shown on television. And ESPN did its best from December 2011 to the NCAA Tournament in March 2012 to keep *The Shot* in the consciousness of basketball fans everywhere. The network ran a commercial that showed Watford hitting *The Shot* and fans rushing the court.

"I've been seeing it a lot," Watford said early in the week before the rematch with Kentucky, following a practice at Assembly Hall. "At this point it's kind of over with. You just move forward to the next game. I don't really watch it."

But in the same breath, he admitted that you don't have to try very hard to see the highlight clip shown somewhere.

"ESPN does a great job of broadcasting it every time I watch 'SportsCenter,'" Watford said.

Watford said in the days that followed *The Shot*, he was treated like a rock star. He was inundated with emails, phone calls and texts.

"I heard from people I hadn't heard from in forever," he said. "It was crazy. Things have been kind of different since. At that point, I knew it was time to move on. Once you enjoy it, you move forward."

As much as Indiana fans and Watford, in particular, enjoyed seeing *The Shot* go in on replay time after time after time, it got a little old for the Kentucky folks.

Doron Lamb called out Watford on a radio show saying that "it was a lucky shot."

After Kentucky beat Iowa State to advance to the Sweet Sixteen, UK freshman Michael Kidd-Gilchrist went off about the ESPN commercial of Watford's shot that the network was using to promote the NCAA Tournament.

"I hate that commercial," Kidd-Gilchrist said. "We're going to get them back."

When Kentucky coach John Calapari heard what Kidd-Gilchrist had said, he tried to lessen the potential bulletin board material by referring to the fact that his player doesn't turn 19 until September.

"Youngest freshman in the country," Calipari said. "They say stupid things."

Early in the week before the rematch, Calipari did his best to downplay revenge as a motivating factor for the rematch.

"Let's not worry about four months ago," Calipari said he told his team. "It doesn't matter now. We haven't talked about it in any of the meetings. It's not like, 'OK, we've got another shot at these (guys).' It's none of that.

"We've got a team in front of us. They can beat us. We know that. They've already beaten us. So we'll have to play a terrific ball game."

Still, Calipari would make it a point to thank ESPN prior to the second IU-Kentucky game for showing it so much because his players were clearly getting tired of watching it. Whether it served as motivation for them or not, Calipari didn't know, but there was no question that the ESPN clips kept *The Shot* always on their minds.

Asked about that first game with Indiana the day before the two teams met for a second time in Atlanta, Calipari referenced the ESPN clip.

"I know they made one really good shot at the end of the game, because I've seen it on commercials about every 15 minutes," Calipari said.

In response, Crean said he enjoyed watching it every time it came on the screen.

"It goes in every time," Crean said. "Every time. Never changes. It still goes in every time. And there's still a hand up in front of him. There's still a great pass from Verdell. There's still a great screen from Cody Zeller. And every time it goes in."

Watford said seeing the clip, for him anyway, always made his heart smile.

"It's just one of those things and one of those moments I will always be really proud of," Watford said. "It's something that no one will ever be able to take away. At the same time, it's now a moment that is in the past, and I want to live in the present. So as much as I enjoy thinking about it, I also know I need to move past it, too."

Ernest Watford, Christian's father, said on the night of the second IU-Kentucky game in Atlanta that he believed *The Shot* changed his son in many positive ways.

"I think it gave him a lot of confidence and it changed him in that way," Ernest Watford said. "But most of all I think it changed the dynamic of our team, and it proved to our players that all of the hard work they had been putting in since the end of last season was finally beginning to pay off."

In the NCAA's second round in Portland, Will Sheehey knocked down a shot in the closing seconds to put the Hoosiers up by two in come-from-behind fashion against VCU. Indiana then survived a 3-point miss at the buzzer by VCU's Rob Brandenberg from the vicinity of where Watford's shot had gone down against Kentucky.

The result of that shot compared to Watford's shot successful one wasn't lost on the 6-9 forward from Birmingham, Alabama.

"It just shows you how close things can be in this game," Watford said. "That shot seemed to hang in the air forever, while my shot was a lot quicker. I just have to thank God that my shot went in. He's the one who deserves all the glory for that."

⁃   ⁃

In the press conferences the day before Indiana faced Kentucky in Atlanta, Tom Crean talked about the Kentucky team his Hoosiers were about to face.

"We know we've got a major, major task in front of us in playing this Kentucky team," Crean said. "We know how good this South Region is. We knew that from the time the brackets came out, and Kentucky is considerably better than what they were when we played them when they were No. 1 in the country, and they were really good then. Their team is clicking on all cylinders. Their team defense is phenomenal. Their individual play has improved, which has made their offense better.

"They're extremely, extremely well coached, and I think Coach Calipari has done a phenomenal job of not only making that team better, but making that team with so many young guys very, very cohesive and absolutely committed to sharing the basketball. I think that's a big part of why they're successful."

At the same time, he was quick to point out that his team had improved since then, too.

"Our success comes from many of the same things," Crean said. "We've improved. Our young men are getting tougher mentally and physically all the time. We've been through some great battles this year, some that we were successful in and some that we weren't and we learned from. But they've continued to take every game for what it is, which is the most important game on their schedule.

"When you're coming off what we've dealt with the last couple of years, you have no choice but to treat every game as the most important game. If you do that enough, it leads to moments like this, for these guys to play in an environment like this."

Crean was asked about how much he could take from the first time the two teams had played.

"We don't de-emphasize it, but we don't overemphasize it," Crean said. "There's similarities. First and foremost, it gives players confidence. So play a team like Kentucky, there's a lot of different stages that you've got to go through, and belief is a big part of that because they're so good. You have to literally believe you can win the game, because they have the ability to come in and throw those first couple blows and punches in a game, and they're hard to recover from.

"If you don't believe you can win, it's a lot harder to recover from that. So I think those things play into it. But there are definitely certain things from the game that stand out, that are still very, very tangible for us. There are some things where they've improved. There's certain parts of our game plan that are still in play, and there's others that we've changed."

"So I think it's like any other game you would play, and then playing them again in an environment like this or a Big Ten Tournament, you keep learning not only from that game, but from all the other games that you've played, and it becomes a product of all those experiences."

The first time the two teams played, Anthony Davis was in rare foul trouble and Terrence Jones was basically lost in space. He never got into synch and admitted later it was one of his poorest games ever.

Crean was asked how he would approach those matchups the second time around.

"I think we prepared for both of them to be on the floor the last time," Crean said. "I don't think you prepare differently. You prepare for the very best. You prepare for a lot of the best we've seen from Kentucky and show it to your team. We don't want to spend a lot of time showing clips of people that didn't play them right or didn't come in with that mindset that they could beat them. You want to show their team at their best.

"You're probably right, they have not played much without Davis. I don't think—as good as each individual player is on the team, I think it's a great credit to John and the way that no matter who's there, no matter who's not there, they continue to play at a really high level."

Crean said people forget just how good of a defensive team Kentucky had been during the year. He said everyone focuses on the offense, but the defense was big, too.

"I don't think that defensive field-goal percentage is an accident," Crean said. "I think they're really, really good. Their individual defense is strong because of their talent and athleticism, but he's got them playing team defense in such a strong way. Again, you prepare for the best of it. You have contingency plans for your own team. You don't really base it on if two or three guys are going to be in foul trouble. That can drive you nuts."

One of the points that was made over and over during the tournament was that Indiana was one of the least experienced teams in the field. Forget that Kentucky was mostly freshmen. Still, since no IU player had been to an NCAA Tournament game prior to the trip to Portland, at least one media member wanted to know how important the lack of experience might be.

Hulls said he thought the experience in Portland was enough.

"I mean, there's other guys who have more experience out there, but we feel like we're just as good as anybody in this tournament," Hulls said. "Once that first game was out of the way, the first-game jitters, we were able to play our game, and as long as we can do that, we'll be all right."

Watford was asked about how much the two teams had progressed since the first meeting.

"I feel like we're playing with a lot more confidence than we were playing with back then," Watford said. "As far as Kentucky, they're gelling a lot better. They were kind of young. The season was at the beginning. They're getting their chemistry together. So they're a lot better basketball team."

80   03

The game itself lived up to its billing.

Some say the first half, in particular, may have been the best half of basketball in the entire 2011-12 NCAA Tournament by any two teams.

Indiana had an early lead at 9-7, but Kentucky was up 16-11 five minutes into the game. The Wildcats stretched their lead to nine at 31-22 at the 9:58 mark.

But IU just kept chipping away. When Christian Watford hit a 3-pointer with 5:04 to play in the half, the game was tied at 37.

Remy Abell dribbles in front court against Kentucky.

Cody Zeller scores inside against Kentucky.

Two more Watford baskets would make it a 43-39 Indiana lead before the 'Cats stormed back. Two Watford free throws got Indiana to within one at 48-47 with 34 seconds to play in the half before Doron Lamb hit two foul shots with 7 seconds to play to make it 50-47.

Watford missed a 3-pointer at the other end, but a crazy half of basketball was in the books. Watford had scored IU's final eight points of the half and 11 of Indiana's final 13.

In the second half, Kentucky held a six- to eight-point lead for the first 10 minutes and would build it up to 13 at 79-66 with 8:54 remaining. But a little over three minutes later, Indiana was right back in it when Zeller scored on a tip-in to cut the lead to five at 82-77.

The Wildcats, however, would win this one at the free-throw line. Fourteen of Kentucky's final 16 points were free throws. The Wildcats simply couldn't miss, and IU's only hope was to put them on the line and hope they did.

Final score: Kentucky 102, Indiana 90.

Kentucky ended the game 35-of-37 from the free-throw line, 94.6 percent. Indiana made 13-of-17 from the line.

Indiana had five more field goals, but it wasn't enough because of Kentucky's ability to shoot free throws.

Watford had 27 points for IU and Zeller had 20. Hulls had 12 points and nine assists. Kidd-Gilchrist had 24 points and 10 rebounds to lead Kentucky.

The game stories and columns following the game told a similar story. Indiana put up a valiant effort but simply came up a little short against a really good Kentucky team.

Dustin Dopirak of the *Bloomington Herald-Times* had this to say in his game story the next day.

ATLANTA — With his head firmly tilted toward the floor, Jordan Hulls shuffled all the way to the final seat on Indiana's bench and waited to enter the postgame handshake line until there was no postponing it any further.

It was as if he just wasn't ready for it to end. Really, none of the Hoosiers were.

But on Friday night — really, early Saturday morning — Indiana's magic season of rebirth came to a close against the team the Hoosiers had beaten in December to announce their return to prominence. No. 4-seeded Indiana kept up with No. 1 Kentucky throughout a maniacally paced and brilliantly played NCAA South Regional semifinal at the Georgia Dome, but the Wildcats' length, athleticism and ability to draw fouls was too much in the long run, and they advanced to the Elite Eight with a 102-90 victory in front of a crowd of 24,731 that was largely partisan to their side.

Still, the campaign that ended in Atlanta is one that will long be remembered in Indiana lore. Just four years after the program was decimated and a year after their third straight 20-loss season, the Hoosiers reached the Sweet Sixteen for the first time since 2002, won 27 games for the first time since the 1992-93 season, and defeated three AP top-5 teams in the regular season for the first time in school history.

And in the Hoosiers' final game, they went down swinging as hard as they had all year.

"The Indiana men, and I mean quote me, the Indiana men, mighty men, as I've learned from my brother-in-laws and the way they describe their players, the Indiana mighty men, they gave it all," an emotional coach Tom Crean said in his postgame press conference. "They left it all on that court. I'm proud of what they did."

Said freshman forward Cody Zeller: "It's tough to lose like this. We came in planning to win it. That's why this one really hurts."

Jordan Hulls drives for a shot against Kentucky.

Victor Oladipo takes it to the basket against Kentucky.

The biggest reason they didn't was fouls and what Kentucky did with them. Indiana outshot Kentucky, making 36 of 69 field goals (52.2 percent) compared to the Wildcats 31-for-64 performance (48.4 percent). However, Kentucky went to the line 37 times and hit 35.

Crean hinted he thought the free-throw differential was a tad unfair.

"When they make 22 more free throws and take 20 more, I don't know if I could've imagined that," Crean said. "I wouldn't have imagined a game like this having a free-throw discrepancy of 20. It is what it is. We did a lot of good things. They shot 20 more free throws. That's the game."

How much of that was officiating and how much of that was simply Kentucky's length and strength inside is difficult to tell. The Wildcats were often able to break the Hoosiers down off the dribble and draw fouls deep in the paint.

"They're great drivers," Zeller said. "They were attacking pretty hard throughout the game. Late in the game they had to foul just to

try to close the margin a little bit. But they got to the bonus pretty early, and that really helped them out pretty well."

The top of my story the next day in the *Indianapolis Star* went like this:

ATLANTA — It was a game in terms of energy, excitement and environment that felt more like a Final Four matchup than a No. 1 and No. 4 seed playing in the Sweet Sixteen.

But the game that brought Indiana's magical season to an end will be remembered simply for the things IU couldn't do.

It couldn't stop Kentucky's dribble penetration and it couldn't stop the Wildcats from making the unguarded 15-foot free throw.

Kentucky consistently scored at will off the dribble in the Wildcats' 102-90 victory over Indiana on Friday in the NCAA South Regional semifinals at the Georgia Dome.

"They drove the ball to the basket hard and when they didn't finish, they got some timely rebounds," said IU's Christian Watford. "We just couldn't get stops when we needed them. It was as simple as that."

Bob Kravitz's column summed up the feelings of a lot of Indiana fans who were proud of the way their team went toe to toe with the eventual national champions when the teams met that night in the Sweet Sixteen.

ATLANTA — Disappointing?

Yes.

Of course.

The end to any season brings disappointment and even tears, buckets of them, and there were surely plenty of both in the Indiana locker room after the Hoosiers' 102-90 Sweet Sixteen loss to Kentucky on Friday night. This was an epic game played at an amazingly high level by both teams, far and away the best game so far in this NCAA Tournament.

A disappointment?

Hardly.

"As I said to my team, there's always sadness, tremendous sadness, but there's a lot more sadness when you realize your team had something left and didn't give it all," IU coach Tom Crean said.

"The Indiana men – and quote me, the Indiana men, these mighty men – they gave it all. They left it all on that court. I'm proud of what we did. We don't take the moral victory in any sense, but when you give every ounce of fight you have, you can move forward."

Think about it: The first three years, the Hoosiers won six, 10 and 12 games, 28 total. This year, they won 27 and got within two victories of an unlikely Final Four.

They beat three top-five teams.

They earned a fourth seed in the NCAA Tournament.

They reached the Sweet Sixteen.

Will Sheehey dunks on Kentucky in IU's Sweet Sixteen game in Atlanta.

And they reinstalled IU basketball as one of the elite programs in the country.

Not bad for a season's work, especially after three miserable years of 20-plus losses.

Despite the ultimate outcome Friday night at the Georgia Dome, this was, by any measure, an extraordinary achievement. This group got as much from itself as humanly possible. And in the process, it put Indiana basketball back on the map.

The Sweet Sixteen loss is disappointing, true, because the Hoosiers had raised the bar so high. At the beginning of this season, most IU fans would have been thrilled with 18 to 20 wins and an NIT performance. But then there was the winning streak to start the season, and those three victories over No. 1 Kentucky, No. 2 Ohio State and No. 5 Michigan State, and soon this group was on its way, growing exponentially each and every week.

How does Crean fail to win Big Ten Coach of the Year?

Can somebody please explain?

The team's internal growth was magnificent: Jordan Hulls, from a meek facilitator to multidimensional point guard; Christian Watford, from mystery man to NBA-quality talent; Victor Oladipo and Will Sheehey, from freshman gym rats to sophomore contributors. And on and on the list goes.

And that Zeller kid, Cody, had a whole lot to do with making everybody better.

From minimal expectations to crazy dreams of competing for a Final Four.

That's how far they came.

This rematch? They don't get more delicious than this Sweet Sixteen IU-Kentucky matchup, unless you're Bob Knight and you'd rather not mention either school's name.

We're not just talking about rivals, but basketball royalty. Kentucky is second all-time in national titles with seven. IU is tied with North Carolina for third with five. Nobody wanted to see the Alabama-LSU football rematch; everybody wanted to see the IU-Kentucky rematch. Interest was so great, organizers opened additional sections of the Georgia Dome to accommodate fans.

The two sides have gone back and forth. Kentucky coach John Calipari first saying his 'Cats got beat by a "lucky" shot, then saying Thursday his team should have lost by 20 points. Meanwhile, close friends Calipari and Crean have been tweaking each other, Crean noting how much he loves watching the commercial featuring Watford's buzzer-beating 3-pointer.

"It goes in every time," he said earlier this season. "It never changes."

Please excuse me for stating the blatantly obvious: This was an extraordinary basketball game played by two teams who played at such a high level offensively, you could see either one competing for a national title. They went back and forth at each other like heavyweights, IU running its sets, Kentucky finding mismatches and living on dribble penetration and isolations.

The first half? Simply stated, one of the greatest halves of college basketball we can ever remember. Offensively, anyway. If you're a defensive coach, with the missed rotations and the like, it was a nightmare. On both sides.

It was 50-47 Kentucky at the half, and the score didn't even do the quality of play justice. Even as the officials insinuated themselves into the game, sending Kentucky's Anthony Davis and IU's Zeller and Hulls to the bench with two early fouls, the play-making and shot-making were remarkable.

The Hoosiers shot 58 percent from the field, Kentucky 49.

And these were largely contested shots.

But in the end, there was too much Darius Miller, coming off the Kentucky bench and hitting 3-point shots. There was too much Michael Kidd-Gilchrist, who is reportedly ready to make himself available for the NBA draft. There was too much of everybody, and way too many made free throws, the Wildcats hitting an amazing 35-of-37 from the line.

Have any questions about Kentucky's worthiness as a national champion?

If ever they were going to get knocked off, it was Friday night by an IU team that is playing at its highest level all season.

The Hoosiers accomplished one thing they enjoyed in the December game: They got center Anthony Davis in early foul trouble. But they weren't able to turn Kentucky over like they did in the first game. They weren't able to keep Terrence Jones under control, as they did in the first game. They weren't able to hold serve on the boards, where Kentucky eventually asserted its size and strength.

Too big, too strong, too tough.

"They're great drivers," Zeller said of the Wildcats. "They're attacking pretty hard. Once they got into the bonus and got there (to the free-throw line), they were knocking them down."

So this is where the run ends, the whole enjoyable and unlikely Indiana NCAA Tournament run, ending where we all figured it might end: In the Sweet Sixteen, at the hands of the dominant No. 1 overall seed, Kentucky.

Disappointing? Sure.

A disappointment, though? Not a chance.

ဢ 03

A true measure of the Indiana basketball team could have been taken from the scene in the postgame locker room after Kentucky had ended IU's season.

There were tears. Lots of them. There was an outpouring of disappointment and grief. The national pundits and most everyone in the other 49 states may not have believed that Indiana could beat Kentucky for a second time in the same season, but these guys absolutely did.

The plane ride home the next day was the same way. A lot of quiet kids filled with disappointment. At some point they would look back at this 27-9 season with a sense of pride. But it was too close right now. This one was going to take some time to get over.

IU play-by-play announcer Don Fischer said there was no phoniness in any of the outward feelings these guys expressed. It was very real.

"I think those kids were truly disappointed in not being able to beat Kentucky a second time," Fischer said. "And if you watched how they played that ballgame, they never gave up. They fought their tails off the whole way down to the end. Even though Kentucky continued to get to the free-throw line in that last five minutes on a consistent basis, they were doing everything they could to try to pull that game out."

Fischer said the team brought fun and pride back to Indiana basketball again.

"This team had a lot of pride and really enjoyed playing with each other. That much was really obvious," Fischer said. "But you could tell on the plane ride back home the next day that there was a real disappointment in not having accomplished their goal.

"I really think this team thought they not only could get to the Final Four, but they'd have a chance at winning the national championship. That's the kind of confidence level they had. And it wasn't anything cocky, it wasn't anything arrogant. It was simply a true belief in what they felt they could have accomplished."

Chapter 26

When the 2011-12 season ended, the immediate attention turned to what Indiana basketball was going to look like in 2012-13.

If everyone returned, Indiana would be loaded. All five starters from the three NCAA Tournament games would be back.

A big-time incoming freshman class, dubbed "The Movement", would be ready to make its splash in the college basketball world. The names Kevin 'Yogi' Ferrell, Hanner Perea, Jeremy Hollowell, Ron Patterson and Peter Jurkin had been bantered about as the players who could put Indiana basketball back on the map again.

Obviously the 2011-12 team didn't get that memo and hit the fast-forward button. But now with the program re-established as one that could compete for Big Ten championships and deep runs into the NCAA Tournament again, adding that talented class would just improve IU's chances exponentially.

There was also a player like Maurice Creek whom Indiana basketball fans still hoped could be a solid contributor. Creek, who missed the entire 2011-12 season with a torn Achilles injury, would return as a junior with two full years of eligibility remaining.

In other words, the future of IU basketball looked extremely bright.

And then the national pundits started weighing in, and a red bulls-eye was firmly affixed to the Indiana program.

Just hours after Kentucky was crowned the 2012 national champion, national college basketball writers started coming out with their preseason top 25 picks for the 2012-13 season.

ESPN.com ranked Indiana No. 1. *USA Today* followed suit. NBC Sports wasn't far behind. Eventually, The Sporting News made it a foursome when it made the same pick. Two others, Yahoo Sports and CNNSI.com, also would make the same claim.

Now, of course, all of those picks were based on everyone coming back, and they were made in April. Hoosier Hysteria isn't until October, and IU's schedule wouldn't begin until mid-November. Translation: It was way too early to be making predictions.

But if nothing else, the rankings were a validation that the Hoosiers were back in the conversation. Even if the Hoosiers didn't turn out to be No. 1 come November, you would think that much attention in April would at least get them ranked in the preseason top five. If not the top five, you would think the top 10 would be a given.

And let's put that into perspective. For the first three years under Tom Crean, Indiana was barely being predicted to crack the top 10 of the Big Ten.

But what if Indiana was the preseason No. 1 team in the land? The last time that happened was in the 1979-80 season when the Hoosiers had a freshman guard named Isiah Thomas and a couple of guys named Ray Tolbert and Mike Woodson in the starting five. The year after, Indiana would hang its fourth national championship banner.

If it's not No. 1 but just top five, that would be the first time that IU had debuted in that spot since the 1992-93 Indiana team was No. 4 in the preseason poll. The season before that, Indiana was No. 2 to open the season. Those teams had guys like Calbert Cheaney, Greg Graham, Damon Bailey and Alan Henderson in the lineup.

The last time Indiana was simply a top 10 team to open the season was Kelvin Sampson's second and final year at Indiana when the Hoosiers were No. 9 in the country in the preseason poll.

But again, the important thing isn't so much that Indiana was being considered in the loftiest of ranking spots, but rather that Indiana was even being considered.

Being a top 10-ranked team would mean a lot of things, but most of all it would mean Indiana was indeed back from the ashes. After the 27-9 showing from the year before and a final No. 13 ranking in the *USA Today*/Coaches poll there was little doubt that would be the case. But the preseason ranking would simply provide validation of that point.

As good as all of that sounded, Indiana basketball fans were skeptical about getting ahead of themselves.

There were two reasons for their concern: rumors that Christian Watford and/or Cody Zeller were considering leaving Indiana in this offseason to enter the NBA Draft.

Watford seemed the most likely. When I spoke to his father, Ernest, the night of the second IU-Kentucky game, he said his son would definitely be exploring his options with regards to the NBA once the season was over. He didn't say he was leaving for sure, but he didn't say he was coming back, either.

Anyone who knows Watford knows that since arriving on campus in 2009 he had talked about getting to the NBA. And most believed if he could elevate his status high enough that he would be ready to bolt for the pros.

I remember when Kirk Haston decided to leave after his junior season in 2001. He had just led the Big Ten in scoring and was second in rebounding and his stock was likely as high as it would ever get. He was named All-American after averaging 19 points and nearly nine rebounds per game. He was being advised that he would be selected in the middle of the first round (which he eventually was by Charlotte with the 16th pick overall) and he opted to leave.

That one made sense. Watford didn't. None of the NBA mock drafts had the IU senior-to-be in the vicinity of the first round. A few had him as a late second-round pick, but most didn't have him ranked in the top 60 players who were draft-eligible.

But Watford was giving it some thought and looking for someone, anyone, to give him a glimmer of hope that he could be drafted.

Zeller, on the other hand, was a much different prospect. Most mock drafts had him being selected in the top 10 of the first round if he decided to come out. With Zeller though, there was more reason to believe he would stick around at least one more season. First of all he liked college and had thoroughly enjoyed his first season at Indiana. Second, he was good friends with a lot of the guys coming in as freshmen in 2012-13 and had been outspoken at one time about looking forward to playing with them. Finally, he was well-grounded and came from a family that believed strongly in the benefits of an education.

But in early April, both Watford and Zeller were said to be exploring their options. What their ultimate decisions would be would have a lot to do with IU's lofty preseason rankings. If Watford were to leave, IU could still survive it and be ranked high, just probably not No. 1. If Zeller left, all bets were off.

Fortunately, the Hoosier Nation didn't have to wait too long to get their answers.

On April 10, 2012, both Watford and Zeller announced they would remain in school and play for the Hoosiers in the fall. As the news was going out on Twitter and other social media, you could hear the Hallelujah Chorus playing in the background from the Hoosier Nation.

All of a sudden, dreams of being a top five-ranked team in fall of 2012 were inching ever closer to reality.

Watford, who made the NCAA South Regional All-Tournament team, will return to IU as the leading returning scorer in the Big Ten with 1,287 points. As a junior he scored just over 450 points and averaged 12.6 points per game. If he were to duplicate that effort his senior season, he would finish with more than 1,700 career points, which could rank him in the all-time top 10 in Indiana history. The No. 10 spot is currently held by Brian Evans with 1,701 points.

"I'm looking forward to the opportunity to complete my degree and to continue restoring the winning tradition at IU," said Watford.

"I believe in Coach Crean and our staff, and I am eager to lead my new teammates and build on what we started."

Crean said Watford was playing some of his best basketball at the end of the season. He had 27 points in the Sweet Sixteen loss to Kentucky.

"Christian really ended the season on a high note on the biggest stage and is building off that," said IU coach Tom Crean. "He is going to have the opportunity to be a leader and have an even greater impact on the program and his game, but more importantly, he will earn his degree from IU."

Zeller was the Big Ten Freshman of the Year and an honorable mention *Associated Press* All-American. He averaged 15.6 points and 6.6 rebounds and shot 62.3 percent from the field. That ranked fourth in the nation.

"I grew up hoping that one day I would get the opportunity to play in the NBA, but at this point, I'm not ready for my college experience to be over," Zeller said. "Coach Crean and my family were very supportive and helpful as I made my decision. My college experience at IU this year has exceeded my expectations, on and off the court."

Crean said he sat down with both Watford and Zeller and tried to help them make the best decisions they could make. He contacted NBA people to get their takes and then passed on those results to the players and their families.

"I didn't try to convince them to stay, I just tried to help them in any way I could to make the best decision for them," Crean said.

When Zeller announced he was staying, Crean talked a little bit about what a special player the soon-to-be sophomore continues to become.

"Cody is a player who, along with his unique skillset, makes everyone around him better," Crean said. "He is going to have great opportunities ahead of him, yet his demeanor, work ethic and his desire to be a great teammate never waver. He will have the opportunity to be as good as any player in college basketball."

      ⁞    

The day that Zeller signed to play basketball at Indiana—Nov. 11, 2010—was a red-letter day in recent Indiana basketball lore.

November 9, 2011, however, wasn't far behind.

That's the day The Movement signed to play basketball for Coach Crean and the Hoosiers.

As I wrote the next day in the *Indianapolis Star*, The Movement was now officially a season away from playing basketball at Indiana University.

Indianapolis' Broad Ripple High's Ron Patterson, one of the five members of the Hoosiers' class of 2012 who signed his letter of intent November 9, coined that phrase on his Twitter account the year before.

It described a class, ranked No.2 in the nation by rivals.com and scout.com, that IU fans expected to collectively revitalize the program.

"We're going to Indiana to hang banners," Patterson said.

It was a sentiment shared by his future teammates throughout the day.

Hanner Perea, a 6-8 power forward from La Lumiere School in LaPorte, Indiana, was the first to sign. He was the highest-ranked player in the class at No. 16 nationally at the time of their signing.

"We know there's going to be a lot of pressure on us to succeed because of our class ranking, but I don't think any of us really care about that," Perea said. "We've all played together in AAU in the past, and we all know what we can do. We know we can have something special at Indiana."

One of the interesting aspects of the IU class was that the five players conceivably could be on the court at the same time.

Park Tudor (Indianapolis)'s Kevin "Yogi" Ferrell, ranked No.17 in the nation by rivals, is a point guard who can run the floor, make the extra pass and be a vocal leader. Patterson, ranked No. 131, is a shooting guard who can get to the rim. Lawrence Central's Jeremy Hollowell, ranked No. 48 in the nation, is a 6-7 small forward who is very athletic.

Perea, described by his high school coach as having freak athletic ability, is the power forward, and Peter Jurkin, a 7-0 center, is the man in the middle who can alter shots on defense. Jurkin, from United Faith Christian Academy in Charlotte, North Carolina, is the only player in the class not ranked nationally. But with Tom Pritchard graduating, Jurkin was expected to be first in line to receive the backup center minutes behind Cody Zeller.

The formation of the class began in early August 2010, when Jurkin gave his commitment. A week later, Patterson got on board. Perea became the third player in the class in late October, and Ferrell followed in November shortly after Zeller signed to play at IU. Hollowell was the final player to commit, in mid-March 2011.

The only player who Indiana really wanted that got away was eventual *Indianapolis Star* Indiana Mr. Basketball Gary Harris of Hamilton Southeastern. Harris chose to play for Tom Izzo at Michigan State.

Still, with or without Harris, there was clearly a movement headed toward Bloomington.

Patterson said he was confident the group would play together in college. He said they shared a family kind of camaraderie. He said that was where The Movement came from, too.

"I was just thinking one day about how we could be so good in the future and looking at the guys we had coming in. And I just thought it was a movement," Patterson said. "We're a very confident group."

Ferrell signed at his school at 11:45 a.m. along with teammate Paul Bayt, who is headed to Manhattan. Ferrell says he can't wait to get to campus and begin working on his primary goal.

"When I think about what could be, I think about getting that sixth (national championship) banner," Ferrell said of a program that won its fifth NCAA crown in 1987.

"What I like about our class is their determination to win. I've played with all of these guys for a long time, and I know that when we step out on the floor we give it our all. And I know we'll do that in college, too, and we'll get it done."

Yogi's father, also named Kevin Ferrell, said there would be plenty of pressure on this class to be successful.

"They're going to be asked to do quite a bit, and I think (Coach Tom) Crean is going to ask them to do quite a bit," the elder Ferrell said. "It's his job on the line. I think the IU fans are kind of fed up with the way things have been going, and they're going to demand that we win. So I think from the kids' perspective, they're going to do more than any other group has ever done."

Of course, the elder Ferrell's comments were made in November before the 2011-12 Hoosiers had tipped for their first game of the season. Had he been able to reference the 27-9 record and Sweet Sixteen appearance, he might have felt a little differently about what Indiana fans thought about the program.

Still, his thought process and lofty expectations for The Movement were clearly in line with what Indiana fans and the players in that particular class were all thinking, as well.

❧　☙

At his press conference the next day to talk about the players who had signed with the Hoosiers, Crean tried to put the significance of the class of 2012 into perspective.

"The biggest thing, putting this in context, back in 2008, whether it be May, whether it be June, when we realized that we were in for the fight of our life in the sense of where we stood inside of the program with having to absolutely build a team that year, we knew this day was coming," Crean said. "Where this year was going to come and this was going to be imperative because the thing we kept talking about is we're going to have to start over again.

"Nobody wanted to do that. We knew at that point we were starting over at Indiana, and with all the young men that we signed in that class, we knew this day was going to come. One of the main reasons that we decided to recruit every class on its own merit, at that point the rising seniors, the rising juniors, the rising sophomores, the rising freshmen, was so that we wouldn't have to start over from scratch."

Crean said this class was particularly special.

"Needless to say, to have a class like this at Indiana was way beyond our imagination and our dreams at that point in time," Crean said. "There's no way around it. We're very thankful that we were able to get in on so many players at a young age and get to know them and get to know their families and their coaches and their programs.

"Get them to start coming to Indiana, get them to start coming to a building like this, get them comfortable not only with the coaches and with the players, but like I mentioned, everybody else around. Get them around this Hoosier Nation, get them around this campus, get them around this atmosphere and that's what happened, that's what happened. It's happened that way over the last couple of years."

As he looked back to just the previous two classes, Crean was extremely happy with the way things had worked out. Obviously the current freshman class had Zeller, Austin Etherington and Remy Abell. The one before that had Victor Oladipo and Will Sheehey. Three of those five would eventually start all three NCAA Tournament games for Indiana in 2011-12.

"I look back, for what we might not have been able to recruit in Victor and Will's class, I wouldn't trade those two for anybody in it, because those two have come in and been fantastic," Crean said. "Obviously last year's class was paramount, with Cody and Austin and then Remy signing late, but this was the impact class. We knew it was going to have to be a big one.

"Early on we realized there were probably going to be some people out there that didn't want to be a part of a big class, but we had no way around it. I am so thankful for the people that joined this wanting to be a part of this because it's a dynamic group, it's an explosive group, it's an exciting group and we are absolutely excited and just blessed to be able to bring people like that into the program and get to work with them on a day-to-day basis."

Crean said he's looking forward to getting started with this group in the summer of 2012.

"I think it will be a two-way street, we'll be excited, they'll be excited and there will be many days where they'll be wondering 'what did I get myself into?'," Crean said. "But when it's all said and done and they grow up to be the young men that their families want them to be, much like the other guys here, it'll all be worth it.

"We're very excited about it. Obviously Calbert can't have a lot to do with the recruiting, can't have anything to do with it off campus, but when they're on campus, Calbert's as good as it gets and that's really, really important, too. When you not only have somebody of his quality and character, but then they look in the rafters and look in here and see what he's done in his career. I'm fortunate and blessed to be around a really great organization and staff, we all work really well together. I think the recruits see it and that's what's exciting about this."

Here's what Crean had to say about each player in the movement individually:

Kevin 'Yogi' Ferrell: "Yogi brings so many intangibles. What you are looking for in players is you're always looking for their tools. What kind of tools do they have and what kind of skills do they have inside of those tools? Where can you really build their skills up? The tools, that's what they have. When Yogi comes in, part of his tools are his charisma, his fearlessness, he's absolutely relentless when it comes to winning, and he puts winning first. His change of speed, change of direction, his ability to shoot the three, his ability to play in transition, his ability to shoot the pull-up, now he's adding the ability to get that broad jump at the basket and go up and explode in and around people and he'll continue to get that. He's getting stronger. He's been somebody that's been on the scene for a long time, even longer than we've been here, so it seems like he's actually older than he is and he plays older than he is. I think that's going to really fit in when he gets here, but you just put him right up at the top of the list when you talk about a guy that's been coached to win year round."

Hanner Perea: "He's got an edge. We saw a game last year, he had already committed, against Rakeem Christmas and Illinois. Rakeem was ranked one or two in the country as a center. It was two grown men going at one another, and it was not for the fainthearted. There was a lot of talent on the floor, but Hanner Perea has an edge about him. That's the grit, when you start to think about some of these guys and you talk about recruiting grit, Hanner Perea brings grit and he's got an explosiveness. He's one of the greater athletes in the entire class, let alone our class. We're really excited about the upside of him. He's a hard worker, he's a willing worker, he's a great young man and really, really excited to be coming to Indiana. We feel really good with that. I think he's going to make the game easier for others in different ways. Some of it's going to be with his energy, his defense, his ability around the bucket, his ability to rebound the ball, but he's going to become a very capable scorer for us in the time that we have him. We see that potential coming, again, another guy that's really well-coached year round."

Jeremy Hollowell: "Jeremy is one of the more improved from-tenth -grade-on players that there is, because he keeps adding things to his game. He has a quiet demeanor, he's quiet on the court. He's not a showy type of player, he's not a flashy type of player, but he's got the tools and the skills. When you talk about short-space quickness, when you talk about explosiveness, feel for the game, just loves to be in the gym, those kinds of things help him a great deal. He keeps growing and his game keeps expanding. He can get to the rim. That's the versatility that really strikes me, when you start to think about that. It's going to take some time, and I think he's committed to it this year and I know (his coach) is committed to getting him to this point, but he's got to defend with the same exuberance that he can play offense with because that's what it's going to take for him to be successful here, and when he becomes the two-way player that he's capable of being, I mean Katie bar the door, not to use an old corny statement, he's going to be really good, really good, but he's got to get all those things."

Ron Patterson: "It goes back to the athleticism, the explosiveness, the willingness. He's got a motor that's really second to none. His hustle, his energy, especially on the defensive end, his desire to get to the basket. He knows what his improvement measurements have to be, we know what they have to be, he needs to continue to do that this year for his team to win and he'll get better along the way. When all their seasons are over, then we'll really dive in to what they need to have here. He's got a motor that's as ready as it gets. Now getting the skills and the fundamentals and all those things inside that motor, decision making, those are the things that he's got to continue to really work hard on. But, again, there's a young man that continues to get better and better. You can't really put into context a young man that has a plus-12 wingspan. I've never coached one, recruited one, let alone met one other than him. Maybe there is one, but I've never met one. When he stretches out and plays with that length, it's a sight to behold."

Peter Jurkin: "I think the upside of Peter is as high as anyone because he's, again and you could see it at a young age, great timing, a presence in the court, outstanding athlete, there's been a couple of growth spurts for him not only in height but in his weight and his body has continued to change. There's no question that last year set him back with the injury and then it came back, but I think there's a guy that will have an impact this year nationally because he's playing with another great player on his team. I think they'll get a lot of attention. I think people will see, if he can stay injury-free, that this guy really has a chance. He's developing a perimeter jump shot to a degree, he's probably not comfortable taking it yet, but he runs the floor. The thing that Peter and Hanner do on the front line is they change the game for us unlike anybody we've had to this point. Not unlike anybody other people have had, but what we've had in our time at Indiana. You can work on a lot of things, but you can't work on height, length, energy and edge. Everything else you can get, those guys bring that."

ꗗ   ꗍ

I caught up with Rick Greenspan in May 2012 and asked if he'd like to participate in this book. I gave him the opportunity to speak candidly about what went wrong with the decision to hire Kelvin Sampson but he declined. Rick was always someone who would take the high road. He wasn't someone who was about to throw people under the bus after the fact. I'm convinced that Greenspan knows where all of the bodies are buried, but those thoughts are going to remain with him and not become public.

Greenspan is now the athletic director at Rice. I asked him if he had seen Watford's shot to beat Kentucky. He said he watched it from his home in Houston.

"I thought it was a magical moment, and it seemed like the stress and strain of the previous years had been lifted," Greenspan said. "Beating Kentucky is magical but beating them in Assembly Hall after some rough years was a very special moment."

I also wondered if after watching IU's memorable 2011-12 season from afar, if he had any special pride knowing that he was the person who hired Tom Crean in April 2008.

"I am proud of the accomplishments of Coach Crean and his staff," Greenspan said. "The Indiana basketball job requires a CEO, an individual that is absolutely committed to all facets of the program: student development, recruiting, public relations, fundraising, community service, academics, etc. It is rewarding to see see that Tom has been successful in all of these areas and the university and program will benefit for many years under his leadership."

ᔥ   ᔥ

What the 2011-12 IU season proved is that you can come back. It is possible to rise from the ashes. That is clearly what transpired in Bloomington.

To do so, there had to be patience, hard work and dedication. And the Indiana basketball fans deserve more than a little credit. Throughout his first four years at Indiana, Crean has consistently called out the Hoosier Nation in postgame press conferences and speaking engagements throughout the state, thanking them for standing behind the program. Even in its worst times, Indiana basketball was still playing before 15,000 plus in the 17,000-seat Assembly Hall.

It's not something that was lost on IU's players, coaches or former players.

"After the Kelvin Sampson fiasco, I was expecting things to be rough for a while, but I never thought it was going to be as bad as it was," said Joe Hillman, a member of the 1987 national championship team, the last team to hang a basketball banner in Bloomington. "The one thing I remember most of all the struggles was how well the IU fan base supported the team. Fans kept filling Assembly Hall, and the atmosphere was unreal for a team struggling.

"The players were doing a great job of representing IU and playing hard which made it easier to watch, and you could tell the coaching staff was working hard because the players were improving. They just weren't getting the results they expected."

Verdell Jones III, one of the senior leaders on the Indiana team that brought IU basketball back to relevance again, was a player who at times in his career drew the ire of Indiana fans because of some ball-handling struggles, in particular. But even Jones had nothing but good things to say about Indiana's fan support.

"Our fans are second to none, and there's no way we could have accomplished the things we were able to accomplish without their support," Jones said. "But when you've been here a while and you see how important basketball is to so many people, you start to understand it. Like Coach Crean said when he first got here, 'It's Indiana.' That's really all you need to know."

‽   ∾

With Zeller and Watford not going anywhere, the core of the returning Indiana team in place and a star-studded cast of players arriving with The Movement, Indiana basketball should be fun to watch in the 2012-13 season and beyond.

The more success this group has, the farther in the rearview mirror the ugliness of what transpired under Kelvin Sampon's watch will become. For Indiana basketball fans, it can't happen soon enough.

While IU fans will always feel a debt to players like Kyle Taber, Brett Finkelmeier, Daniel Moore, Tom Pritchard, Matt Roth, Verdell Jones III and Kory Barnett, to name a few, it will be the star players of 2011-12 who will hold a special place in Indiana history, as well.

And to think it all happened thanks to a simple flick of the wrist by Christian Watford on that early December day in 2011. How he was able to hit nothing but net with that massive gorilla draped on his back with its forearm around his neck, we'll never know.

But along with Keith Smart's shot that won a national championship, Watford's shot against Kentucky will forever be remembered as *The Shot* that brought Indiana basketball back to relevance.

Index

Chapter 9

120, "After all the turmoil Hoosiers get it right", Bob Kravitz, *Indianapolis Star*, April 2, 2008.

Chapter 13

Page 155, "Record Suffered; Pride Didn't at Indiana", Gene Wojciechowski, *ESPN.com*, March 13, 2009. (Reprinted with permission from ESPN.com)

Chapter 14

Page 169, "Creek's blown out knee spills blowout victory", Terry Hutchens, *Indianapolis Star*, Dec. 29, 2009.

Page 171, "Crean bemoans his team's lack of toughness in loss", Terry Hutchens, *Indianapolis Star*, Jan. 25, 2010.

Page 172, "Crean takes new tone after Iowa debacle", Chris Korman, *The Herald-Times*, Bloomington, Jan. 25, 2010.

Page 174, "Forward-thinking Hoosiers would rather forget this season", Bob Kravitz, *Indianapolis Star*, March 12, 2010.

Chapter 15

Page 177, "IU's Biggest Recruit", Jeff Rabjohns, *Indianapolis Star*, Nov. 12, 2010

Page 180, "Zeller heads to IU", Todd Lancaster, *Washington Times-Herald*, Nov. 12, 2010

Page 182, "Zeller will announce today but there is no word for whom", Dustin Dopirak, *The Herald-Times*, Bloomington, Nov. 11, 2010.

Page 183, "Advice to Zeller? Be selfish, be happy", Bob Kravitz, *Indianapolis Star*, Nov. 11, 2010.

Page 187, "Ferrell commits to IU, Crean", Jody Demling, *Louisville Courier-Journal*, Nov. 25, 2010.

Chapter 16

Page 196, "Jones spurs IU to 60-57 win over Minnesota in return", Terry Hutchens, *Indianapolis Star*, Feb. 3, 2011.

Page 198, "Indiana Can Hold Head High", Ben Smith, *Fort Wayne Journal Gazette*, March 11, 2011.

Page 200, "It's time for Hoosiers to start showing some progress", Bob Kravitz, *Indianapolis Star*, March 11, 2011.

Chapter 18

Page 217, "Tom Crean's response to IU's secondary recruiting violation", Terry Hutchens, *Indianapolis Star*, *Hoosier Insider Blog*, Oct. 12, 2011.

Page 220, "Hoosier Hysteria spirits run high for start of Indiana University basketball", Kyle Neddenriep, *Indianapolis Star*, Oct. 16, 2011

Page 223, "Zeller brings Indiana new offensive strategy", Terry Hutchens, *Indianapolis Star*, Oct. 28, 2011.

Page 227, "I'm picking IU to go 19-12 in the regular season. What's your pick?", Terry Hutchens, *Indianapolis Star*, *Hoosier Insider Blog*, Nov. 7, 2011.

Chapter 19

Page 233, "IU shows its tough enough", Rick Bozich, *Louisville Courier-Journal*, Nov. 28, 2011.

Chapter 20

Page 244, "Hoosiers' record — 10-0 — says it all", Rick Bozich, *Louisville Courier-Journal*, Dec. 18, 2011.

Chapter 22

Page 268, "Ahead of schedule, this IU team is NCAA bound", Bob Kravitz, *Indianapolis Star*, Feb. 10, 2012.

Page 271, "IU making wise guys' predictions look dumb", Rick Bozich, *Louisville Courier-Journal*, Feb. 16, 2012.

Chapter 23

Page 283, "These IU seniors finally have a year to enjoy", Bob Kravitz, *Indianapolis Star*, March 5, 2012.

Page 285, "IU's victory painful", Bob Kravitz, *The Indianapolis Star*, March 9, 2012.

Chapter 24

Page 293, "IU hits on all cylinders", Terry Hutchens, *The Indianapolis Star*, March 16, 2012.

Page 298, "Cinderella or not, Rams remain eager", Chris Foster, *Daily Press*, Newport News, Va., March 17, 2012.

Page 299, "VCU press could bring nightmares for Hoosiers", Bob Kravitz, *Indianapolis Star*, March 17, 2012.

Page 302, "Sweet Shot, Sweet 16", Terry Hutchens, *Indianapolis Star*, March 18, 2012.

Chapter 25

Page 315, "IU's dream season comes to a close, 102-90", Dustin Dopirak, *The Herald-Times*, Bloomington, March 24, 2012.

Page 317, "Defeat, not repeat", Terry Hutchens, *Indianapolis Star*, March 24, 2012.

Page 317, "Fight to the finish", Bob Kravitz, *Indianapolis Star*, March 24, 2012.

ᏰᏫ ᏣᏃ

About the Author

Terry Hutchens knows Indiana University basketball. For the past 15 years he has worked as the IU football and basketball beat writer for the *Indianapolis Star*. He covered Bob Knight, Mike Davis, Kelvin Sampson and now Tom Crean.

Overall, Terry has worked as a sportswriter for more than 35 years including the last 21 at the *Indianapolis Star and Indianapolis News*.

Five times in the last six years and four years in a row, Terry has been honored as Indiana's Sportswriter of the Year by the National Sportscasters and Sportswriters Association.

This is Terry's fourth book. *Let 'Er Rip*, chronicling the Indianapolis Colts' improbable run to within one game of the Super Bowl, was published in 1995. *Hep Remembered*, a book about former IU football coach Terry Hoeppner, who died from the effects of brain cancer in 2007, was published later that year. *Never Ever Quit*, a Christian inspirational book that he wrote along with Jane Hoeppner, the widow of Terry Hoeppner, was published in 2009.

Terry and wife, Susan, have been married 26 years and live in Indianapolis. His oldest son, Bryan, is a senior at Wabash College studying financial math, and his youngest, Kevin, is a freshman at Belmont University studying music.